Embracing
Watershed
Politics

Embracing Watershed Politics

Edella Schlager
AND William Blomquist

UNIVERSITY PRESS OF COLORADO

© 2008 by the University Press of Colorado

Published by the University Press of Colorado
5589 Arapahoe Avenue, Suite 206C
Boulder, Colorado 80303

 The University Press of Colorado is a proud member of
the Association of American University Presses.

The University Press of Colorado is a cooperative publishing enterprise supported, in part,
by Adams State College, Colorado State University, Fort Lewis College, Mesa State College,
Metropolitan State College of Denver, University of Colorado, University of Northern
Colorado, and Western State College of Colorado.

∞ The paper used in this publication meets the minimum requirements of the American
National Standard for Information Sciences—Permanence of Paper for Printed Library
Materials. ANSI Z39.48-1992

Library of Congress Cataloging-in-Publication Data

Schlager, Edella, 1960–
  Embracing watershed politics / Edella Schlager and William Blomquist.
    p. cm.
  Includes bibliographical references and index.
  ISBN 978-0-87081-909-4 (hbk. : alk. paper) 1. Watershed management—Political as-
pects—United States. 2. Integrated water development—United States. I. Blomquist,
William A. (William Andrew), 1957– II. Title.
  TC423.S33 2008
  333.73—dc22
                        2008017090
Design by Daniel Pratt

17 16 15 14 13 12 11 10 09 08   10 9 8 7 6 5 4 3 2 1

Contents

Preface

The modern "watershed movement" constitutes a broad and ambitious experiment in natural resource governance. Watershed initiatives are forcing a reexamination of several *fundamental components of resource management*, including: who should be involved in making management decisions; at what geographic locations should the decisions (and decision-making processes) be based; and which evaluation criteria should be used to determine appropriate water uses and management philosophies?

FRANK GREGG, DOUGLAS KENNEY, KATHRYN MUTZ, AND TERESA RICE

(1998, EMPHASIS ADDED)

Who gets to participate in decision making and how, on what scale and with what processes and through what organizational forms, and toward what ends and with what means of evaluation and change are fundamental components, indeed, and the focus of this book. They are fundamental questions of resource management, and they are the fundamental questions of *politics*. Politics is not only "who gets what, when, and how" as it has been famously described (Lasswell 1958). It is also *who decides* who gets what, when, and how, and *how we decide* such things.

So much has been written about watersheds: their importance, their complexity, their rediscovery as a focus of natural resource management and environmental protection. A fair amount has been written, too, about the management of watersheds and the kinds of institutional arrangements that would be best suited to the task. Much of that writing prescribes one or another organizational approach (such as an integrated watershed management agency or basin commission) or decision-making style (collaborative, consensus based, etc.) as essential or at least desirable to that task. Most watersheds, though, at least in the United States, have not conformed to such prescriptions and are instead governed and managed through complex, polycentric mixes of private and public bodies, of general-purpose and special district governments, of jurisdictions that lie within the watershed and jurisdictions that spill beyond it.

Our primary purpose in this book is not to criticize the institutional prescriptions that others have recommended but to try to explain the more complicated reality of the political watershed. Of course, we are not interested in providing merely a justification for existing institutions; we will have some prescriptions of our own along the way. We are, however, interested in combating a couple of viewpoints that surface from time to time in writing about watersheds—that one best way (meaning some form of comprehensive integrated management) exists for governing watersheds and that if we could just get rid of the politics we could manage the watershed so much better.

The one-best-way theme surfaces anew with each water era in the United States. Supporters of the National Resources Board and its river basin committees, created in 1934, argued that finally the United States would realize the value of integrated planning and comprehensive development of river basins, leaving behind the fragmented, haphazard approach practiced to that time (Derthick 1974). Two and a half decades later, river basin commissions were heralded as the best way to accomplish river basin management, replacing the fragmented, uncoordinated practices of the previous water era. As a 1960 report of the Senate Select Committee on National Water Resources explained: "For this new type of approach the term 'comprehensive development' is suggested. By it we mean the application of integrated multipurpose design, planning and management" (Senate Select Committee on National Water Resources 1960, Print #31:2). And, again, contemporary efforts at watershed planning and management through watershed partnerships claim that one of their prime advantages over earlier efforts is their broad focus on managing all dimensions of a watershed (Sabatier et al. 2005).

In addition, the tone of frustration with political considerations is clear in some of the reflections of commentators (especially from the physical sciences) who have contributed their thoughts on natural resource systems generally or watersheds in particular. Watershed management efforts "face numerous obstacles, more social than hydrologic" (Kraft et al. 1999, 10), and their success often depends on "the degree of political commitment to the objectives by those who have authority to act. Regrettably, science can offer no help in this problem" (Pereira 1989, 54). Particularly in the United States, the governmental structure exhibits problems of "overlapping areal jurisdiction, dispersed functional responsibilities, and ineffective coordination . . . heightened by traditional interunit and intergovernmental tensions" (Nakamura and Born 1993, 812), with agencies and programs sometimes operating at cross-purposes (Behrman 1993, 11; U.S. EPA 1995, iii; Duncan 2001). Other water problems have remained unaddressed because they do not fit within established programs, so no agency or unit of government is charged with responding to them (Kraft et al. 1999). While they remain unaddressed, they grow worse.

These are important and valid criticisms by thoughtful and respected colleagues, and there is plenty of empirical support for them. The differences between political boundaries and watershed boundaries complicate many aspects of water resources management, and the existence of multiple governments and organizations with differing jurisdictions, powers, and portfolios creates opportunities for delayed and uncoordinated action. Left unanswered by this critique of the past and present, however, are three other questions that we think are important. First, how has watershed management (particularly in the United States) emerged despite this complex system, and what does it look like? Second, why do these polycentric and complicated arrangements exist—is there any logic to why people have constructed organizational and inter-organizational relationships in these ways, and if so what is it? Third, how can individuals working on watershed management under these circumstances better understand the institutional environment that surrounds them, why it is the way it is, and what to do? (In particular, we imagine the situation of a person who has assumed a position of responsibility for managing a watershed, whose education and experience heretofore have been primarily in science or engineering, and who is looking for some practical help as well as a broader understanding.) Addressing these questions is a way of taking watershed politics seriously, of rightly viewing those political issues as "fundamental components of resource management."

In this book, we also discuss political considerations as they affect watershed governance. Our approach as political scientists is somewhat different, at least in style, but in substance too. Instead of being stymied by political issues, we concentrate on them and the challenges they present. We do so for a variety of reasons.

For people to govern watersheds well requires that they make collective choices. People, organizations, interest groups, and governments, all of whom represent different interests, values, dreams, and aspirations, must collectively decide how to govern the shared resources and uses of watersheds. Collective choices are ultimately political choices. Thus, governing watersheds well requires embracing politics. Fortunately, watershed politics does not have to be blindly embraced; rather political science and, more broadly, political economy provide explanations, analyses, and prescriptions to assist watershed governors. The explanations and analyses, grounded in political theory, transaction costs, local public economies, and federalism, provide us with an understanding of why watershed governance is almost always going to involve many overlapping, sometimes cooperative, sometimes competitive governments, organizations, and associations. Such organizational and institutional complexity is likely even if cooperative and problem-solving orientations dominate among the participants in a watershed.

These literatures also provide prescriptions for good governance, which we will focus on and highlight. In our reading of the watershed literature we believe that political explanations and analyses are largely missing, and, consequently, so too are the prescriptions arising from such analyses. Finally, in engaging in a political economy analysis of watershed governance we hope to begin to reorient the policy debates surrounding watersheds from the search for the one best way to govern to the exploration of what forms of governance are possible in what types of situations and how institutional and organizational complexity can be better managed.[1]

We begin in Chapter 1 by constructing the physical and institutional setting within which watershed governance occurs in the United States. Watersheds are complex adaptive systems, and as such they exhibit certain characteristics and dynamics that present particular challenges for their governance and use. Institutional arrangements, such as those in use in a watershed, can also be thought of as complex adaptive systems. Viewing both watersheds and institutions as complex adaptive systems provides opportunities not only to compare and contrast them but also to consider their relation to one another in a context where neither is privileged conceptually over the other.

In Chapter 2, we examine three eras of water management in the United States. Each era represents efforts at a nationwide scale to realize comprehensive integrated watershed management. In examining these eras we focus on the conceptions of the physical and institutional settings of watersheds, governance problems emerging and existing in watersheds, and means of addressing those problems. The fundamental political issues were similar across eras; however, how they were addressed differed, except in two important respects. The preferred mode of decision making was consensus, and plan implementation was voluntary. Such organizations are relatively weak and unable to realize integrated management. In the end, we argue that searching for the best way to manage a watershed is not as productive as examining how watershed management unfolds in practice and why.

In Chapter 3 we consider issues that are fundamental to politics. Those issues involve determining whose interests count in decision making, the strengths and limitations of different forms of decision making, and different institutional mechanisms for holding decision makers accountable. All of these issues require people to make choices that result in governing structures that are not always fair, that sometimes neglect important interests, and that are imperfectly accountable. These choices and their implications may sometimes be so difficult and divisive that people have trouble devising institutional arrangements that would allow them to better govern watersheds. We illustrate the difficult political choices that public officials and citizens must make in a case study of the Platte River watershed.

Beginning with Chapter 4, we construct a political economy analysis of watershed governance. In that chapter we assume that people are boundedly rational and make choices and take actions in a world of transaction costs. Bounded rationality and transaction costs place constraints on the types and structures of institutions and organizations that people can devise in order to achieve shared goals and desired outcomes. In order to cope with transaction costs, boundedly rational individuals construct multiple, overlapping organizations that separately address limited goals and problems that would otherwise be impossible to achieve in a single, watershed-scale, general-purpose government. We illustrate our theoretical argument by applying it to a case study of the Columbia River Basin and the Northwest Power Planning Council.

In Chapter 5, we refine and further flesh out the analysis from Chapter 4 by focusing on values. In constructing governing arrangements, people must not only make trade-offs among transaction costs but also make trade-offs among efficiency, fairness, and responsiveness. Organizations that may be responsive to their members' needs may not be very efficient in producing desired goods and services, for instance. We use the local public economies literature to explain how devising a diverse set of organizations with different missions and at different scales in a watershed may allow people to realize differing and sometimes conflicting values. The San Gabriel River watershed in Southern California provides us with the empirical example to apply our argument.

In Chapter 6, we turn to issues of scale and the relationships among governments and organizations at different levels extending from those that are wholly within the watershed to those that extend beyond the watershed. One of the sustained critiques of polycentric governance is that it is fragmented and uncoordinated. We use the literature on federalism to explore cross-scale linkages and relationships among governments, and how those relationships can be structured to support coordinated and complementary efforts on the one hand, and how they can dampen and discourage destructive competition among governments on the other. We use the Delaware River Basin Compact to further explore these issues.

In the concluding chapter, we review lessons from the case studies that were used in the previous chapters. In the similarities and differences among the cases, we find examples of the broader themes raised in the other chapters and in the book overall—the complex dynamics of water resources and human communities, the multiple scales and goals that are relevant to water resources management, the limited ability of people to address multiple scales and goals through integrated decision making and organizations, and the rationale underpinning the multi-organizational, polycentric, even federal style of governance seen in watersheds in the United States. Although it can seem a less congenial and rational place than the ideal integrated and scientifically managed watershed, the political watershed has the modest virtues of being real and attainable. Embracing the political watershed is thus not so much a matter of ardor as of acceptance.

NOTE

1. We illustrate our arguments using several case studies of watershed management efforts. They include the Santa Ana and San Gabriel watersheds, the Platte River Basin, the Columbia River Basin, and the Delaware River Basin. We selected these case studies for a variety of reasons. First, although these watersheds are located across the United States from the northeast to the northwest and points in between, policy makers and citizens, no matter their location, were confronted with similar types of political challenges in governing watersheds. Second, the cases represent watersheds at a variety of scales, from those wholly within a state to those spanning numerous states. Third, the cases represent a variety of issues and challenges, from endangered species, to water quality, to drought management, to water supply, to habitat protection, and so on. Fourth, the cases represent a variety of institutional arrangements. The Platte River Cooperative Agreement is an administrative agreement among Colorado, Nebraska, Wyoming, and the U.S. Department of the Interior to recover endangered species. The Northwest Power Planning Council was created by an act of Congress to integrate power planning and development and fish and wildlife protection on the Columbia River. The Delaware River Basin Compact was the first interstate river compact to include the federal government as an official member. And the two watersheds within California represent local entities assembling watershed governance from the ground up.

Embracing
Watershed
Politics

1

Complex Landscapes

WATERSHEDS AND INSTITUTIONS

Every watershed has a physical landscape—a complex terrain of landforms, water resources, vegetation, animals and their habitats, human beings and the structures they have built. Every watershed has an institutional landscape, too—a complex but largely invisible terrain of rules and organizations that govern and affect human choices about the making of decisions, the use of resources, and the relationships of people to nature and one another. This book considers the institutional landscapes of watersheds, not in isolation from the physical world but in connection to it, recognizing that watersheds have both physical and institutional landscapes.

Institutions are political—not in the limited sense of Democratic or Republican, conservative or liberal, or labor and so forth, but in the larger sense of involving choices about who may participate in decision making and how, what actions can be taken and under what conditions, what issues fall into which jurisdictions, and how and by whom current actions and past decisions can be examined, critiqued, and modified. Political scientists are fond of saying that politics is about power, which is true. "Power," however, is not necessarily employed in this book as the word is used in ordinary conversation, where it makes many people uncomfortable and suspicious. Politics is about power because politics is about who can do what and when and under what conditions and under what limitations. In that broad sense, politics is about all of us in all the landscapes of our lives. Politics is even part of how people relate to nature, and so it matters in watersheds.

Without question the institutional arrangements in most watersheds in the United States are complicated. There are nongovernmental components (associations, councils, trusts, etc.) as well as governmental ones. The governmental components are themselves complex, being embedded in a political system that features the separation and sharing of powers as well as federalism and its web of intergovernmental relations. Furthermore, neither governmental nor nongovernmental elements of the institutional landscapes of watersheds remain fixed for long. Organizations and the rules governing them change. Like their physical counterparts, institutional landscapes shift, sometimes almost imperceptibly and at other times dramatically.

How, then, to understand the institutional as well as the physical landscapes of watersheds? Much has been gained recently in understanding the physical dimensions of watersheds and other ecosystems by viewing them as complex adaptive systems. That view can be applied also to understanding institutions relating to watersheds. First we will summarize briefly the view of watersheds as complex adaptive systems, and later in the chapter we will connect that view to the understanding of institutions and what these complexities mean for organizing the management of watersheds.

COMPLEX ADAPTIVE SYSTEMS I: ECOSYSTEMS AND WATERSHEDS

The idea and study of complex adaptive systems emerged in connection with rising interest in ecosystems. A significant literature on ecosystems as complex adaptive systems has developed (Holling 1978, 1986; Walters 1986;

Lee 1993; Grumbine 1995; Gunderson, Holling, and Light 1995; Stanley 1995; Carpenter 1996; Haueber 1996; Lackey 1998; Levin 1999; Low et al. 2003). The concept of complex adaptive systems is encapsulated elegantly by Low and colleagues (2003, 103), who write that "complex adaptive systems are composed of a large number of active elements whose rich pattern of interactions produce emergent properties which are not easy to predict by analyzing the separate system components." The connection between complex adaptive systems and ecosystems is that ecosystems also consist of multiple interacting elements, the conditions and behavior of which change over time in ways that can yield unpredictable shifts and outcomes.

Ecosystems, Watersheds, and Complex Adaptive Systems

The literature on ecosystems has had many points of overlap with the literature on watersheds. Watersheds fit the conception of ecosystems noted above and are often employed as examples of ecosystems (but this is not a one-to-one match since a watershed may be home to multiple ecosystems and a given ecosystem could contain more than one watershed). Although the ecosystem literature is not entirely about watersheds and not all contributions to the watershed literature include a discussion of ecosystems, each concept has contributed to the development of thought about the other.

When analysts and policy advocates try to apply the ecosystem concept to actual settings, they often use watersheds as examples. Ecosystems can be difficult to identify in a way that finds agreement among many people. As Ruhl (1999, 519) stated provocatively, "The term 'ecosystem' is much like Darwinism and Marxism, in that everybody 'knows' what it means, but after not very much discussion of the subject it turns out everybody's meaning differs to some degree." Barham (2001, 183) connects this difficulty with ecosystems to the attention that watersheds receive: "Setting precise boundaries around an 'ecosystem' has proven difficult. . . . For planners and policymakers in the public arena, the result has often been the adoption of the watershed or catchment basin as an ecosystem proxy. Watersheds, defined by the ridgetops that separate drainage basins from one another, provide ecosystem boundaries that are not as open to dispute in terms of their physical location." Ruhl too advocates watersheds as proxy ecosystems for exactly this reason: "It is imperative . . . that policy decision makers undertake a concerted effort to agree upon a single predominant controlling factor for ecosystem delineation. Of the realistic candidates for that purpose, watersheds stand out as the most suitable [and] most viable planning unit available" (1999, 521–522). With some satisfaction, then, Ruhl observes that "the use of watershed based planning as a foundation for ecosystem protection has grown steadily throughout the 1990s to the point of predominance" (522).[1]

Watersheds thus are not merely examples of ecosystems; they are seen by advocates of ecosystem management as near-substitutes for ecosystems and as an appropriate physical landscape on which to put ecosystem management concepts into practice.[2] Although we will have much more to say about the matter of watershed boundaries, it suffices here to note that the topographical manifestation of watersheds has pragmatically reinforced the conceptual link that already existed between watersheds and ecosystems.

Accordingly, the literature on complex adaptive systems may be seen as relating not only to the broad category of ecosystems but also to watersheds as ecosystems. Writing about watershed management projects in language compatible with the language of complex adaptive systems, Kerr and Chung (2001, 539) observe:

> Spatial interlinkages related to the flow of water are inherent in watersheds. Water pollution upstream may harm downstream uses of land and water, while conservation measures upstream may benefit downstream use. Coordination or collective action is often required, which may be difficult because benefits and costs are distributed unevenly. . . . Since the extent of such complexity will vary by case, a project that works in one location may not work well in another. Subtleties in underlying differences can make it difficult for researchers to understand causal relationships governing project success.

The closing sentences of that observation underscore the roles of uncertainty and surprise that characterize complex adaptive systems, including ecosystems and watersheds. The difficulties of predicting watershed or ecosystem behavior are not merely a matter of intellectual curiosity: they are vitally connected with the challenges of management. We therefore turn to the topic of uncertainty and its relation to the understanding of complex adaptive systems such as watersheds and ecosystems.

Complex Adaptive Systems and Scientific Uncertainty

"Uncertainty" is used in several contexts. Often it signifies a lack of complete information (insufficient data). Sometimes it means the presence of "noise" or risk due to the stochastic, or randomly varying, nature of some process. Underlying these standard or familiar definitions of "uncertainty" is an "assumption that we know or believe we know the basic cause-and-effect relationships—the system structure—in . . . whatever we are studying" (Wilson 2002a, 333), we just lack enough data to be more precise and accurate, or our predictions contain errors because of variability in the system. We might call these kinds of uncertainty "system uncertainty."

By contrast, "scientific uncertainty" involves more than a lack of reliable data. Scientific uncertainty involves a lack of knowledge or absence of agreement among scientists about the nature of the resource system and its dynamic behavior, about what elements of the system are the best indicators of its overall condition, and about what changes in those indicators mean. By themselves, more or better data would not necessarily diminish or eliminate this kind of uncertainty.

Because the problem of scientific uncertainty has been discussed in the context of complex adaptive systems, people may think uncertainty is the same as complexity. As Emery Roe has usefully and clearly articulated, however, uncertainty and complexity are distinct. "Issues are uncertain when causal processes are unclear or not easily understood. Issues are complex when they are more numerous, varied, and interrelated than before" (2001, 111). Seeing this distinction helps avoid a misconception that underlies standard modern (often engineering-based) approaches to environmental management; namely, that the accumulation and integration of additional information will allow us to understand the complex processes better, which will reduce the uncertainty. Roe continues:

> It is commonly said that, since ecosystems are complex, many of their causal processes are uncertain, which in turn requires learning more about these processes if the ecosystems are to be managed more optimally. Hence, the implicit notion is that complexity leads to uncertainty, which, if reduced, would allow for more complete management. . . . As ecologists remind us, it is also true that a deal of uncertainty remains, even after scaling down from the ecosystem to the site, where presumably the components are fewer if not less varied or interrelated. (2001, 111–112)

Uncertainty of this type is particularly troublesome for understanding or managing complex adaptive systems (Holling 1986; Lee 1993). Ecologists have struggled for some time with the challenge of being able to describe and predict ecosystem processes (Jordan and Miller 1996). With respect to the management of ecosystems in particular, Carpenter (1996, 118–119) observed that "a host of scientific uncertainties about the behavior of ecosystems under anthropogenic and natural perturbations continue to frustrate statistically reliable biophysical measurements and ecologic understanding."

Wilson (2002a) contrasts the Newtonian world of controllable non-adaptive systems with the ecosystem world of complex adaptive systems. A problem with the latter is the pervasiveness of nonlinear relationships, making it difficult to trace the particular course of movement of one object in the system and, from that information, predict the reactions of other objects. In Carpenter's words, "Almost all real systems, and certainly all ecosystems, are nonlinear (small change in a parameter can lead to a sudden large change in behavior)" (1996: 134). Past approaches to managing ecosystems have typically assumed "relatively complete (if stochastic) biological knowledge operating in a Newtonian world" (Wilson 2002a, 342). Actual experiences (more bluntly, observed failures) in ecosystem management suggest that the Newtonian view does not apply readily to complex adaptive systems, and perhaps not at all.

Why is scientific uncertainty of this sort particularly associated with complex adaptive systems such as ecosystems? The literature on uncertainty in ecosystem management discusses at least three distinct but interrelated reasons: differential rates of change among system components, scale differences, and disturbance processes.

The factors that make up a complex adaptive system such as an ecosystem typically change at different rates. Species populations within the system change at different rates. A host of ambient environmental conditions connected with ecosystem conditions (e.g., temperatures, air or water quality, soil composition) change at different rates. Anthropogenic impacts on the system (e.g., harvesting behavior or technologies) change at different rates as well. In and of themselves, differential rates of change present a complexity problem rather than an uncertainty problem. The uncertainty problem arises from the fact that in a complex adaptive system, elements respond to changes in other elements so the differential rates of change yield alterations that are not mere linear extensions of trends. Relationships and effects are contingent. "State shifts" occur among system elements as the configuration of other elements changes. Thus, a one-degree temperature change in combination with one configuration of ambient conditions produces little effect on a species population, but an additional degree of temperature change occurring in combination with a slightly different configuration of other ambient conditions produces a crash or a surge in that population, which triggers shifts in other populations, and so on.

Interactions and effects also occur across space and time scales in complex adaptive systems. Problems are not always fixed to specific areas, nor can a change of condition in one portion of the system be automatically "scaled up" to predict system-level effects (Gunderson, Holling, and Light 1995, 531). In part because of heterogeneities within resource systems, the effects of a condition change in one part of the system may be relatively insulated from the rest, whereas the same change occurring in a different part of the system translates more directly into system-level transformations. Discontinuities in the relationships between system elements and system effects make it "very difficult to extrapolate results from one scale—frequently the plot scale—to higher spatial scales" (Swallow, Johnson, and Meinzen-Dick 2001, 451).

Furthermore, particularly in the ecosystem context, system processes are interrupted by disturbances. In biological systems, these include effects of infestation and disease, natural disasters, and shifts in the ambient environment. In the case of natural resources, such as water, disturbance processes clearly include droughts and flooding but also climate change and even landscape transformations caused by events such as earthquakes (which in addition to effects such as tidal waves have been known to alter the courses of surface streams and the geologic features of aquifers). Disturbance processes introduce an element of uncertainty—not merely complexity—into the challenge of resource management. Combined with the natural variability of the resource systems themselves, uncertainty allows for "unknowable responses, or true surprises [due to] the self-organizing, ever-changing character of ecosystems and their response to perturbations that are unprecedented (at least to the current ecosystems)" (Carpenter 1996, 120). Rapid and adverse changes may occur for reasons that are unforeseen and poorly understood.

Natural variability, the presence of disturbance processes, and the lack of understanding of the causal processes underlying the resource system mean that additional data—the usual solution recommended by standard modern approaches—will not always or necessarily reduce the uncertainty or make the problem more tractable. Jordan and Miller (1996, 110–115), for example, describe some ecological situations (e.g., the Everglades, Yellowstone National Park) where, in theory, "further study and data collection should help improve ecological predictions, but where in practice, improvement in predictions is unlikely."

In complex adaptive systems, there are changes in conditions that are not trends, but there are also changes in conditions that *are* trends. Among other things, scientific uncertainty with respect to complex adaptive systems means that we lack a clear way of knowing which changes are trends and which are not.

Despite all this, ecosystems are not completely beyond our comprehension and their behavior is not entirely random. But our ability to see and understand the order and predictability of complex adaptive systems is different: we can observe patterns that repeat within systems over time even though they do not repeat in exactly the same way each time, and sometimes system or subsystem conditions shift in ways that set into motion a different set of patterns. Understanding those patterns is useful science. Still, that science may allow us only to make qualitative and conditional predictions rather than quantitative and precise ones (Wilson 2002a, 335), and that affects our decision making.

Elements and Implications of Uncertainty in Contemporary Watershed Management

Much of the literature on complex adaptive systems has dealt with biological ecosystems, such as fisheries, that "may be uniquely vulnerable ecosystems" (Carpenter 1996, 132). Professionals engaged in the study or management of non-biological resource systems, such as watersheds, may wonder whether the difficulties described above affect them too. There are two reasons for answering yes: (1) the frequent use of watersheds as near-substitutes for ecosystems, as noted already, and (2) some recent and emerging issues in watershed management. These issues are the incorporation of species and habitat protection into water management, the river restoration movement, and the greater recognition of human-environment interactions.

The promotion of integrated watershed management has meant incorporating the protection of biological systems (most often riparian and aquatic species and their habitat) into the set of management priorities and tasks. Some of this has been a response to, and embracing of, the integrated water resources management literature's advocacy of drawing together all water uses. Some of it has been forced by public policy—such as species listings under the Endangered Species Act, habitat protections stipulated in natural resource conservation plans, site-specific litigation—which is part of the institutional landscape in almost any watershed. By whatever means, ecosystem considerations have become a more common element of watershed management.

The incorporation of ecosystem protection and/or recovery tasks necessitates some replacement of engineering-based hydraulic water management with a broader, less precise, and less controlled approach. Borrowing Wilson's language, integrated watershed management exchanges the Newtonian world, where water was understood as a physical mass—to be captured, diverted, stored, and delivered in particular quantities with required qualities at specific locations and times—for a new and more uncertain world in which water retains all those physical properties and yet is a habitat at the same time.

Over the same period that ecosystem elements have been integrated into watershed management, other ideas have emerged and been adopted concerning the physical dimensions of the water resource. Stream and river channel restoration—ripping out concrete channels and returning streams to meandering courses with soft beds—is being undertaken in a number of locations and advocated in others as a means of re-balancing flood control objectives with other considerations, such as reduced runoff and erosion and enhanced groundwater replenishment. Restoration efforts also have been supported by communities rediscovering the economic and aesthetic value of waterfronts and stream courses. Wetlands are being constructed and restored to achieve in situ water quality improvement in preference to standard divert-and-treat methods. As sound as these water resources management ideas are, they do reduce the engineering-based control of the physical water resources in a watershed.

Of course, the presence of human societies in the watershed adds another complex adaptive system component. Carl Walters, the early advocate of adaptive ecosystem management, pointed out that focusing resource management on the physical landscape alone overlooks "the socioeconomic dynamics that are never completely controlled by management activities." The presence of human beings in the watershed creates the potential for unexpected dynamic responses as well. Walters (1986, 2) analogized the human-environment relationship to a "predator-prey" relationship and cautioned us not to limit our attention to the "prey," "because the predators don't sit still either." (In the watershed context, see also Swallow, Johnson, and Meinzen-Dick 2001.)

The trends described above can be illustrated using a particular watershed. In March 2003, a federal district court ordered the U.S. Fish and Wildlife Service to designate a critical habitat protection area within the Santa Ana River watershed in Southern California for the Santa Ana sucker, a fish native to several Southern California streams but now found in dramatically diminished numbers and in only a few stretches of the river. The Santa Ana sucker has been a subject of considerable attention within the watershed in recent years (especially since its designation as a threatened species in 2000), and a recovery plan was developed through the collaborative efforts of the Santa Ana Watershed Project Authority and the Orange County Water District in consultation with the U.S. Fish and Wildlife Service and the California Department of Fish and Game.

The Santa Ana River watershed is already an intensively managed resource system, with dense networks of physical facilities and institutional arrangements developed to address flood control, wastewater treatment and disposal, drinking water quality, the allocation of water supplies across subwatershed basins and communities, restraint of water use and assignment of water rights to individuals and organizations, and the conjunctive management of surface water flows and storage with groundwater yields and storage. In large measure, those management approaches reflect an intent to minimize variability of flows and reduce vulnerability to familiar (though unpredictable) hazards of drought and flooding by maximizing the ability of agencies to store, release, move, and deliver water within the watershed while maintaining water quality parameters within limits needed to serve human consumptive purposes.

The additional feature of managing the watershed in order to avert the elimination of the sucker, and even try to restore the sucker population, is affecting the watershed management challenge in ways not yet fully calculable. Urbanization of the watershed landscape and changes in river

*The Santa Ana
River Basin.*

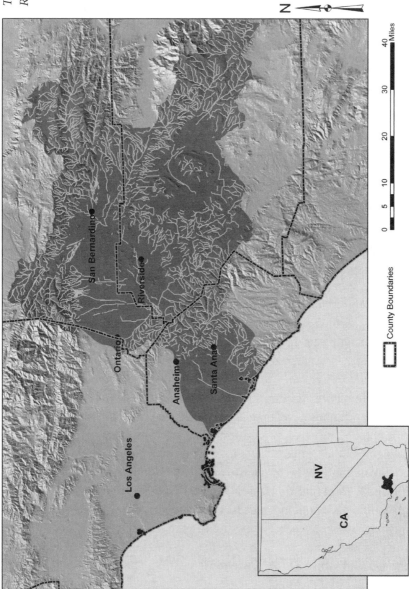

water quality are the most frequently mentioned causes of the decline in the sucker population and its current threatened status, but in fact no one is certain whether those factors alone have caused the decline, or whether and how they have interacted with other causes. After all, the sucker has vanished from all other urbanized Southern California streams in which it was once found but has remained in certain stretches of the Santa Ana River, which is sometimes described as the most urbanized watershed in North America. In addition to puzzling over why the sucker population continues to decline in the Santa Ana (and, just as intriguing, why it has survived there despite dying out everywhere else), scientists have yet to determine exactly what water quality and riverbed conditions the sucker requires in order for its decline to be arrested and its recovery to begin.

No consensus exists, therefore, on what the indicators or targets for sucker recovery policy should be. What is almost certain is that the water quality and river condition indicators and targets that will be appropriate for the goal of sucker protection and recovery will differ from those indicators and targets that have been developed and used for the flood control, conjunctive management, wastewater treatment and disposal, and drinking water protection practices in the watershed to date. Combining the policies and practices for species and habitat protection with the current and long-standing watershed management practices will add complexity but also increase uncertainty, that is, greater prospects in the watershed for surprise, for unanticipated population shifts and other state changes.

The Santa Ana River watershed has been changing from a hydraulically managed watershed, where the emphasis was on physical control of the water, to a watershed that also has to be managed as an ecosystem, with all that implies in relation to complex adaptive systems. Even though the particular circumstances of each watershed are distinct, in some respects the case of the Santa Ana River illustrates how watershed management has been changing in the United States and elsewhere for the past couple of decades, adding not only to its complexity but also to its uncertainty. These changes raise important questions. How do these changes relate to decision making within and about watersheds? What kinds of institutional arrangements might people use when attempting to manage and protect watersheds as complex adaptive systems? Answers to these questions require us to consider the uses and properties of institutions.

COMPLEX ADAPTIVE SYSTEMS II: WATERSHEDS AND INSTITUTIONS

The view of watersheds as ecosystems—and of both as complex adaptive systems—has substantial and far-reaching implications for decision making. Those implications have ramifications of their own for the kinds of organizational and governance structures human beings devise and employ. Most importantly, the creation and adaptation of decision-making arrangements bring the kinds of political considerations we mentioned at the outset into the heart of the watershed.

Uncertainty, Complexity, and Decision Making

Complex adaptive systems pose a substantial challenge to twentieth-century engineering-based decision models, such as rational-comprehensive decision making. With its requirements for specification of objectives, evaluation of alternatives, and selection of the alternative that achieves the desired objectives at least cost, rational-comprehensive decision making presumes that underlying system processes and cause-effect relationships are understood. In the face of scientific uncertainty, this presumption may not hold.

Not only does rational-comprehensive decision making (or any comparable approach) require predictions of the system-level effects of alternative actions, it also requires agreement on which indicators are valuable for assessing system-level effects. As already noted, however, scientific uncertainty implies a lack of consensus over what elements of a system are the best indicators of its overall condition. It also implies a lack of agreement on what a change in one or more of those indicators at any particular time signifies. Under such circumstances, the selection of policy "targets" becomes especially unclear, and so does our understanding of how alternative policy actions relate to those targets. Furthermore, if resource managers focus their attention on a few selected policy targets, undesired and undesirable results may occur as other elements of the system shift in unanticipated ways (Carpenter 1996, 147).

In addition to challenging our ability to pursue comprehensive decision making generally, scientific uncertainty poses problems for the role of science itself in policy making. When underlying system structures are known (or believed to be known), remaining uncertainties result from lack of data or from insufficient specification of the stochastic processes at work. Those kinds of uncertainty can be reduced by directing scientific effort toward the problem, with a justified confidence that science will facilitate or improve comprehensive decision making. But in the protection and management of complex adaptive systems, where our uncertainty concerns the underlying system processes themselves and we do not entirely understand the basic relationships that make up the system or drive its transformations over time, both the scientific problem and the policy problem are not just harder—they are different.

Wilson (2002b) points out that much of environmental policy making and management (at least in the United States) is performed through the delegation of authority to regulatory agencies. This is done with the underlying presumptions that science will be employed in regulatory decision making and will also be available to check or correct regulatory errors. In light of uncertainty about system processes and cause-effect relationships, science loses some ability to provide policy makers with specific predictions through its usual methods of professional criticism and consensus development (Jordan and Miller 1996, 97, 108) or to check the mistaken exercise of policy-making authority.

This change in the role of science and in its relationship to decision making poses two serious problems. One is that science's eroded role in guiding decision making opens the field for the use of regulatory instruments to serve other political and economic purposes, including the ability of some interests to use scientific uncertainty as an excuse to delay action (Caldwell 1996, 394; Wilson 2002b, 6). Another problem is "error proneness," as scientific uncertainty expands the prospects for regulatory decision making to produce misguided or maladaptive policies.

In the effort to manage and protect complex adaptive systems, failure to recognize and acknowledge uncertainty can magnify the error proneness of management efforts. Low and colleagues (2003) have observed that decision makers tend to underestimate the uncertainty and overestimate their understanding of problems. This makes error correction even more important. Error correction depends upon error detection, and as Caldwell (1996, 404) points out, "Uncertainty unacknowledged is a factor that handicaps efforts to discover whether error has occurred." Wilson (2002a, 332) adds that failure to acknowledge uncertainty, or pretending it does not exist, lessens our ability to develop and implement management practices that have learning elements deliberately designed into them, exposing us to more "catastrophic" errors that can result from an incomplete understanding of the resource system.

With this catalog of difficulties, it is important to insert a caveat. Just as uncertainty does not mean that natural systems behave randomly or are incomprehensible, uncertainty additionally does not mean that scientific research on natural systems is useless to policy makers. Despite its limits and imprecision, science concerning complex adaptive systems such as ecosystems has value. Even this limited vision "is far more valuable than a sense that the future is totally unpredictable and not subject to influence" (Caldwell 1996, 400).

Instead, the limited vision that is possible with respect to complex adaptive systems "is the basis for forward-looking adaptive management" (Wilson 2002a, 339; see also Walters 1986). In light of the contemporary tasks of watershed management (integrating species and habitat protection, restoring streams and constructing wetlands, and taking more seriously the dynamic and adaptive human communities within watersheds), adaptive management warrants consideration in the watershed context. Lee (1993) has argued this point effectively. (See also Swallow, Johnson, and Meinzen-Dick 2001, 451.)

Adaptive management has high information requirements too, of course, but of a different sort than those required by a comprehensive decision-making model. In the management of complex adaptive natural resource systems, the general predictions underlying policy actions must be closely and continually compared with observations of the resource system. Furthermore, this close monitoring and comparison will need to be done at multiple scales and with respect to multiple indicators.

Arrangements are therefore needed that will enhance information collection, error detection, and the opportunities for adaptation. Further advances are difficult if scientists and policy makers do not engage questions of organization—such as what institutional arrangements may be able to counteract unacknowledged uncertainty, closely check general predictions against actual physical conditions, and "substitute for the hoped for role of science" (Wilson 2002b, 6) as a check on decision making. These questions about organizing decision making are of great interest to political scientists and others in the social sciences. The physical complexity of watersheds, and certain characteristics of people and institutions, however, will frustrate any effort to identify and follow a best way to organize the governance and management of watersheds.

Decision Making, Governance, and Institutions

Noting the inapplicability of the Newtonian paradigm to complex adaptive systems, resource economist James Wilson has stated the implications broadly but emphatically: "We have wrongly characterized our knowledge of the natural environment and, consequently, have viewed the uncertainty and learning problem as if it were a typical engineering problem. As a result, we have created institutions and administrative procedures ill adapted to a solution of the conservation problem" (2002a, 351). Those ill-adapted institutions and procedures include efforts at comprehensive regulation through integrated agencies.

In the preceding section, we discussed the applicability of comprehensive decision making in complex adaptive systems. Some readers may have perceived this to be a kind of straw-man approach, since the model of rational-comprehensive decision making has been subject to so many thorough critiques in the latter half of the twentieth century that it appears to have few remaining advocates. Yet, we believe the desire for comprehensive decision making still holds significant attraction in the literature on integrated ecosystem management and integrated watershed management, even if obliquely. Comprehensive decision making is implicitly associated with the notion of an integrated decision-making apparatus. Advocacy of integrated decision-making organizations, such as unified river basin agencies or watershed authorities, is often justified in terms of the need for comprehensive decision making that encompasses all affected interests and addresses all interrelated resources within a watershed or ecosystem.

Other authors whose work we find useful for anyone contemplating the complexities of watershed management are skeptical of using an integrated decision-making organization for the management of complex adaptive systems. Their rationale appears to comprise three common themes—recognizing scale diversity, reducing error proneness and promoting learning, and overcoming limitations on human information-processing capabilities.

In complex adaptive natural resource systems, organizations of multiple scales may be useful to gather and exchange information about resource conditions (e.g., Berkes 2006). Gunderson and colleagues (2002, 262) observed that "resource systems that have been sustained over long time periods increase resilience by managing processes at multiple scales." Such arrangements are likely to include relatively small local organizations that can focus on particular locations or subsystems, thereby approaching a complex adaptive system as being modular or decomposable, made up of smaller albeit interrelated elements (Simon 2005).

The argument for smaller local organizations attending to particular subsystems does not presume that uncertainty disappears at small scales— in other words, it is not a "complexity" argument in disguise. Rather, it acknowledges that complex systems are usually composed of subsystems, and subsystem levels are more nearly amenable to close monitoring and to the development of improved understanding of patterns of activity. Especially for geographically extensive systems with multiple and heterogeneous local subsystems, smaller organizations are likely to be better suited to monitoring and managing those local conditions, noticing changes rapidly, and notifying others of them. Of course, small local arrangements are not all that is needed (Costanza et al. 2001, 8). Overlapping organizations at larger scales can serve as forums for communication across local subsystems and as a check on local structures that behave in ways detrimental to other subsystems (Low et al. 2003, 106).

A second theme is the importance of reducing error proneness and promoting learning, an effort that may be aided by some degree of duplication and redundancy of organizational structures. In the kind of adaptive management that has been advocated for complex adaptive systems like ecosystems (Walther 1987; Lee 1993), the real key to progress is learning. Learning is likely to be maximized and accelerated in a diversified institutional setting where multiple interventions are being undertaken and compared within the same system simultaneously with opportunities to exchange results and observe others' experiences (Wilson 2002a, 345–347; see also Holling 1986; Ostrom 2005).

We noted in the preceding section the danger of limited attention to a few selected indicators of system conditions, but this is exactly what a comprehensive organization trying to monitor and manage a complex system will be prone to do. Polycentric structures of overlapping organizations— networks, federal systems, and other multiple-organization arrangements— are one organizational option that can increase the likelihood of checks on the persistent maintenance of maladaptive policies and practices. Such safeguards might exist within a single comprehensive resource management agency as well, but a century of organizational behavior research suggests that more nearly centralized organizations are susceptible internally to distortions of information and communications that can allow poor policies and practices to persist for undesirably long periods.

It may therefore be especially important to avoid organizational integration where information distortions and losses may cascade into dramatically erroneous decisions and actions. Low and colleagues (2003, 103) cite Landau's (1969, 354) critique of integrated hierarchical structures: "Organization systems of this sort are a form of administrative brinksmanship. They are extraordinary gambles. When one bulb goes, everything goes." More directly in relation to the ecosystem management challenge, Wilson (2002a, 347) adds: "Perhaps the only reasonable institutional response to this problem is to maintain independent (nearly decomposable) local governing units. Their ability to probe different policies and to remain skeptical without great cost is one of the few ways there might be to constrain persistent maladaptive policies, or viewed more positively, to assure the continuing evolution of the institution." Ludwig, Walker, and Holling (2002, 23) agree, employing the metaphor of a raft (representing institutions for managing ecological systems) withstanding unexpected or unpredictable waves or shifts of weight (representing the changeability of complex adaptive systems):

> Another possible response to disturbance might be to restructure the raft itself. If it were constructed of several loosely coupled subunits, then excessive weighting or a strong disturbance might flip one part of the system but leave the rest intact. Such a structure might not require as much vigilance as the single raft, and it might be able to withstand a greater variety of external disturbances. On the other hand, if the bindings that link the subunits become stiff, then the structure may become brittle and, hence, more prone to failure.

The concept of decomposability and the metaphor of the single raft bring us to a third theme, which is the limited information-processing and decision-making capabilities of single systems, a theme that applies concepts such as bounded rationality (a characteristic of individuals) to organizations. The problems of limited understanding and cognition may not be solved merely by the often-prescribed organizational fix of "scale matching," that is, creating organizations to correspond with the boundaries of a complex resource system (Gunderson, Holling, and Light 1995, 531). Herbert Simon (1996, 178) advocated "nearly decomposable" rather than centralized organizational structures to deal with complex systems, balancing the need for close interaction and specialized expertise against the need for communication and integration. Because of the complexity of systems and the uncertainty associated with large numbers of adaptive components in multiple relationships that vary continuously and discontinuously over space and time, "no one individual or group could hope to adequately address the learning problem" (Wilson 2002a, 341). With particular reference to managing water resources, Gilbert White (1998, 25) has reflected that "truly comprehensive analysis" is challenging. He maintains that "the constraints of professional training and competence, the limits of organizational authority and the ignorance of the outcomes of many actions, past and future, impede the balanced formulation of all potential solutions and options in dealing with such aims as efficient use of water for food production, or for transportation, or for ecosystem health."[3]

Managing and protecting complex adaptive resource systems are challenging enough even if human uses, interests, and values are not at stake. The addition of human beings brings an additional set of multiple scales (Lebel, Garden, and Imamura 2005; Berkes 2006). Just as the physical dimensions of a watershed or other ecosystem appear at different scales, so do the multiple human uses and behaviors that occur in a watershed, complicating further the tasks of decision making, monitoring, and enforcement (Adger, Brown, and Tompkins 2006). Once we contemplate individuals and communities interacting with the natural resources within a watershed, the "how" questions about decision-making arrangements are compounded by "for whom" questions (Hooghe and Marks 2003, 241). When we think about how to make decisions and for whom, boundary issues (e.g., who belongs "in" and who does not) are not only complex but take on added intensity. The implications of these complexities for water resources management were conveyed well by Blatter and Ingram (2000, 464):

> Common goods such as water are multidimensional (drinking, shipping, power generation, irrigation, recreation, ecological functions, economic development, et al.). For this reason, [a single principle] does not work very well as an instrument to define the one best size of a geographical area for governing water. Instead of applying economic criteria or

markets to the task of creating boundaries, a political process of trading values off against one another must take place. It is necessary to determine the most important function(s), create the government structure(s) corresponding to these functions, and find some mechanisms to deal with the interdependencies and spillovers between these functions.

As countless authors have observed, human communities have rarely been organized to coincide with ecosystem boundaries or even the more visible boundaries of watersheds. As a result, "achieving coordination often requires *reconciling* socially defined boundaries like villages with physically defined boundaries like catchments. . . . Organizing collective action along strict hydrological boundaries is difficult" (Swallow et al. 2004, 1, emphasis added). The communities that matter most to people, and where established decision-making structures already exist, typically are either smaller than the watershed or straddle watershed boundaries. Neither form of organization is likely to displace the other, and reconciling them adds further complexity to the task of institutional design.

Neither a single decision-making principle nor a single organization at a single scale is therefore likely to suffice. As a result, institutional arrangements suited to decision making about complex adaptive systems may themselves need to exhibit some features of complexity and adaptability (Berkes 2006). The cases we describe in this book provide a few illustrations of how complex institutional arrangements have evolved in watershed contexts in the United States.

In the uncertain world of complex social and ecological systems, institutional richness may be preferable to institutional neatness. Multi-scale institutional arrangements, including small and local organizations linked horizontally with each other and vertically with larger-scale organizations, may be able to achieve (1) close monitoring of local (subsystem) conditions; (2) representation of diverse interests associated with different physical components of the system as a whole; (3) error correction when management practices undertaken with respect to one element of the system create unanticipated negative effects elsewhere in the system; and (4) opportunities to communicate and exchange information across subsystem elements and to discuss subsystem interactions and system-wide conditions without necessarily trying to manage all parts of the system with a comprehensive organization.

In a useful article distilling decades of theoretical development about the organization of governing jurisdictions, Hooghe and Marks (2003) have distinguished between "Type I" and "Type II" governance structures. Type I structures are *constituency-defined multi-service or multi-function organizations*—that is, general-purpose governments, such as a municipality, that encompass a defined group of residents and provide an array of services (police patrol, trash pickup, parks, and so on). In the United States, Type I governance structures typically exhibit the familiar branches of government, with a legislative body, a judicial forum, and an executive capability. Type I structures may be nested—cities and counties encompassed by states, states within a nation, even regional and international organizations arranged in meso or supra levels—but they do not overlap horizontally (i.e., the territory and population of one city or state does not extend into those of another city or state), and each Type I jurisdiction is a multi-function mechanism for governance within its own domain. Type I governmental structures facilitate bargaining and trade-off decisions (e.g., whether to devote more resources this year to policing or to street maintenance).

Type II governmental structures are *functionally* defined, and their boundaries vary from one service or function to another. Type II structures are established at whatever geographical scale may be suited to funding and delivering a particular service—hence, a library district or regional transportation authority covering a metropolitan area, an irrigation district serving a collection of farmers, and so forth. These structures do not necessarily feature legislative, executive, and judicial branches—rarely in the United States do Type II structures have a judicial function, for example. Type II governments can and often do overlap horizontally, and many may operate in the same location because their functional responsibilities are distinct (Hooghe and Marks 2003, 236–240). They have the advantages of flexibility in jurisdictional size and specialization of function. On the other hand, because of that specialization they are usually not engaged in trade-offs or bargaining among service priorities. Conflicts involving their policies or performance generally must be resolved in the judicial systems associated with Type I structures.

Although these governance forms "represent very different ways of organizing political life," Hooghe and Marks point out the compatibility and complementarity of the two:

Type I governance reflects a simple design principle: Maximize the fit between the scale of a jurisdiction and the optimal scale of public good provision while minimizing interjurisdictional coordination by (a) creating inclusive jurisdictions that internalize most relevant externalities and (b) limiting the number of jurisdictional levels.

Type II governance also limits the transaction costs of interjurisdictional coordination, but it does so in a fundamentally different way, by splicing public good provision into a large number of functionally discrete jurisdictions. (2003, 241)

In most (perhaps all) watersheds or other ecosystems, combinations of Type I and Type II governance structures will exist, additional ones may be created and existing ones modified, and the relationships among them adjusted from time to time. Overall, then, the institutional arrangements in a watershed may themselves be thought of as a kind of complex adaptive system (perhaps more accurately, a complex adaptable system) composed of multiple elements at differing scales and operating both independently and interdependently.

For reasons already noted—scale differences, disturbance processes, the importance of reducing error proneness while increasing error detection and learning—complex adaptable systems of institutions may be well-suited to the management and protection of complex adaptive natural resource systems. Swallow and colleagues (2004, 2) have reached such a conclusion with particular reference to the management of watersheds:

The scale at which the physical environment is optimally managed may not correspond to any one decision-making body in a community. In that case, collective action within existing institutions or through the creation of new institutions becomes critical for managing watershed resources. Decisionmaking does not have to be embedded in only one body at one level, but different management responsibilities can be devolved to different bodies. These options vary according to the size of the watershed, the populations occupying the watershed, and how the scale and interaction of resource flows affect people.

Returning to our watershed example, fortunately for Santa Ana River water users and for the Santa Ana sucker, that watershed already has developed a network of institutional arrangements that includes relatively small sub-watershed communities and agencies and some watershed-scale rules and organizations. Water quality is already monitored intensively in the watershed, and river flows are managed under rules that were agreed to by upstream and downstream organizations and made part of a stipulated judgment enforceable in court. The two largest groundwater basins in the watershed are governed by court judgments and by agencies that try to manage the basins' storage capacity while balancing annual yields with demands. There are numerous special water districts and municipal water and wastewater utilities in the watershed that look out for their local concerns and monitor their conditions. There are five larger water districts that acquire supplemental supplies for those smaller districts and utilities and engage in several planning and resource management activities. And there have been two forums for watershed-scale communication and coordinated action—the Santa Ana Watershed Project Authority mentioned earlier, which is a joint-powers agency of five water districts within the watershed, and the Santa Ana River Watershed Group, a nongovernmental entity convening organized stakeholders and interested individuals to discuss issues of concern within the watershed and seek cooperative solutions.

There is in the Santa Ana River watershed a rich mix of Type I and Type II organizations. Rather than impeding effective management, this institutional richness may aid policy making in the Santa Ana River watershed as its components adapt to the complex tasks of managing for ecosystem survival and stability.

COMPLEXITY, CHOICE, AND POLITICS

Institutional arrangements are human creations; they are matters of choice. There have been recommendations to try to match organizational boundaries to watershed boundaries and create comprehensive jurisdictions since the time of John Wesley Powell. Relatively few examples of comprehensive watershed or river basin agencies exist, however, and even where watershed-scale entities have been created, they are intricately interconnected with smaller and larger jurisdictions of both Type I and Type II characteristics.

The impressive empirical analysis reported by Lubell and colleagues (2002) found that collective action in America's watersheds is being attempted and accomplished instead through literally thousands of "watershed partnerships" and network-style structures involving numerous private and public organizations of varied sizes and functions. Why is this so? Why have we so rarely chosen to create comprehensive organizations based on hydrological boundaries? Is the partnership approach merely the path of least resistance? Are watershed stakeholders relying on these complex, polycentric arrangements because it is too difficult to create the comprehensive watershed agencies that, deep down, they really would prefer?

The final report of the National Watershed Forum, held in 2001, is interesting in this regard. After three days of meetings, the hundreds of participants—some of the Americans most intensively involved in watershed management—generated several pages of "key recommendations and findings." These included five pages of findings and recommendations concerning watershed governance, organization, and participation. Not one of those findings or recommendations called for the establishment of more centralized and comprehensive watershed-scale agencies. Rather, most of the recommendations emphasized maintaining a variety of organizations at a variety of scales while enhancing their exchange of information and coordination of activities (National Watershed Forum 2001, 15–17, 37–38).[4] Indeed, the participants recommended the establishment of even smaller, sub-watershed "stream teams" to monitor local conditions more closely. Altogether, the forum's findings and recommendations displayed an intriguing congruence with the analysis in this chapter about the relationship between nature's complex adaptive systems and humans' complex adaptable systems. Even individuals closely involved in and committed to watershed management did not recommend the creation of integrated watershed agencies, and they were inclined toward greater organizational complexity rather than less.

Nature has many complex adaptive systems—watersheds, continents, lakes and seas, prairies, tropics, wildlife habitats, and so forth, from the micro to the intercontinental scale. Human beings still have to choose how (and around what) to organize their activities. We do not get to just let nature do the choosing for us, pointing to topographical boundaries or other physical features as a way of defining communities of interest and crafting decision-making processes. Despite their importance and visibility, it is not clear why watersheds or river basins should have primacy in the shaping of human decision-making systems.

Furthermore, even if people chose to organize decision-making arrangements around watersheds, that would hardly be the end of the choices to be made. For good or ill, nature's watershed boundaries have been altered by human actions in many cases all over the planet. So even if we zero in on watersheds and river basins, we still have to choose how to bound the decision-making arrangements. Is Los Angeles in the Owens Valley or not (not *should* it be, but *is* it)? Is Denver in the Colorado River basin or not? Are San Diegans in the Sacramento River watershed? Should San Franciscans get to participate in decisions about the Hetch Hetchy Valley? One could pose an almost endless list of such questions, and they are not idle ones—they must be addressed in order for watershed management to proceed. As Walther (1987, 443) observed, the effort to establish integrated resource management in any location confronts "institutional environments that are ruled by culture, politics, and tradition and that have a history." Communities of interest already exist in and for many watersheds, and topographical features do not go far in telling us who they are or how they should be involved.

Who is "in" and who is "out"? Who gets to decide what we are going to do? How do we decide? These are political questions, and they are inescapable no matter what natural boundaries we try to employ and no matter what organizational structures we try to construct. Michael McGinnis (1999, 499) sagely observed: "Watershed policymaking is both a scientific and a political enterprise. The mythical separation of politics from administration will not suffice in watershed policymaking because of the diverse values held by policymakers and the scientific uncertainty endemic to physical sciences in this policy area." In the chapters that follow, we will explore the politics of watershed policy making and management as it has evolved in the United States (primarily), with particular attention to the choices that have been made about how to connect institutional landscapes with physical ones.

Complex systems of institutional arrangements can appear chaotic to some observers—and understandably so. The institutional landscape of a watershed, like its physical and ecological landscape, can be and often is complicated. Although there are ways to make sense of that landscape (such as the distinction between Type I and Type II structures), we understand that institutional arrangements in a watershed are likely to be complicated and, on initial view, even confusing. Institutional complexity in a watershed can be viewed as an intrinsically undesirable trait to be minimized, an intrinsically desirable trait to be maximized, or a phenomenon that is intrinsically neither good nor bad but a fact of life and where the extent and kinds of complexity will vary from one watershed to another. Those variations to greater or lesser degree will reflect the physical, biological, and human terrain. In some ways they may work well to reduce environmental damage and achieve sustainable human-environment relationships, and in other ways, poorly. Because our goal is not to prescribe a best way to organize water resource management, we do not have a model organization to hold up before our readers.

Instead, we proceed to the remaining chapters, operating from the premise that there may be sound reasons for institutional complexity in the watershed, but the questions of what institutional forms that complexity takes and how institutional arrangements operate are empirical ones. They are also political questions—it is not only a physical watershed, it is a political one too. Questions about the institutional landscapes of watersheds are questions about the social and political tools people use to govern and manage themselves and their relationships to one another and to nature.

NOTES

1. That observation coincides with Milon, Kiker, and Lee's comment (1998, 37) about the rise in attention to ecosystem management during the same decade: "Within the past decade ecosystem management has become a central theme in state and federal environmental resource management and a powerful issue in environmental policy debates. A recent survey [Yaffee et al. 1996] showed that more than 600 projects related to ecosystem management are underway around the U.S. Under the Clinton Administration, a high level of federal commitment to an ecosystem management approach has developed despite many obstacles."

2. "A watershed is a complex ecosystem" (Brandes et al. 2005, 87).

3. In a comparison of two cases, for example, Slaughter and Wiener (2007) found that the concentration of decision making in a single agency was less effective in detecting and solving complex problems in a watershed than polycentric arrangements in another one.

4. Participants even suggested *replacing* watershed coordination teams organized at the federal and regional scale with ones organized along state boundaries (National Watershed Forum 2001, 37). Since almost no state boundaries in the United States match watershed boundaries, this recommendation is a notable departure from the watershed management literature's emphasis on superseding traditional political jurisdictions in favor of regional-scale entities.

2

Watersheds, Politics, and Institutions

PAST AND PRESENT ASSESSMENTS

The principal thing that experience suggests is that pragmatism is the best policy: it leads to the most effective regional organizations.

MARTHA DERTHICK (1974, 226)

The research and policy literature on watershed management expanded rapidly from the late 1980s to the present, as has the number of initiatives undertaken in the United States to create watershed-based efforts at resource management. The concept has shown great appeal among academics and policy makers (Walther 1987, 439; Milon, Kiker, and Lee 1998, 37) and has spawned considerable activity (Kraft et al. 1999; Lubell et al. 2002).[1] It is not an exaggeration to characterize this combination of publications and actions as a "watershed movement." The "movement" is not so much a formally organized effort as a burgeoning literature of academic and practitioner recommendations to organize water resources management around watersheds rather than around the discrete water resources—streams, lakes, aquifers, wetlands—they contain (e.g., Harkins and Baggs 1987; U.S. EPA 1991; Bates et al. 1993; Doppelt et al. 1993; Goldfarb 1994; Naiman 1994; U.S. Coastal America Organization 1994; MacKenzie 1996; Newsom 1997; Gregg et al. 1998; Hinchcliffe, Thompson, and Pretty 1998).

Despite the rapid increase in the number of writings about watershed management over the past twenty years, the idea of watersheds (or river basins) as the appropriate units for resource planning and management is hardly new.[2] Each of the different water management eras Sabatier, Weible, and Ficker (2005) identify, from the beginning of the twentieth century to the present day, includes an emphasis on watershed management. The watershed is considered the appropriate scale for organizing water resource management because all water sources and uses within a watershed are interrelated. Not only are the water resources in a watershed related to one another, but they are intertwined with land and other natural resources. Accordingly, the uses and conditions of any natural resource within a watershed may (and very likely will) affect the others (see Pereira 1989, xv–xvi; Bates et al. 1993, 93; Kerr and Chung 2001, 539).

As Derthick (1974) has noted, the scale issue has a close counterpart: that of coordination. Given the variety of water and land resources within a watershed and the multitude of uses made of them, what would be the best way to coordinate and manage such complexity? The answer, according to a number of scholars (see Holmes 1972; Goldfarb 1994; Adler 1995; Kenney 1999; Sabatier, Weible, and Ficker 2005), varies by time period or era. Each era is characterized by a distinct management approach or suite of approaches, which at the time was argued to be the best approach, especially compared to the approaches that preceded it. As time passed, that best approach became subject to sustained criticism for its failure to address new and pressing issues or realize cherished values, and was eventually transformed, with new approaches promising to address the many pitfalls of the previous era. For instance, Sabatier, Weible, and Ficker (2005, 36–38) argue that the "Environmental Era" replaced the "New Deal Era" as environmental values came to the forefront along with distrust of federal water agencies and their commitment to realizing environmental values. In turn, the "Environmental Era" has been replaced by the "Watershed Collaborative Era" as citizens and local organizations attempt to gain greater access to decision making and efforts center on holistic management approaches.

Thus, one common way of reading the historical record is as a constant search for the best way to govern watersheds, with the one best way redefined as circumstances change.[3] Each era does not represent a sweeping away of previous management approaches as much as a grafting of new strategies and policies to old ones. The current era, the "Watershed Collaborative Era," has certainly not seen the abolition of the specialized federal and state water quality agencies and programs that emerged during the "Environmental Era," just as new agencies and programs in the "Environmental Era" did not replace the large federal water development agencies that blossomed during the "New Deal Era."

Even though each era is characterized by a new best approach to managing watersheds, that new best approach is often a blend of idealism and pragmatism. Idealism appears in the consistent desire to create a comprehensive, integrated watershed authority, and pragmatism emerges by settling for the approach that is feasible at the time and comes closest to the ideal. In 1972, for example, the National Water Commission recognized the desirable qualities of a federal corporation like the Tennessee Valley Authority (TVA), but realized that such a form was unlikely to be adopted, and instead recommended the federal-interstate compact commission as the preferred form for water resources planning and management (National Water Commission 1973). It was the most comprehensive and integrated form thought politically feasible.[4]

This chapter examines this underlying set of political issues during three eras: 1933 to 1965, or roughly from the New Deal to the formal creation of river basin commissions with the passage of the 1965 Water Resources Act; 1965 to 1980, the period covering the creation, operation, and dissolution of the river basin commissions; and the 1980s to the present, covering the emergence of the watershed movement and the creation of many different types and forms of watershed collaboratives.[5] The overall period covered, from 1933 to 2007, encompasses the major concerted efforts to realize in practice comprehensive, integrated watershed management in the United States.[6] We choose to focus on three broad time periods for clarity and economy. We wish to explore how elected officials, public managers, and water users were regularly confronted with and repeatedly addressed a variety of political concerns. Whether examining a single era or multiple eras, the constancy of political issues remains.[7]

Although there are distinctions among the eras, in this chapter we focus on their underlying unity. That unity centers on politics: they all share a common set of political issues and concerns that policy makers and citizens alike struggled with. The common political challenges include the motivation for pursuing integrated management; the scale at which water should be managed; who should participate in decision making; what values, benefits, and goals are to be realized; and the obstacles that limit achievement of comprehensive, integrated watershed management.[8] Explicitly drawing out the common and enduring political issues and questions turns attention away from the search for the one best way to manage watersheds and instead centers it on the ever-present challenges of realizing a range of conflicting and compatible goals and values in the context of complex adaptive and adaptable biophysical and social systems. The eras are characterized by a common set of political issues; they differ in the answers adopted.

As Goldfarb (1994) has noted, the contemporary watershed movement has its roots in the unified river basin management movement. That movement unfolded over much of the twentieth century, ending in the 1980s when the Reagan administration dissolved the Title II river basin commissions. The centerpiece of unified river basin management had been basin-wide programs with multipurpose storage projects. Prior to 1965, the president, Congress, and federal water agencies experimented with different forms of river basin planning and management, typically centering on a board or council, located either in the Executive Office of the President or among cabinet departments, and individual ad hoc river basin planning committees. These experiments had little direction from the president or Congress, except for the short-lived National Planning Board, and they were criticized for failing to realize comprehensive management plans or tight coordination among federal agencies (Derthick 1974, 136).

The Title II river basin commissions changed that. Created by the 1965 Water Resources Act, the commissions were composed of representatives from federal water agencies and the states located in the respective basins. Each commission was granted a director with an independent budget and a small staff to oversee day-to-day operations and support planning activities. The commissions were guided and supported by the Water Resources Council, located in the Executive Office of the President. Overall, commissions lagged in their planning activities; many produced general studies of their river basins, but few produced detailed documents identifying specific water projects and none was able to prioritize projects (Derthick 1974).

By the time most of the river basin commissions were formed and operational—in the mid-1970s—their time had perhaps already passed. In 1980, Wengart wrote: "As a major governing concept in water policy, integrated river basin development is in trouble. In the public mind, it is being superseded by concerns for environmental improvement, protection of ecosystems, and the complex problems of water pollution control" (1981, 9). Citizens were increasingly concerned with environmental values not readily captured by the kinds of traditional management activities and traditional water projects on which the commissions focused.[9]

Even though the commissions were dissolved at the beginning of President Reagan's first term, the federal government, state and local governments, and citizens did not abandon the hope of "watershed" management. Attention turned during the 1980s from more ambitious (from an engineering and financial standpoint) river basin projects to a more modest "best management practices" approach, and from the federal government to state and local governments as the locus of watershed planning, with federal agencies such as the EPA strongly encouraging such activity as an important approach for addressing non-point sources of water pollution.

Thus, within each era some ideas and approaches prevailed, which provide points of contrast even as we recognize the consistency of certain political issues and challenges. For each era we can characterize dominant ideas and directions concerning (1) why integrated management should be pursued; (2) at what scale and (3) by what means water resource activities would best be organized in order to achieve integrated management; and (d) the goals and values to be achieved via integrated management. We begin with the issues and ideas motivating efforts toward integrated management.

MOTIVATION FOR INTEGRATED MANAGEMENT

A given across all three time periods is that the diverse dimensions of a watershed, natural and human, are intertwined, making integrated management necessary. What differed over time were the types of watershed interactions emphasized and in need of integration and coordination. Earlier periods focused on the interaction among water development projects within a single basin. Later periods focused on the interaction among the biophysical dimensions of a watershed and how to minimize the environmental impacts of water development projects and other destructive uses of river basins.

River Basin Development, 1933 to 1965

The beginning of this era was marked by the Great Depression and an unprecedented federal response to realize economic recovery on a national scale. One of the centerpieces of economic recovery was massive investment in public works, particularly large-scale, multipurpose water projects. Not only did the construction of the projects provide jobs for thousands of people, but improved navigation, flood control, water for irrigation, and hydropower spurred economic development and recovery. The major federal water development agencies, the Army Corps of Engineers and the Bureau of Reclamation, had been established decades earlier and, over time, had been authorized to engage in the planning for and construction of multipurpose projects (Holmes 1972). What was missing were plans for comprehensive river basin development and institutional mechanisms to ensure that the water development programs of the federal agencies fit within and were coordinated with the comprehensive plans. As Holmes (1972, 13) argued, "New Deal planners were very intent on avoiding the accusation of maintaining a pork barrel composed of ill-planned, jerry-rigged projects." Integration was vital for ensuring that the many water projects to be built were complementary and coordinated, promoting comprehensive development of the waters of a river basin. At the scale of the project, multiple uses required coordination; at the scale of the river basin, multiple projects needed coordination. Thus, integration, as discussed below, centered on experimenting with a variety of coordinating mechanisms, all of which were found wanting, providing considerable justification for new forms of river basin management.

River Basin Commissions, 1965 to 1980

By the 1950s, criticism of river basin development identified a lack of both comprehensiveness and integration. The lack of comprehensiveness centered on two issues. First, most multipurpose water projects provided water, electricity, and flood control for irrigation districts and rural communities. Increasingly, representatives of urban areas demanded that a larger range of uses be incorporated within existing and new projects, particularly municipal and industrial water supplies and recreational opportunities. Second, most of the benefits of multipurpose water projects were directed to a narrow range of constituents—farmers and residents of rural areas, primarily located in the western United States. Critics of the federal water agencies wanted to see the benefits of water projects extended more equitably across the United States and include uses valued by urban residents.

The lack of integration also centered on two issues. First, critics argued that the Army Corps of Engineers and the Bureau of Reclamation managed to avoid close coordination and integration of their water activities. On a number of occasions the two agencies engaged in public squabbles over who was to plan and develop particular projects in a river basin, such as the King and Kern Rivers development, in which the Army Corps of Engineers won out over the Bureau of Reclamation (Knott and Miller 1987, 154). In other river basins, public conflicts were avoided by the two agencies' carving up of different portions of a river basin. For instance, the bureau was allowed to build irrigation projects in the upper Missouri River Basin, and the corps was allowed to build several main-stem dams to regulate flooding and provide navigation improvements (Knott and Miller 1987, 154). Second, the lack of integration extended to who was allowed to participate in river basin planning and development. Many federal agencies with interests in a river basin—such as the National Park Service, the U.S. Forest Service, and the Federal Power Commission, among others—resented the Army Corps of Engineers' domination of decision making (Derthick 1974, 137). They were joined by states and localities who also sought more active participation in river basin planning (Holmes 1972). In the end, Congress and the president attempted to respond to these criticisms through the passage of the Water Resources Act of 1965, which attempted to centralize and integrate river basin management to an extent never seen before or since, as will be discussed below.[10]

The Watershed Movement, 1980s to 2007

The motivation for integration over the past two decades is distinctly different from the previous two eras. No longer were public officials, managers, and water users faced with the challenges of integrating new multipurpose projects into river basins. Rather, they were confronted with integrating a host of environmental values into water management. Thus, the focus moved from attending to interactions among multiple-use projects across a river basin to the environmental effects of the previous seventy-five years of river basin development.

The lack of comprehensiveness and integration of water management activities in previous eras was largely blamed for many environmental problems. The lack of coordination among water resource programs established a relatively lax management setting in which agricultural, industrial, and other forms of development flourished to the detriment of the condition of the nation's water resources (McGinnis 1999, 497). Furthermore, environmental water programs—such as contamination prevention and remediation, wetlands protection, and species preservation—were adopted in an incremental and uncoordinated fashion that failed to recognize the connections among these programs and the water problems they were meant to address (Mann 1993; Behrman 1993, 11; U.S. EPA 1995, iii). Finally, the incremental and uncoordinated programs created barriers to citizen participation. The presence of multiple governmental units and agencies operating within any given watershed, each carrying out some program or policy that affected only one portion of the overall water environment therein, discouraged active public participation. Citizens found it difficult to know or learn where to find information, whom to contact or how, and how to participate effectively (Nakamura and Born 1993, 812). In the end, "the need to integrate across traditional program areas (e.g., flood control, wastewater, land use) and across levels of government (federal, state, tribal, local) [led] natural resource management toward a watershed approach" (U.S. EPA 1995, iii).

Across each of the eras, the need for comprehensive, integrated management was clearly articulated, whether its purpose was to coordinate river basin development or environmental restoration. What was also clear to advocates in each era was that management in previous eras was "fragmented," "piecemeal," "inadequate," "myopic" (Milon, Kiker, and Lee 1998, 38), and the like. Thus, within each era, the promise to finally realize comprehensive, integrated management was made.

SCALE OF ORGANIZATION

Across each of the eras, elected officials, public managers, and citizens supported management at the river basin or watershed scale. As the Environmental Protection Agency has noted, however, a watershed can mean many things, because "watersheds occur on a range of scales from the subnational or regional (e.g., the Mississippi watershed) down to local scale (e.g., the watershed of a small creek)" (U.S. EPA, 1995, 1–8). How a given watershed was defined, and therefore the scale at which watershed management should occur, differed over time, ranging from a regional meaning of watershed to a local meaning of watershed, as described by the EPA.

River Basin Development, 1933 to 1965

The scale of comprehensive integrated management during the era of river basin development was distinctly regional. Early plans and projects were developed for the main stems of major rivers—such as the Tennessee, the Colorado, the Columbia, the Mississippi, and the Missouri. Comprehensive planning centered on the main stems of rivers, with little attention paid to tributaries. A prime example of a main-stem focus is the development of the Colorado River. From the Colorado River Compact, an agreement initially adopted by the seven basin states in 1922 that allocated the water of the river among the states, to the Boulder Canyon Act of 1928, in which Congress directed the Bureau of Reclamation to build and operate the major projects that would allow the basin states to realize the compact's water allocations, to later acts and developments, attention centered almost exclusively on the main stem, leaving the basin states to do what they would with the Colorado's tributaries. Only in the last decade, as severe drought has persisted over much of the basin and as tension has risen among the basin states over one another's water use, have some states attempted to extend basin-wide management to include tributaries.

River Basin Commissions, 1965 to 1980

As suggested in the previous section on motivation for integration, this era began with formal efforts to engage in more comprehensive and integrated management efforts than what occurred during the era that preceded it; this period includes a more comprehensive view of scale. The emphasis remains on regional river systems, as river basin commissions are organized around such systems, but planning and management extend to encompass tributaries (Holmes 1979). The planning process established by the 1965 Water Resources Act included Type I plans that provided a broad overview of the water resources, problems, and challenges occurring within the basin and Type II plans that addressed specific problems and solutions all within the context of Type I plans. The specific problems and solutions often focused on tributaries (Derthick 1974). For instance, the Ohio River Commission, as part of its Type II planning process, included instream flow studies on different tributaries, such as the Monongahela River (Holmes 1979; Joering 1980).

The Monongahela River, although certainly a tributary of the Ohio River, is a major river in its own right, highlighting the flexibility of the terms "watershed" and "river basin." In practice, the boundaries of river basin commissions were hydrologically based, but whether they encompassed a single major river and its tributaries or multiple rivers with no single major drainage largely depended on the desires of the states that formed the commissions. Contrast the Ohio River Commission with the New England River Basin Commission, which encompassed twenty-eight river basins, sixteen of which were either interstate or international (McCrea 1980). Thus, efforts were directed toward comprehensive planning at scales that encompassed major rivers and their primary tributaries.

The Watershed Movement, 1980s to 2007

Sabatier, Weible, and Ficker (2005) argue that the primary distinguishing feature of the Watershed Collaborative Era is the active participation of a wide variety of stakeholders, most notably local citizens, in watershed governance. We would add one more—the scale of organization.[11] Watershed collaboratives are organized at the scale of streams or segments of smaller rivers. They are intrastate and, in a number of instances, intracounty. These streams and stream/river segments were rarely, if ever, considered in the previous two eras; they were simply too small. They are now the focus of active planning and management. Watershed management at the local scale is viewed favorably because it is ecologically meaningful, and "the health of an entire watershed can be measured by the health of the aquatic ecosystem" (McGinnis 1999, 498).

The scope of management during the first two eras centered on regional-level watersheds with some attention paid to major tributaries. Once the federal government removed itself from river basin planning and plan funding, such efforts faltered. Watershed planning and management fell to the states, where its scope and purpose substantially changed. Local watershed planning focused on addressing serious water quality degradation of streams and stream segments.

ORGANIZATIONAL BASICS

How to organize planning and management of watersheds was constantly debated and experimented with over time. Who should participate, how should decisions be made, and how will implementation occur? Although organizational form varied, decision-making and implementation processes remained remarkably similar.

River Basin Development, 1933 to 1965

The organization of comprehensive integrated river basin management consisted of variations on two distinct forms. The first, more centralized form, which lasted for a decade, was a congressionally created or funded organization under the direct control of the president. The second, voluntary form consisted of a committee of cabinet-level secretaries and their staffs who consulted with each other on river basin activities by agencies within their departments.

The centralized form, which at different times in its incarnation was named the National Planning Board, the National Resources Board, and the National Resources Committee, assisted the president in planning the many public works projects (water projects being the most important) for recovering and rebuilding the economy (Holmes 1972). Over the ten years of its existence, from 1933 to 1943, its membership varied. Sometimes it only consisted of three "non-aligned" experts from the business or university sectors who were trusted to give the president sound advice. At other times it consisted of three "non-aligned" experts and the secretaries of war, interior, agriculture, and labor (Holmes 1972, 14–18). Much of its water project planning was conducted by a water committee whose makeup reflected that of the board's, three "non-aligned" experts and representatives from the Departments of War, Interior, Agriculture, and Labor. The committee developed river basin plans and studies of water projects for congressional adoption based on basins as entire units. This committee, in turn, relied on regional committees to investigate and develop plans and proposals for specific river basins. The regional committees usually consisted of field representatives of the major federal agencies, although on occasion, state representatives were invited to participate (Holmes 1972).

The National Resources Board exercised a variety of powers that supported its efforts at comprehensive, integrated river basin development. It had the authority to review and revise the six-year construction plans of the Army Corps of Engineers and the Bureau of Reclamation, and it eventually gained authority in conjunction with the Bureau of the Budget to review the two agencies' budgets and to prioritize projects slated for construction. Overall, the board exercised powers that allowed the president to provide some direction and coherency to river basin development (Holmes 1972, 18).[12]

In 1943, Congress abolished the National Resources Planning Board (Holmes 1972, 22). The secretaries of agriculture, interior, and war and the head of the Federal Power Commission voluntarily created the Federal Interagency River Basin Committee as a coordinating mechanism, although it had no central executive supervision. It largely mimicked the structure of its predecessor with a central committee and numerous regional committees organized around specific river basins. And, like its predecessor, participants were federal government political appointees, public managers, and experts, although state representatives were occasionally invited to participate. Unlike its predecessor, however, it could not develop integrated river basin plans, nor could it settle conflicts among different federal agencies. These limitations were largely due to its decision rule, consensus, and the manner in which the regional river basin committees were organized. Consensus decision making led to logrolling, with federal agencies carving up river basins and basin projects among themselves. Furthermore, regional committees were convened only after agencies had created project proposals or after a single agency invested extensively in planning for a particular river basin, making any type of integrated planning across agencies virtually impossible (Holmes 1972, 38). Not surprisingly, both the national and regional committees were regularly criticized for their inability to coordinate the activities of all federal agencies in a coherent manner. Also, federal agencies resented the dominating position of the Army Corps of Engineers on many of the regional committees, and states actively pressed for a more central role (Derthick 1974, 135–137).

River Basin Commissions, 1965 to 1980

By the end of the 1950s, reports of study commissions were piling up, all urging greater centralization and coordination of river basin development (Holmes 1972). One particular report, issued by the Senate Select Committee on National Water Resources in 1960, spurred action. It envisioned a looming water crisis that could only be adequately addressed through centralized and coordinated river basin planning and by the expansion of existing agency programs to encompass water quality, municipal and industrial water supplies, recreation, and fish and wildlife protection and enhancement (Holmes 1972, 41).

The 1965 Water Resources Act attempted to realize more centralized and coordinated river basin planning and management largely by formalizing the practices of the previous era. The act created a Water Resources Council located in the Executive Office of the President. As a cabinet-level council, the council consisted of the secretaries of agriculture, army, interior, HEW, and the Federal Power Commission, with the secretary of the interior as the chair. Its primary tasks included developing regular national assessments of regional water supply and demand, establishing river basin commissions, reviewing river basin plans, and developing more standards for project evaluation besides just cost-benefit analyses, among others (Holmes 1979, 256). It operated on the basis of consensus.

The Water Resources Council would only agree to the creation of a river basin commission upon a state's request and with the concurrence of all states in the basin. The commissions consisted of a federal representative appointed by the president who oversaw the commission's staff and who was to coordinate the other federal members of the commission. The other federal members consisted of representatives from each federal agency with an interest in the water resources of the basin. Also, each state appointed a representative. In practice, participation in commission activities was much broader. Many commissions created and relied on citizen advisory committees to assist in developing both Type I and Type II plans. The citizen advisory committees consisted of local government officials and representatives from voluntary associations and civic groups.

Commissions were forums for coordination and planning, not independent decision makers. Operating on the basis of consensus, each commission was responsible for preparing and updating comprehensive plans.

No government was responsible for carrying out the plans unless they were adopted by the legislatures of the states (Derthick 1974, 138–140; Holmes 1979, 256). No state ever adopted a commission plan, and, in fact, most commissions labored under the twin burdens of inadequate staff and funding and the rule of consensus to even develop plans. Those commissions that did develop plans largely put together wish lists of projects, unable to prioritize among them (Derthick 1974).

Derthick (1974, 151) argues that states were reluctant partners in joining and participating in commissions. States that did participate did so for defensive reasons, protecting their interests from the adverse actions of either the federal government or other state governments. In other words, commissions were valuable to the extent they provided states with veto power that they otherwise would not have been able to exercise.

The Water Resources Council and the river basin commissions were different from the coordinating committees of the 1950s in some important respects. The commissions' operations were not solely dependent on federal agencies; rather, they had an independent federal representative appointed by the president who was supposed to coordinate the federal agencies and settle conflicts among them. Furthermore, commissions had their own staffs and some funding to carry out their planning work. Also, participation was considerably broader. Federal employees were just one of several groups participating instead of the only participants. State and local officials and citizens participated on commissions and in commission activities. In other respects, the Water Resources Council and the river basin commissions replicated the weaknesses of their predecessors, namely, consensus decision making, which inhibited the development of comprehensive integrated river basin plans and voluntary implementation. Components of plans would be realized only if federal or state agencies agreed to adopt and implement them.[13]

The Watershed Movement, 1980s to 2007

Sabatier, Weible, and Ficker (2005) argue that watershed partnerships and collaboratives arise, in part, as a reaction to three defining characteristics of environmental regulation—the fragmentation of environmental programs across many different agencies, inadequate opportunities for citizens to participate in decision making, and the contentiousness of adversarial legal proceedings. The organizational forms adopted to address the three challenges distinguish collaboratives and partnerships from the committees, councils, and commissions of earlier eras.

Fragmentation and limited participation are addressed through the same mechanism—the identification and inclusion of stakeholders of all types—citizens, nonprofit organizations and civic groups, business associations, government officials at all levels—representing the full range of interests, including water quality, water quantity, land use planning, agricultural policy, wildlife management, and habitat protection and restoration. As the EPA succinctly states: "All parties with a stake in the specific local situation should participate in the analysis of problems and the creation of solutions," and "The actions undertaken should draw on the full range of methods and tools available, integrating them into a coordinated, multiorganization attack on the problems" (U.S. EPA 1991, 1).

Once a broad range of stakeholders is convened, they work with facilitators to elicit and share information about resource conditions; development and its impacts within the watershed; the beliefs, interests, values, and concerns of all participants; possible courses of action to remedy perceived problems; and so forth. The partnerships exercise little formal authority; rather, they provide a forum in which management plans and projects are discussed and revised and eventually turned over to the public-sector agencies for implementation (Sabatier et al. 2005).[14] Accordingly, consensus decision-making processes are supposed to be used to develop goals, plans, and projects. Consensus decision making is viewed much more positively than in previous eras, when it was largely considered a tool used by federal and state agencies and state governments to protect their interests and their turf by vetoing plans and projects. Consensus decision making is the key to successful partnerships because it allows for people from diverse and conflicting backgrounds to sympathetically learn with and from each other and to search and find common ground on which to build collective action.

The movement's impact on policy makers is evident in the considerable amount of activity to promote watershed-scale planning groups, councils, interagency coordination efforts, collaborative watershed partnerships, and the like. At least some, and perhaps most, of this activity has occurred in response to federal and state initiatives (Goldfarb 1994). That activity has been promoted in several ways by the national government, although it is occurring mostly at the regional and substate levels (Gregg et al. 1998;

Nakamura and Born 1993; Sabatier et al. 2005). McGinnis (1999, 498) reports that "17 federal resource agencies and state governments officially have embraced some form of watershed approach" and that more than 200 watershed groups have been created in California alone. Kenney and colleagues (2000) identified 346 watershed partnerships in the western United States. Sabatier and colleagues (2005) believe that total is an undercount as they found 150 in California and 60 in Washington. A survey by Yaffee and colleagues (1996) found more than 600 ecosystem management projects—many of them watershed projects—in the United States.[15]

In one of the few large-n empirical studies of watershed partnerships, Leach and Sabatier (2005) examine the keys to success of partnerships and in so doing reveal strengths and weaknesses of these informal advisory bodies. Leach and Sabatier randomly sampled 47 of 150 identified watershed partnerships in California and 29 of 60 partnerships identified in Washington. They used three measures of success: (1) reaching agreement on issues, goals, implementation actions, and management plans; (2) implementing projects; and (3) perceived effectiveness of partnership actions (Leach and Sabatier 2005, 241). Many of the partnerships reached agreement on issues and goals with fewer developing implementation actions and management plans. Partnerships in which members believed their watersheds were in crisis were more likely to reach agreements, as were partnerships with higher levels of trust, particularly those that were in existence for three years or more. Of the seventy-six partnerships, only thirty-six, or 47 percent, had attempted to implement projects. Project implementation largely depended on funding and the age of the partnership. Finally, partnerships that implemented projects and that were infused with trust and norms of reciprocity were evaluated more positively by their stakeholders (Leach and Sabatier 2005, 250).

Watershed partnerships can point to a number of successes. The inclusiveness of membership and consensus-based decision making result in participants viewing partnerships as highly legitimate forums for engaging in conversations, discussions, and arguments over problems, goals, and solutions to watershed problems. Such legitimacy is built through growing levels of trust, as widely divergent participants come to know one another better and discover common ground. Furthermore, given the extensive participation of federal, state, and local officials,[16] they hold promise of supporting and encouraging intergovernmental coordination. As Lubell and colleagues (2005, 288) note, however, the success of watershed partnerships ultimately rests in results, and at present it is unclear whether collaboratives improve environmental conditions in their watersheds.

Collaborative, and even primarily nongovernmental, watershed arrangements have had achievements. An important question remains regarding whether such achievements represent proof of concept—that is, whether they validate the collaborative partnership as an organizational type—or have been instead due to particular circumstances in certain locations at certain moments. Leaning more toward the latter interpretation, Woolley and McGinnis (1999, 591) surmised:

> If watershed organizations succeed . . . we expect that this will be due
> to several special conditions. First, it could be because the actual range
> of interests or ideas represented in the organization is not very broad
> or deep. This can be the case of some watersheds that are not very large
> or organizations that do not incorporate a very wide range of kinds of
> economic activities. Second, successful cooperation could be because the
> "facts" about the condition of the watershed are clear and uncontested
> and point unambiguously to a set of actions that must be taken, but this
> is rarely the case. Third, it could be because the organization is not, in
> fact, truly voluntary, in the sense that it operates under a more or less
> explicit threat of external intervention by some other governmental level.

Gregg and colleagues (1998) employed more optimistic language but reached a similar substantive conclusion:

> While broad governance issues . . . are at the core of the watershed move-
> ment, most individual watershed initiatives are much more pragmatic,
> concerned with finding and implementing solutions to localized prob-
> lems. In fact, one of the strengths of watershed initiatives is their ability
> to focus their activities directly at the most pressing natural resource
> problems of particular watersheds, often operating outside of normal
> governmental processes and free from the constraints of inflexible man-
> dates or program requirements.

Both sets of authors, then, share the view that successful watershed efforts are often *not* comprehensive, *not* integrated, and *not* legitimized with formal authority but focused on particular concerns that are deemed to require separate and immediate attention.

Even Lubell and colleagues (2005, 289–290), who argue that watershed partnerships represent a quiet revolution in watershed management, are cautious. They state:

> The collaborative approach to watershed management is not a magic bullet that addresses all situations at all times or that will even be appropriate most of the time. . . . [W]e recommend that the collaborative approach to watershed management be used as a method for resolving environmental and socioeconomic problems only when there are high stakes, high social distrust, high governmental distrust, and high knowledge uncertainty. Collaborative approaches are particularly useful for addressing issues that perplex command-and-control institutions, such as nonpoint source pollution and habitat destruction. Collaborative approaches are probably not justified when existing institutions are already adequate.

In other words, watershed partnerships should be used as a last resort for particularly problematic watershed settings.

Most watershed-scale arrangements established thus far have been on what Nakamura and Born (1993, 808) call the "weaker" end of the spectrum: watershed discussion forums, advisory bodies, interagency agreements to collaborate on research, and the like (see Lubell et al. 2002). These typically have little capacity and no authority to take formal decisions, only advisory decisions; implementation largely rests with their governmental partners; and they do not have the ability to sanction entities within the watershed whose behavior fails to conform to plans.

Over the past seventy-five years, comprehensive integrated watershed management efforts have taken a variety of organizational forms, from a national planning agency in the Executive Office of the President and its regional river basin committees to the hundreds of watershed partnerships and collaboratives currently in existence. Not only have organizational forms differed over the eras but so too has participation. During the river basin development era, participation was largely restricted to experts in the federal agencies in charge of planning and building water projects. Participation broadened over time to eventually include state officials formally seated on river basin commissions, and with watershed partnerships, participation was actively sought for all stakeholders representing a wide variety of interests. Although organization forms and participation varied, decision rules and implementation processes did not. The dominant decision rule was consensus, and plan implementation was largely voluntary, relying on the support and cooperation of individual government agencies. In the earlier eras, both practices were singled out as the primary sources of failure of comprehensive integrated management (Derthick 1974; Holmes

1979). Whether consensus decision making and voluntary implementation will also spell failure for many of the watershed partnerships is an open question, although there is nothing distinct about the structure of such partnerships to suggest otherwise.

GOALS AND VALUES OF INTEGRATION

The goals, benefits, and values to be realized by engaging in comprehensive, integrated watershed management varied over each time period, particularly biophysical goals. Biophysical goals center on uses made of a watershed, such as water for irrigation, protection from flooding, low-flow regulation to protect water quality, or the protection of rich riparian habitat. In contrast, overall political and socioeconomic goals and values tended to remain stable, varying by the emphasis placed on the different dimensions of the overall goal. For example, protecting and enhancing democracy runs throughout each era, but what democracy means and how it should be realized changes over time.

River Basin Development, 1933 to 1965

The biophysical goals of this era were clear-cut. Large-scale water projects were to realize either singly or in combination the goals of navigation, flood control, irrigation water, and hydropower. These biophysical goals were stepping-stones to accomplishing pressing political and socioeconomic goals. Large-scale public works projects were the keys for realizing both short-term and long-term goals. In the short term, such projects put many people to work and pulled the nation out of the Great Depression. In the long term, water projects supported regional economic development— plentiful and inexpensive power and water spurred investment in agriculture and industry and flood control protected such investments.

Furthermore, multipurpose water projects realized economy and efficiency through several avenues. Multipurpose water projects avoided water waste by capturing and storing river flows and floodwaters that would otherwise be lost to the oceans. And, only those projects that were efficient, or cost-effective, were built. The federal water agencies were required to subject their plans and projects to cost-benefit analyses.

More than efficiency and economy, though, multipurpose water projects protected and enhanced democracy by ensuring an equitable distribution of benefits. Navigation projects and improvements and publicly owned and operated power projects protected the average citizen from railroad and power trusts, granting them ready and affordable access to the transportation and energy they needed to raise and ship their products to markets (Holmes 1972, 13).[17] Overall, large-scale water projects were viewed as examples of how science and technology could be used to transform nature to enhance people's lives (Holmes 1979, 77). In other words, they were socially transformative.

River Basin Commissions, 1965 to 1980

The biophysical goals of this era included all of those from the previous era—navigation, flood control, irrigation water, and hydropower—plus many others, such as municipal and industrial water supplies, water quality protection and enhancement through low-flow regulation and dilution, recreational areas and opportunities, and protection of areas of natural beauty. Like the previous era, these many goals were accomplished primarily, although not exclusively, through the construction and operation of multipurpose water projects and their careful placement (Holmes 1979, 111). These projects were not necessary to spur regional economic development as much as they were needed to respond to rapidly growing urban populations, a booming economy, and increasing demands for recreational opportunities by greater numbers of affluent citizens.[18]

Attempting to realize a wider variety of goals, some of which were in direct conflict, in an economical and efficient manner required something more than cost-benefit analysis. Additional techniques were necessary. The Water Resources Council developed and advocated the use of multiple objective planning processes. River basin objectives would be identified and weighted; multiple alternatives, both structural and nonstructural, for achieving objectives would be identified and evaluated. The best combination of alternatives for achieving the objectives would be selected. The goal was to move beyond justifying each project through cost-benefit analysis and toward achieving the *optimal* use of water and land resources in a basin by selecting the best combination of projects and activities (Holmes 1979, 267).

The optimal development of river basins required greater participation and consent from a broader cross-section of policy makers and citizens. No longer could critical development decisions rest largely in the hands of federal government experts. Participation in decision making was expanded by the composition and functioning of river basin commissions. Notably, state representatives took seats alongside federal representatives as voting members of the commissions. Some commissions also actively relied on a variety of citizen and science advisory groups to provide assistance and input to planning processes (Harrison 1980; Joering 1980). Commission meetings governed by consensus allowed the major state and federal actors to meet together, to share information and problems, to learn about interests and activities, and to eventually agree on specific goals, thereby transforming relations among participants who previously found themselves at odds with one another (Joering 1980). Consensus-building processes supported cooperation and eventually coordination (Joering 1980).

The Watershed Movement, 1980 to 2007

The biophysical goals of the previous eras largely rested on reengineering river systems to meet human needs. The biophysical goals of the watershed movement era are notably different. They entail reengineering human uses to restore and protect the natural processes of watersheds and the environmental services those processes provide. Reclaiming watersheds involves placing water back in the stream, operating dams to mimic the natural hydrographs of rivers, preventing non-point source pollution from degrading water quality, protecting and restoring wetlands, and so forth. These biophysical goals are not only different from those of earlier eras, but they directly challenge them and seek to reverse their effects.

Socioeconomic goals also differ from previous eras. Science replaces economics as the primary guide for action. Basic scientific information about different dimensions of a watershed guides the selection and adoption of projects. Economic decision making, even cost-benefit analysis, is still used to justify projects, but different sorts of projects, such as dismantling dams. Also, environmental services, such as water cleansing and flood control provided by wetlands, are valued and compared to the costs of replacing such services if the wetlands are destroyed.

But most importantly, the partnerships support democracy. Just as multipurpose water projects were viewed as experiments in democracy, enabling people to pursue productive livelihoods and so become active and contributing citizens, watershed partnerships are also viewed as experiments in democracy, but a different type of democracy. Partnerships support the practice of direct democracy, allowing citizens to make decisions that directly affect their lives rather than allowing those decisions to be made by experts. Partnerships engage citizens in self-governance, allowing them to take control of their lives and their communities. In so doing, partnerships also forge a new identity among residents of a watershed. No longer are these residents only citizens of a town or a state; they are citizens of a watershed with all the benefits and responsibilities that entails for ensuring good governance.

Each era differed in the goals and values pursued, but advocates in each era repeatedly pointed to the transformative powers of comprehensive integrated watershed governance.

CONCLUSION

Nationwide efforts toward comprehensive, integrated watershed management in the United States have a long and rich history—from large-scale river basin commissions organized by federal law to watershed partnerships organized around smaller, intrastate watersheds. While engaging in such efforts, policy makers, public managers, interest groups, and citizens have repeatedly struggled with answering fundamental political questions. How watershed management unfolded depended on how the questions were answered.

During the river basin development era, the goals were to stimulate economic activity and regional economic development by investing in large-scale multipurpose projects. Participation in planning, development, and construction was limited to government experts who built and operated the projects. Decision making and plan implementation changed over time. Initially, the president, through the National Resources Committee, created by executive order, exercised some control over the development of integrated river basin plans and negotiated with Congress and the federal water agencies over plan implementation. Once Congress eliminated the National Resources Committee, planning floundered on the consensus decision processes of the Federal Interagency River Basin Committee.

Frustration over the limited goals, limited participation, and weak decision-making processes of the river basin development era eventually led to a search for a better way to manage river basins, and a new comprehensive integrated watershed planning and management effort unfolded. Answers to the political questions incrementally changed. Goals and values changed by adding municipal and industrial water users and recreational enthusiasts as beneficiaries of water projects. Decision-making processes changed by formalizing the processes of the previous era into a formally constituted council in the Executive Office of the President that oversees the river basin planning processes of the river basin commissions. Although the council consists only of cabinet secretaries, participation in planning is extended to states, local governments, and citizens through the constitution of the commissions and their use of citizen advisory committees. Furthermore, a federal representative, independent of the federal water agencies, serving as commission chair and controlling an independent staff and budget, was believed to be sufficient to bring the federal agencies on board in developing and supporting integrated river basin plans. Decision-making processes remained the same, however; at all levels, decisions were by consensus, and implementation of plans was voluntary. In the end, most commissions functioned no better at developing and implementing integrated river basin plans than did their predecessors (Derthick 1974).

The watershed movement emerged not only in reaction to the dismantling of the river basin commissions but primarily in reaction to the excesses and shortcomings of more than a decade of environmental regulation (Sabatier, Weible, and Ficker 2005). In some ways, advocates of watershed planning were justified in their harsh criticism of the status quo approaches to water resources management as "fragmented," "piecemeal," "inadequate," "myopic" (Milon, Kiker, and Lee 1998, 38), and the like. Not only were no formal efforts at comprehensive integrated management occurring among the water development agencies (with the dissolution of the council and commissions), but federal efforts appeared all the more fragmented because of the addition of numerous environmental programs spread across different federal agencies, with no attempt to coordinate them either. Consequently, the search for comprehensive integrated management begins again, but in a distinctly different manner.

The answers to the political questions are not just incrementally different, as was the case in the transition between the river basin development and river basin commission eras, but qualitatively different. The overarching goal is ecosystem health to be achieved by mitigating the effects of decades of watershed development. Achieving ecosystem health is a complex process requiring considerable time and information about such things as non-point pollution sources and the structure and function of ecosystem processes. Not only are the goals qualitatively different but so is participation. Although government employees are primary participants, so too are the many citizens and representatives of different nonprofit and private organizations. However, decision-making and implementation processes remain similar to those from the previous eras. Watershed partnerships constituted of members from a wide variety of interests and walks of life use consensus decision processes to develop common goals and plans, and implementation of those plans is voluntary. Those that succeed are likely to do so in spite of—not because of—such institutional mechanisms. They have the right combination of leadership, constituency support, and resources that allow them to move forward and act.

Historically, efforts at comprehensive integrated watershed management have failed. Not only has there been no one best way, but whatever way was chosen proved neither comprehensive nor integrated. Why? These efforts have all been grounded in relatively weak coordinating mechanisms, which as Derthick (1974, 143) explains, act as a "'forum of peers,' which is less an organization than a meeting place of organizations.... The forum is supposed to foster goodwill, facilitate communication in matters of shared interest, and provide a setting within which mutual adjustments may take place, but it lacks authority or other means for inducing mutual adjustments." Furthermore, particularly in the first two eras, comprehensive integrated planning and management efforts were centrally planned as opposed to responding to pressing needs or problems in particular river basins. Derthick (1974, 227) argues that "for a regional organization to be centrally planned is practically a guarantee that it will be weak and ineffectual." The reasons are many. Centrally planned organizations "imposed" on river basins are not likely to have strong constituent support, nor are they likely to have independent sources of funding. Also, they typically do not interfere with or challenge the authority of existing agencies. For the most part, they simply reflect the interests of their centralized creators, in this case, the president and Congress (Derthick 1974), who were searching for means of coordinating the federal agencies.

Ironically, a somewhat similar argument may be made in relation to many of the watershed partnerships. Their widespread emergence beginning in the late 1980s was not a coincidence. Numerous federal and state agencies viewed partnerships as promising mechanisms to assist them in addressing particularly vexing environmental problems, such as mitigating non-point source pollution and restoring riparian habitats. Congress and state legislatures alike directed agencies to work with local collaboratives, providing technical expertise and funding (Koontz et al. 2004, 8). Although some partnerships are initiated by citizens and others by governments, they all bear the imprint of governments, from statutorily defined environmental goals to participation by government employees. Whether partnerships accomplish integrated management and a more equitable distribution of power among stakeholders will largely be determined by the actions of governments (Koontz et al. 2004, 184).

If most efforts to create comprehensive integrated watershed management end in failure, is watershed management impossible? Our answer to that question is no, and in the remainder of the book we explain why comprehensive integrated watershed management does not occur and how watershed management typically unfolds instead. As we will explore in the following chapters, answers to both questions are based in politics, in the limits to human decision making and transaction costs, and in the political and organizational features of polycentricity.

In the end, we agree with Derthick's conclusion (1974, 230): "[I]n the formation of regional organizations with operating or regulatory functions the *best results* are likely to be achieved *ad hoc*, in response to particular needs that can be shown to require organization on a regional scale and to require it so urgently that the inevitable costs in administrative confusion are worth paying"(emphasis added). In the following chapters, we examine the many different and inevitable choices that people must repeatedly make in governing the different dimensions of watersheds, choices that are likely to keep integrated management elusive.

NOTES

1. The sheer volume of literature on watershed management that has been produced in the last twenty years appears to distinguish this period from previous ones. Derthick (1974), in analyzing regional organizations, including river basin compacts and commissions, theorized at the time that little had been written about the appropriate functions or ideal forms for regional organizations because political scientists have paid scant attention. Much of the recent literature is by political scientists (Lubell et al. 2002; Weber 2003; Koontz et al. 2004; Sabatier et al. 2005).

2. This does not prevent contributors to the literature from having different views of its origin, as the following examples attest. "The concept of watershed-based policymaking is not new. In 1878, John Wesley Powell, head of the U.S. Geological Survey, proposed to Congress that new states in the semiarid West be organized and governed in accordance with the appropriate watershed boundaries rather than straight-line political boundaries. For Powell, the watershed was the ideal medium for a new form of self-governance" (McGinnis 1999, 498; see also Bates et al. 1993, 170–171). "The United States Inland Waterways Commission, appointed in the 1890s to undertake a comprehensive assessment of the nation's interior water resources, 'reported to Congress in 1908 that each river system—from its headwaters in the mountains to its mouth at the coast—is an integrated system and must be treated as such'" (U.S. EPA 1995, 1-1). "The Tennessee Valley Authority became 'an exploratory concept in soil and water management because of its approach to erosion control; "watershed management" was a term first used there and an agency spawned by the approach—the U.S. Soil Conservation Service—was to have a major influence throughout the world'" (Newson 1997, 97). "Since the 1970s, there has been dramatic and imaginative experimentation with new approaches to water and land resources management at the state and local levels. Many of these efforts have reinvigorated the idea that most water resource problems should be addressed on a watershed basis, and have experimented with ways to achieve a more integrated, or at least better coordinated, resources management" (Nakamura and Born 1993, 807). "One of the most striking and innovative characteristics of water management in the 1990s is a renewed interest in local, generally sub-state watersheds as the preferred administrative unit" (Gregg et al. 1998; see also Kraft et al. 1999, 10).

3. Derthick (1974, 3) characterizes the historical record as a series of intellectual fads and fashions.

4. For additional examples, see *Water Resources Activities in the United States: Reviews of National Water Resources During the Past Fifty Years*, printed for the use of the Senate Select Committee on National Water Resources, 86th Cong., 1 sess., 1959.

5. These eras are a modification of those used by Wengart (1981), who also used three eras, nineteenth century to 1933, 1933 to 1965, and 1965 to 1980. We drop his first time period and add the contemporary period of "watershed collaboratives."

6. Prior to 1933, policy makers and technical experts alike expressed considerable interest in comprehensive river basin development. Not until 1933, however, with the creation of the National Planning Board as part of the National Industrial Recovery Act, was there a formal organization charged with coordinating the activities of the different federal water agencies (Holmes 1972). For instance, in the early 1900s a series of high-profile study commissions, such as the Inland Waterways Commission and the National Waterways Commission, issued reports that pro-

posed the creation of bodies to coordinate the work of the several federal water development agencies (Holmes 1972). Also, prior to 1933, the federal water development agencies were all granted powers to engage in planning for comprehensive river basin development. For instance, the Army Corps of Engineers used the Board of Engineers for Rivers and Harbors to review all river basin studies (Horton 1972). However, there was no single person or agency charged with reviewing and coordinating the plans and construction activities of the different agencies.

7. For an excellent analysis of how political issues were addressed in a variety of ways within a single time period, see Koontz et al. (2004).

8. These criteria are commonly accepted in the political science watershed collaborative literature; see Koontz et al. (2004) and Sabatier, Weible, and Ficker (2005).

9. Derthick (1974, 150) quotes Minnesota's commissioner on the Great Lakes and Souris-Red-Rainy commissions as saying: "The Federal legislation is designed not to create independent state planning bodies to take over planning responsibilities which are too much for Federal agencies to carry. They are designed, instead, to supply a basis of state legitimation for the traditional construction activities of the Federal development agencies, i.e., the Corps of Engineers, the Social Conservation Service, and the Bureau of Reclamation."

10. As Holmes (1972) notes, in a five-year period between 1949 and 1955, several congressional and presidential study commissions and committees all recommended greater centralization and integration of federal water resources planning and development. Most recommended the creation of an agency in the Executive Office of the President to oversee coordination and integration, supplemented with river basin committees.

11. A water historian may disagree with both assertions, because most river basin commissions had citizen advisory committees, some of which were quite active in thwarting major water projects (McCrea 1980), and the Soil Conservation Service actively engaged in soil erosion and flood control "treatments" of small watersheds since the early 1940s (Holmes 1972). In neither instance, however, were citizens or small watersheds defining aspects of an era until recently.

12. It is important not to attribute too much power to the president to guide and control river basin development. As Holmes (1972) argues, Congress was largely hostile to the efforts of the president to control the activities of the federal water agencies. "The Corps planning work was set up so that Congress made decisions regarding not only general policies of water resources development, but also the choice, timing, and extent of Federal investment in individual projects. . . . [Congress] . . . considered the President's attempts to subordinate its planning activities to coordinated executive branch plans and policies to be usurpations of congressional power" (Holmes 1972, 21).

13. As Holmes (1979, 278) noted, "Some contemporary observers considered that the proposed Council would only be another version of Interagency Committee on Water Resources (ICWR), the national interagency committee device of the fifties. They asserted that such committees had proven incapable, because of interagency logrolling, of developing water policies and plans responsive to contemporary problems and majority political demands."

14. Others have summarized partnership processes as follows. The processes entail stakeholder identification and involvement, leading to consensus on goals and an identification of actions to be taken to reach them, followed by assignment of responsibilities among agencies and organizations, producing implementation to be accompanied by monitoring and evaluation (see, e.g., Goldfarb 1994; U.S. EPA 1991, 2; 1995, 1–4). A more detailed set of process prescriptions for statewide oversight and coordination (U.S. EPA 1995) included the establishment of basin management plans using rotating five-year cycles for the completion of planning, modeling, permitting, and monitoring among all the watersheds within a state.

15. Case studies can be found in Nakamura and Born 1993; U.S. EPA 1995; Kenney 1997; Gregg et al. 1998; Heathcote 1998; Hinchcliffe et al. 1998; Milon, Kiker, and Lee 1998; Reimold 1998; Bolte et al. 1999; Kraft et al. 1999; Sabatier and Quinn 1999; Tucker et al. 1999; Kenney 2000; Weber 2003; Koontz et al. 2004. Leach and Pelkey (2001) reviewed the literature on watershed partnerships, noting that most studies involved one or a few cases and, from the studies, culled 210 "lessons learned." Grouped into twenty-one themes, the lessons range from funding to adequate scientific and technical information to use of consensus rules (Leach and Pelkey 2001).

16. In a study of national estuary programs by Lubell and colleagues (2002), 60 percent of participants were government officials. In the watershed partnership study by Leach and Sabatier (2005), 57 percent of participants were government officials.

17. Holmes (1972, 13) states: "Multipurpose projects involving public power operations were hailed as 'experiments in democracy,' combining regional economic growth with widespread distribution of benefits among the people."

18. The Water Resources Council and the river basin commissions did not directly and actively engage environmental values; rather, the federal agencies active in both organizations began addressing environmental values because of the National Environmental Protection Act (NEPA). For example, the effects of the NEPA on the Army Corps of Engineers included more public participation, such as well-publicized hearings beginning at pre-planning stages. Also, the corps committed to giving equal weight to environmental values, along with economic and technical factors, and selected those projects that were not merely economically justified but were the best solution to the problem at hand (Holmes 1979, 117).

3

The Essentials of Watershed Politics

BOUNDARIES, DECISION MAKING, AND ACCOUNTABILITY

The political choices that people confront in governing watersheds include deciding how to structure the governing institutions and organizations, who will participate in making decisions, how decisions will be made, and how decision makers will be held accountable. Several watershed writers accept politics as a given but express a weariness with existing political choices and a hope or desire for a different type of politics—a politics that is more reflective, collaborative, and cooperative; a politics that unfolds outside of present governments and dominant political institutions. Even savvy and experienced scholars such as Gregg and colleagues (1998, 26) convey such a sentiment in their discussion of collaborative watershed efforts: "One of the strengths of watershed initiatives is their ability to focus their activities directly at the most pressing natural resource problems of particular watersheds, *often operating outside of normal governmental processes and free from the constraints of inflexible mandates or program requirements*" (emphasis added).

Of course, Gregg and colleagues may merely be pointing out that political decision making can be improved when governance structures better match the watershed setting. (On this point, see also E. Ostrom 1992.) That is certainly a laudable aim, and we do not suggest for a moment that all institutional arrangements are equally good or bad. Political settings and choices may be more or less conflictual, more or less rigid, more or less open and accountable; what they cannot be is nonpolitical. And politics matters a great deal. In the end, policy alternatives are understood—and to a great degree either embraced and implemented or undermined and abandoned—in relation to whom they include or exclude, or whom they affect and how; how decisions are made and by whom; and how decision makers may be held accountable for their decisions. They are understood and accepted or rejected, in other words, on the basis of political considerations. As Scharpf (1997) notes, and as has been amply demonstrated in the watershed literature, policies believed to be optimal, in that they maximize a specific value or two, such as wetland protection or nutrient reduction, are rarely adopted as designed (see also Nakamura and Born 1993, 808). Usually they are modified because of political reasons, and (despite the somewhat politics-weary tone found in much of the watershed literature) that is not necessarily a bad thing.

Our goal is therefore to place some of the political choices that are embedded within watershed management in plain view and discuss them, in the hope that a clearer understanding of the political nature of the watershed will be useful for resource managers and their fellow citizens in recognizing those choices and their implications. In this chapter we focus directly on three sets of political issues—boundaries, decision-making arrangements, and accountability—all of which are unavoidable, even in collaborative efforts to manage watersheds sustainably and scientifically. We hope that the discussion illuminates not only the issues themselves but the necessity and value of being more explicit about them.

The chapter closes with a case study of the Platte River Basin. After more than a decade of conflict over endangered species issues, the governors of the three basin states and the Department of the Interior adopted the Platte River Cooperative Agreement. The agreement commits Nebraska, Colorado, and Wyoming to providing additional water to the river to protect and enhance critical habitat and to mitigate the effects of new water uses on river flows. In developing the agreement and devising a governing structure to implement it, the participants had to make explicit choices about who participates, how decisions are made, and how participants are to be held accountable. The Platte River case therefore provides an illustration of these fundamental political choices at work.

BOUNDARIES: WHO SHOULD MATTER IN WATERSHED DECISION-MAKING ARRANGEMENTS

The hope for a best way of governing watersheds can sound at times like a hope for watershed management without politics—more scientific, rational, and comprehensive, less bogged down by special interests and intergovernmental rivalries. This can be heard to some degree in the language about organizing management around watershed boundaries, because they are "natural" and "real," unlike "political boundaries" that create undesirable "jurisdictional externalities." Other scholars have pointed out, however, that the physical setting is less determinative and perhaps even less a "given" than thought. As Griffin (1999, 509) observed, "One problem with using watersheds as the geographic unit for management is that watersheds may not always be well defined. Omernik and Bailey (1997) report that approximately one third of the coterminous United States may possess physical characteristics that make watershed delineation problematic."

Besides, Brunson (1998, 65) noted: "All boundaries are social constructs, marking human-perceived differences in the nature and identity of places. . . . Even ecosystem boundaries are social constructs in that they reflect the spatial extent of natural conditions that characterize a human-defined categorization within the continuous range of actual and potential conditions." In the watershed context, Woolley and McGinnis are more direct still:

> Each watershed organization faces a boundary identification problem.
> Watershed organizations cannot depend merely on scientific information in the planning process. Each group struggles with a basic political issue—defining boundaries and planning issues. The benefits of the watershed focus—broadly about connections and interdependencies over a relevant geographic area—do not include the elimination of conflict

and contention. Watershed planning, therefore, is always a scientific *and* a political activity. (1999, 591, emphasis in original)

Furthermore, a new batch of boundary questions emerges once one decides to try to organize management at the watershed scale. What is the appropriate watershed scale at which to govern? Should decision-making bodies be organized around small-scale watersheds that feed into larger watersheds that in turn feed into even larger watersheds? Or should a set of governance boundaries be drawn around a large-scale watershed? What about watersheds that have been tied together through human intervention, as is so common in the western United States with its history of inter-basin water transfer projects? Should these artificially linked water resources be governed as a single watershed (and if so, what happened to our notion of watersheds as "natural" boundaries?) or as separate ones despite the canals, pipelines, and pumping stations that connect them? All of these are political questions, ones that the physical setting alone cannot answer. As experienced water resources managers know, topographical maps cannot give us all the answers. Moreover, until decisions are made concerning who is in and who is out of the watershed, and thus who may have access to decision making about its resources and their use, science cannot answer how much water can be used, how much timber can be harvested, and how much land can be developed and in what manner.

Political scientist Deborah Stone (1988) notes that who gets what is as important as how they get it, but defining "who" and "how" is not a straightforward process. Each may be defined in a multitude of ways, and each definition is likely associated with a different notion of equity or fairness. Who, and whose interests, should be represented in watershed decision making has long been debated in the literature. Defining "who" involves distinguishing some people from others. People will predictably and understandably contest the distinctions made, either fighting to get in and be counted or seeking ways to escape and avoid what they perceive as the burden of belonging.

At one end of the spectrum in the debate over who should be included in decision making are Bates and colleagues (1993), who provide some of the strongest statements for the viewpoint that *everyone* affected by or affecting a water resource should be included in decision-making processes, whether located within the watershed or not. They refer to "the whole community" for any given water resource and define it in the following ways:

Western watersheds all implicate more diverse communities than ever before. Today's community of interest is likely to include—in place of the old miner-farmer-rancher-industrial coalition that made western water policy—citizens determined to reduce government expenditures; Indian tribes; residents opposed to continued rapid growth in their geographic communities; environmentalists; citizens who want western rivers, lakes and aquifers managed to guarantee sustainability for their children and grandchildren; recreationists of all stripes; businesspeople whose livelihoods depend on the West's emerging recreation economy; and those who simply believe, fervently, that western rivers should be allowed to retain the incomparable, eternal qualities that provide so much inspiration, reflection, and fulfillment. All of these and other identifiable interests need to be represented in modern water policy, and in most watersheds nearly all of them are clamoring for recognition. They will be heard, one way or another. (Bates et al. 1993, 9)

The essential importance of water places a special value on the manner in which decisions are made respecting its use and availability. The whole community must be considered in those decisions, and all interests must have a meaningful opportunity to participate. (Bates et al. 1993, 182)

For Bates and colleagues (1993, 197), fairness requires that all who are touched by the effects of water use, no matter how separated by time and distance, be involved in a meaningful way in decisions that affect it. All should be allowed to participate and to have their interests represented. Given the importance of water, they conclude, an expansive notion of "who" must be adopted. Their viewpoint is echoed in statements by countless others arguing that watershed management should encompass "all affected interests."

At the other end of the spectrum, Ingram and colleagues (1984) take a less sanguine view of broad-based participation in watershed decision making. Regional decision making at a watershed or river basin scale always bears the risk of overlooking or undervaluing local impacts. Ingram and colleagues (1984) argue that the people who are most affected by watershed uses, which are most often geographic communities situated within the watershed, must be given the greatest weight in decision making. They caution: "It is important to look at consequences from a particularized or localized perspective as well as basin wide. Despite the fact that physical scientists describe river basins as general, interconnected systems, the experience of impacts is often discrete and localized" (1984, 326). Thus, "the appropriate geographic boundaries within which to identify interests in institutional assessments should be drawn from an understanding of the stakes rather than river basin boundaries, subject matter, or other artificially imposed limits" (ibid.).

Furthermore, in those discrete and localized settings that often exist at the sub-watershed scale, decisions about water resources are also decisions about the nature, strength, and future of communities. "Water still symbolizes such values as opportunity, security and self-determination. . . . Control over it signals social organization and political power. . . . Strong communities are able to hold on to their water and put it to work. Communities that lose control over water probably will fail in trying to control much else of importance" (Ingram 1990, 5). Weber (2003) broadens the discussion to include economic considerations. Members of place-based communities often rely heavily on natural resources for their livelihoods. Severely restrict logging in national forests, or substantially reduce irrigation water from federal water projects, and local economies buckle. Thus, for economic as well as political and cultural reasons, local communities situated within watersheds need to be represented in watershed decision-making processes.

Thus far, nothing has been stated that would raise serious disagreement, even though the statements quoted above come to the issue of inclusion from differing perspectives. One could finesse the choice rhetorically: broad inclusion of "all affected interests" sounds good, as does the representation and protection of local communities where the impacts of watershed management actions are felt most strongly. There is a deeper puzzle, however, that is harder to elide once it is articulated more starkly. If we say that "all affected interests" should be included, for instance, what do we mean by someone or some group having an "interest" in the watershed? Does "having an interest" mean living in the watershed? Using resources from the watershed? Visiting the watershed regularly, or even occasionally? Hoping to visit the watershed someday? Caring about the watershed even though one never expects to live or visit there?

To put it even more bluntly, can one "have an interest" in a watershed by just "taking an interest" in the watershed? Can I put myself "into" a watershed by an act of choice or an exercise of will because I want to be included? And would this be a unilateral act on my part, or do others who claim to be connected with that watershed have some say in whether I am "in" or "out"? When we define boundaries, we are saying (whether we acknowledge it explicitly or not) who is in and who is out, who "counts" and how much and who doesn't count at all. In more mundane political terms, who has a vote, a veto, or both, or neither?

With these questions in mind, let us go back to the points raised by Ingram and colleagues on the one hand and Bates and colleagues on the other. Ingram's argument that local communities should be protected in decision-making processes raises some important concerns over the involvement of non-local communities of interest recommended by Bates and colleagues (1993). The potential loss of control and the fate of one's local community, if watershed-scale decision making is opened up to non-local communities, are serious issues with no easy resolution. Even though Bates and colleagues (1993, 195) advocate opening watershed decision making to all who are affected by or interested in the watershed, they also make the case (perhaps unintentionally) *against* involving non-local communities of interest:

> The trade-offs inherent in water decisions can be calculated in broad equivalents: a car wash in Los Angeles consumes the water of a family farm in Owens Valley; a farm in La Paz County is worth two golf courses in Tucson; a subdivision in the Denver suburbs with Kentucky bluegrass lawns uses the amount of water needed to keep a pristine western Colorado mountain stream full of fish; turning down the air-conditioning temperature by two degrees in Phoenix requires releases of water from hydroelectric dams that destroy a season's boating in the Grand Canyon. What does all this mean to the L.A. car wash customer, the Denver lawn waterer, the cattle rancher, the golfer, or the Phoenix resident? It's tough to appreciate the difference one more clean car, green lawn, golf course or cool Phoenician will make. (Bates et al., 1993, 195)

Do those Phoenicians, Angelenos, and Denverites count as "affected interests" who need to be included in watershed decision making for La Paz County, the Owens Valley, and Colorado mountain streams? Those distant urbanites number in the millions, to say nothing of the financial resources under their control. If watershed policy making is opened to all of these affected people who, according to Bates and colleagues (1993), have a hard time understanding the local impacts of their distant choices, why wouldn't they choose to maintain their lifestyles over those of a comparatively small number of farmers or recreational fishers and kayakers? On what basis would we exclude them from participation in decision making about the resources of those valleys? Now the boundary problem can be seen in sharper resolution—who is going to be in the political watershed and who is not is a question with answers and implications that cannot be seen or defined topographically.

Suppose we opt instead to keep the distant nonresidents out of the political watershed. To be "in" the watershed would then mean to be physically connected with it in some direct way—living there, for instance. Critics of giving precedence to the values of local communities of place rightly note that such communities often fail to, or are incapable of, attending to legitimate values that transcend their boundaries (Tarlock 2000b). As Karkkainen (2002) notes, not only are the Florida Everglades and the Chesapeake Bay regional ecosystems to be used and enjoyed by local residents, they are national treasures with national interests attached to them, interests that deserve to be recognized. For every Owens Valley–like tragedy that supporters of the politics of place can cite, supporters of opening watershed decision making to many interests can point to numerous streams and rivers reengineered to serve the narrow economic needs of the local community while thoughtlessly disregarding a host of other values, such as ecosystem protection. In addition, some commentators on the many local watershed collaboratives springing up across the United States have questioned how participatory such efforts really are in practice and how diverse are the interests they represent (e.g., Kenney 2000; Weber 2003). Weber provocatively raises the question of whether some local watershed collaboratives are really just instances of multinational corporations co-opting and coercing local activists (2003, 6), and others have speculated that companies' participation in collaborative local watershed initiatives is driven primarily by their desire to avoid the regulatory "hammer" held by state or (more likely) federal agencies.

Ultimately, debates over who should be included within decision-making processes are debates over which values should be given the greatest weight. Whose values will be served? Some values do not easily or readily correspond to geographical communities or boundaries. Bates and colleagues (1993) argue for a more expansive notion of who should count in hopes of more directly injecting conservation, sustainability, and protection values into policy decisions. Yet, as their own examples illustrate, including nonlocal communities of interest in decision making may lead to unintended and/or undesirable outcomes. Water demands by urban residents or commercial interests may win out over conservation efforts by local watershed residents.

Arguments over boundaries and inclusion often hinge on the outcomes advocates are trying to promote; they are political arguments. If advocates for ecological values believe that local watershed users are also committed to those values, they will argue for excluding nonresident interests whose inclusion would threaten those values (the "keep L.A. out of Owens Valley" argument). On the other hand, if those advocates believe local residents will not promote ecological values, they will argue for including nonresident interests (the "ANWR is a national treasure" argument). Advocates of commercial interests in the consumptive uses of water make the same sorts of arguments, but in the opposite direction.

Dismissing the inconsistency of these stances as hypocritical is too easy, or at least misses the larger point that each stance is connected strategically with a political goal. The famed twentieth-century American political theorist E. E. Schattschneider (1960) nicknamed such strategies "managing the scope of conflict": one set of interests is likely to advocate defining the situation in ways that keep the scope limited and another set of interests will try to define the situation in ways that draw in more participants, each anticipating the effects that the narrower or broader scope will have on the likelihood of their preferences prevailing.

Of course, conflicts and policy choices are not fixed in time. As the social and economic landscape of a watershed changes, so do the impacts of boundaries identifying who matters. Changes in population concentrations or in economic activities bring different values to the fore within a watershed. Many water districts, formed several decades ago by irrigators, now find that a majority of their members are municipal and industrial water users and that most of their water is used in urban areas for nonagricultural purposes. Beyond the watershed, as administrations change in state capitals and in Washington, D.C., different values will be pursued, impacting watershed policies and activities. Neither defining communities of interest broadly nor giving pride of place to local, geographic communities guarantees that a particular set of values will be pursued consistently over time as the watershed setting and its context change.

ORGANIZING WATERSHED DECISION-MAKING ARRANGEMENTS

The choice of decision-making arrangements or, using Stone's (1988) terminology, defining "how" decisions will be made is just as political as deciding "who" matters. All institutional structures for water resources decision making "are likely to have different policy orientations. They are also likely to vary in their accessibility and responsiveness to particular interests, their capacity to generate the appropriate flow of information, and their preference for certain problem solutions" (Ingram et al. 1984, 328).

How should decisions be made? The answer most commonly given in the watershed management literature currently is consensus, in part because of the widespread adoption and experimentation with watershed initiatives that are based on collaborative working groups of officials from government and nonprofit organizations and citizens, who typically use consensus as their decision-making rule (Kenney 2000). Weber (2003, 4) notes the stark contrast between "business as usual" and a collaborative approach to addressing and resolving environmental problems. "Instead of centralized hierarchy, government experts in control, specialized agencies, and layer upon layer of written rules and procedures, GREM [Grassroots Ecosystem Management] is premised on greater decentralization of governance, shared power among public and private actors, collaborative, ongoing, consensus-based decision processes, holistic missions (environment, economy, and community), results-oriented management, and broad civic participation."

Consensus, which requires that all participants consent to a decision or action before it is taken, is viewed positively for a variety of reasons. First, cooperation is emphasized over conflict. Discussion and debate are continued, information is shared, and alternatives explored until no one insists on opposing a proposed solution (Scharpf 1997, 144). Second, the consensus-building process supports the emergence of productive working relationships that emphasize problem solving over staking out a position and defending it at all costs (Kenney 2000). Third, consensus decision making produces more legitimate and acceptable solutions than do other forms of decision making because all participants must consent to a proposal before it is adopted. As Scharpf (1997, 144) notes, "consenting parties cannot claim to be injured." For all of these reasons, consensus exhibits some attractive normative features. Not only does it work to build community as people search for common ground, but it protects individuals' interests from being subjugated to community interests.

Although certainly consensus possesses some attractive features, political scientists have good reasons to be skeptical about consensus, which is in essence a unanimity rule. For reasons that have been explicated theoretically

(Buchanan and Tullock 1962) and observed in empirical settings, unanimity rules are understood as having the potential to impede collective action by empowering each individual with a veto. A single person can hold out for what he views as a better deal for himself or those that he represents. Scharpf (1997, 144) has labeled such situations as joint decision traps "in which the beneficiaries of the status quo can block all reforms, or at least extract exorbitant side payments." In practical settings, consensus-based decision making has led to gridlock, a search for the lowest common denominator that all participants can agree upon, or a "something for everyone" form of distributive policy (Milon, Kiker, and Lee 1998; Coglianese 1999; Coglianese and Allen 2004).[1] As Coglianese (1999, 31) states, "Consensus building shifts the ultimate goal away from reaching a quality decision and moves it toward reaching an agreeable one. A consensus among a select group will not always equate to socially optimal policy."

Gridlock and a something-for-everyone form of distributive policy making become more likely the greater the number of participants and the more diverse their interests. Bates and colleagues (1993, 3) describe current western water policy as "a Gordian knot." Yet it seems a reasonable question to pose whether the meaningful involvement of the interests of every person or group that affects or is affected by a watershed, even those separated by distance and time, would combine with the requirement of consensus-based decision making in such a way as to cut the Gordian knot or pull it even tighter. It can be challenging to imagine a single watershed restoration project that could be adopted and implemented using such an approach, even in a relatively small watershed.

Consensus may be the recommended approach to decision making in watersheds for at least two reasons. One may be that those who advocate it sincerely believe it is the best means of proceeding toward collective decisions. Another may be that consensus has dominated the watershed management literature because any other manner of decision making seems worse. Consensus seems to promise something other than the types of conflicts and risks that would attend other forms of decision making (Kagan 1997; Kenney 2000).[2]

Move away from consensus, and what remains? Alternatives include some form of majority or super-majority voting process. It is not unusual to find decision-making bodies operating with a combination of consensus and voting. Participants attempt to develop consensus positions on issues;

however, if that fails, participants can bring the issue to a vote. The advantages of combining the two decision-making approaches rest in the ability to make decisions even in the face of significant disagreements among participants. Although the normal operating procedure is consensus, which allows participants to avoid overriding the interests of a minority, voting allows decisions to be made when necessary. Scharpf (1997, 144) suggests that this combination of decision rules emerges in settings where the norm of reciprocity operates and participants expect to be in the minority position at varying times. The Fraser Basin Council in British Columbia, Canada, for example, is renowned for its use of consensus decision making, yet consensus is always reached in the shadow of council rules that allow the council president to call for a vote. Presidents have occasionally used the threat of calling a vote as an instrument for moving contesting council members toward a consensus (Blomquist, Calbick, and Dinar 2004).

Although voting has the agreeable quality of allowing collective action to occur, especially among large numbers of people even in the face of conflict, it is purchased at the expense of permitting the exploitation and domination of minority interests (Ostrom 1987). There are a number of mechanisms that attempt to minimize and correct for the possibility of minority exploitation, such as dividing power among several decision-making bodies; separating executive, legislative, and executive powers and allowing them to check one another; and providing opportunities for the independent review of actions and decisions. Discussion of these familiar accountability mechanisms will be further elaborated in the next section. However, there is another limitation of voting mechanisms, especially from the perspective of proponents of consensus decision making. Voting showcases politics, in the sense of bargaining, vote trading, compromising, presenting information about one's positions and actions in the most favorable light, and casting doubt on the veracity of the information provided by one's opponents, and occasionally treating decision making as a zero-sum game—what is gained by one side is lost to the other. All of this is a far cry from the reasoned deliberation and search for common solutions that consensus processes ideally support.

The desire for reasoned deliberation and solutions that serve the public interest may explain why in the watershed literature, prior to the emergence of consensus-based watershed initiatives, attention was and continues to be focused on integrated management. As described in Chapter 2, advocates of integrated watershed management desire to see put in place watershed-scale authorities with broad functional powers peopled by well-trained experts who could develop and implement policies that take into account and manage the many interconnected dimensions of a watershed. Integrated watershed management has been likened to a restoration of rational planning (Walther 1987, 440), a form of decision making in which expert elites draw together information about all alternatives in order to reach reasoned conclusions about which choices will best serve social goals. Decision making would be, using Scharpf's (1997) terminology, hierarchical. Hierarchical decision making eliminates the transaction costs of coordination, whether that involves developing a consensus among decision makers or building support among a majority of officials, and instead allows an expert, either an individual or an agency, to make decisions (Scharpf 1997, 172). The perceived benefits of such an approach are several and are strongest in their contrast to existing decision making that occurs in many watersheds. For instance, fragmented and uncoordinated decisions would be replaced with comprehensive and integrated decisions. Also, decisions would be based on scientific expertise and not on narrow distributive concerns.[3]

The criticisms leveled at this approach include information demands and motivation concerns (Scharpf 1997). Hierarchical decision making makes a number of information assumptions that are rarely met. It presumes that (1) social goals are known with some precision and remain constant over the relevant period (Milon, Kiker, and Lee 1998); (2) the number of social goals to be pursued is limited and those goals do not contradict one another (O'Toole 1993); and (3) decision makers are able to comprehend everything from land use planning to biological systems and their responses to economic and political dynamics (Newson 1997, 311).

Furthermore, hierarchical decision making assumes that authority will be exercised in a benevolent manner. The expert decision makers will pursue the public good and not their own personal goals or the goals of various special interests. Just like voting systems, however, the exploitation or oppression of underrepresented or minority interests can occur in elite rule. Jacobs (1978) vividly recounts the tragic tale of how watershed planning in the Rio Grande systematically worked to the detriment of an "inconvenient" minority of native Latino and Indian farmers in the Española valley north of Santa Fe. Despite procedural guarantees of public hearings and participation, regional watershed planning for the Rio Grande became in effect "top-down planning." The endeavor to make decisions for and about the watershed as a whole led to the diminution of the effects on several small (and relatively powerless) sub-watershed communities.

Ultimately, the search for a more deliberative or a more rational decision-making structure may be a misguided search for a sort of bloodless organization. Consensus holds the promise of reaching sensible and fair decisions without the conflict and strategic behavior characteristic of traditional approaches. Hierarchical decision making allows experts to devise good policies based on science and professional standards of conduct, once again, avoiding the difficult negotiations, compromises, and trade-offs that so often characterize watershed governance. In practice, however, consensus and hierarchical decision making consistently deliver on their promise in relatively simple and conflict-free settings. Move beyond such settings and their shortcomings become immediately obvious, just as do the shortcomings of different forms of voting systems. In other words, choices among decision-making processes are choices among imperfect alternatives (Komesar 1994).

ACCOUNTABILITY IN WATERSHED GOVERNANCE

We turn next to an examination of accountability, which among other things involves reflecting upon whether decision-making authority has been exercised appropriately. Ensuring that authority is exercised appropriately depends on the form that authority takes. If it takes a traditional form, such as a state legislature or a federal agency, well-understood and commonly used forms of accountability will most often be used. Members of a representative assembly are primarily held accountable through elections. Agency employees are held accountable through legislative oversight, professional norms, and organizational directives.

Watershed governance, however, has historically raised challenging and difficult accountability issues because of the remarkable institutional experimentation and innovation that have occurred in the United States over the past several decades. Many of the organizational and institutional experiments do not fit neatly within existing authority and accountability structures. For instance, decision makers may not be public or elected officials; rather they may be what are commonly called stakeholders and may even be community volunteers. How are volunteers and other stakeholders to be held accountable? Weber (2003) suggests that nontraditional forms of accountability must be recognized if institutional innovation is to be encouraged.

Accountability allows for the correction of mistakes and discourages the abuse of power. However, accountability is not an either/or proposition. It has a primary dimension of answerability (Heywood 2004), where some assess the performance of others, and a consequent dimension of responsiveness, where it is possible to challenge and revise decisions and actions that are regarded as unsatisfactory (Romzek and Dubnick 1987; Romzek 1998).

Consequently, accountability can take a variety of forms and political choices must be made about which types are to be used to ensure good governance of a watershed. The different forms of accountability relationships include hierarchical, legal, political, and professional (Romzek and Dubnick 1987; Radin and Romzek 1996). Hierarchical accountability rests on an organization's rules, regulations, and organizational directives as means of holding employees in check. The behavioral expectation according to Romzek and Ingraham (2000) is obedience to regulations and organizational directives. Those who are higher in a hierarchy can use the rules and regulations to direct, guide, and assess the performance of those lower in the hierarchy. Professional accountability relies on individuals internalizing norms of appropriate behavior that are acquired from professional practices, work experience, and training (Knott and Miller 1987; Wilson 1989; Romzek and Ingraham 2000). An individual's actions are compared to the accepted practices of the individual's profession, often by superiors or by professional boards, to gauge whether that individual exercised professional judgment in acceptable ways.

Legal and political accountability relationships call to mind more traditional forms of accountability. Legal accountability rests on laws and constitutions and determining whether a public employee or public official complied with legal and constitutional mandates (Romzek and Ingraham 2000). Oftentimes such determinations are made by courts, through the process of judicial review, but they may also be made by legislative oversight committees. In addition, legal accountability encompasses veto powers. The president may veto an act of Congress, or Congress may override the veto of a president. Finally, political accountability involves responsiveness to key external stakeholders (Romzek and Ingraham 2000). Elected officials are subject to regular elections by their constituents. Public managers maintain political support by responding to their agencies' key constituencies and to important elected officials.

In most settings, all of these accountability mechanisms are present; however, one or two are primary on a day-to-day basis. For instance, employees within many public agencies are subject to both hierarchical and professional accountability mechanisms. Not only are they expected to follow organizational directives, but they are also expected to exercise their discretion in light of professional practices and norms (Wilson 1989). For elected officials, accountability mechanisms are much more likely to be political and legal, and much less likely to be professional and hierarchical. In other words, the types of accountability mechanisms that decision makers are most likely to be subject to depend on their positions and their organizations. Political appointees are less directly subject to the discipline of elections and more directly subject to legal mandates and organizational directives. Judges are directly subject to professional standards of practice and conduct and legal mandates, and not hierarchical accountability relations or political accountability mechanisms.

Romzek and Ingraham (2000) argue that during times of crisis and times of reform, all four types of mechanisms may come to the fore. For instance, as intense conflict erupts in some watersheds over endangered species, the actions of public agencies come under increasing scrutiny. Not only may the watershed science developed by the agencies be sent out for review to professional organizations to determine if the agencies abided by scientific protocols and developed "good" science, often at the insistence of angry stakeholders, but the agencies may be reviewed by congressional committees to ensure that they are following legislative mandates, and executive office science advisory committees may be brought in to examine the conflict.

When crisis or failure occurs and multiple accountability mechanisms respond, it often becomes apparent that each mechanism demands contradictory behaviors. The former director of the Buenos Aires Wildlife Refuge in southern Arizona discovered this in his attempt to protect threatened Chiricahua leopard frogs (Tobin 2004). In the midst of a drought, a water hole that was home to some of the threatened frogs was on the verge of drying up. A University of Arizona researcher gained permission to move some of the frogs to a pond on his property; however, if held in captivity over an extended period of time, adult frogs eat all tadpoles, eventually eradicating the population. Before the frogs perished, the wildlife refuge director wanted to move the frogs to the refuge. Organizational directives and legal mandates dictated that he follow established procedures and seek permission to move the frogs. However, the frogs would have died before the permission process resulted in a decision. Therefore, he decided to move the frogs without permission. He was subsequently removed as director of the refuge and he now may be charged with a federal felony for moving a threatened species without a permit (Tobin 2004).

Part of the conflict surrounding the case of the Chiricahua leopard frogs is over which accountability mechanism should hold precedence. Hierarchical and legal mechanisms require that the director be strictly disciplined and follow the established procedures, regardless of individual situations. Professional and political mechanisms laud the director's actions as prudent and appropriate in the face of certain death for the endangered frogs. In addition to showing that holding public officials, even scientists, accountable is not always a straightforward process, the incident demonstrates that accountability issues involve political choices that cannot be avoided by arguing that all accountability mechanisms must be used. Choices must be made among them. Should an agency be tightly circumscribed by legal mandates and requirements that also provide numerous opportunities for key stakeholders to intervene and challenge agency decisions? Should public employees be primarily guided by professional norms and practices that are more loosely guided and constrained by legal mandates? Should elected officials be primarily disciplined through regular elections, or should they also be subject to the legal mandate that they can only serve for a limited number of terms? Much like defining whose values should matter most and selecting decision-making processes, there is no one correct answer to these questions.

Watershed governance has historically raised accountability issues that extend beyond making choices among different mechanisms and resolving conflicts among competing accountability claims. Because watershed boundaries do not match political jurisdictions, accountability in whatever form it may take becomes problematic as attempts are made to manage at the watershed level. How do, and how should, new forms of watershed governance fit within the existing political system and all of its familiar accountability mechanisms? Such questions have been raised for decades as citizens and public officials have struggled with the many issues and challenges created by watersheds. Writing in 1966 about the river basin commissions then in vogue, Colorado attorney and future U.S. senator Gary Hart wrote in the *University of Colorado Law Review*:

> Regional agencies such as the Delaware River Basin Commission combine legislative, executive and judicial functions. The establishment of such a unique governmental agency to some extent results in destruction of the traditional system of checks and balances. The agency itself is responsible to no electorate and no single legislature. . . .
>
> Much can be said for the creation of regional water resources development agencies with broad governmental powers and some independent status of their own. The same arguments support the establishment of strong regional agencies designed to meet other regional needs. The thesis of this article, however, is that traditional, institutional protections, viz., the basic "checks and balances," must be established concurrently with and in proportion to the authority given regional development agencies.
>
> With the administrative and legislative recognition of the river basin as the fundamental water unit, attention must be given to the revolutionary possibilities for regional water resources development which this suggests. What kinds of agencies will supervise and manage this development, and what powers will they have? What relations will they bear to existing forms and structures of government—the federal system of government in this country? It is not too soon to begin consideration of such serious questions. (Hart 1966, 46–47)

Hart's comments remain relevant, although the context has changed from mid-twentieth-century basin commissions to early twenty-first-century collaborative watershed bodies. According to Tarlock (2000b, 79–80), a critic of watershed initiatives, one reason for the growing popularity of informal collaborative processes for addressing watershed problems is that collaboration offers an alternative to the rigidities and limits of governmental management. Weber (2003, 4) more explicitly makes that point: "GREM [Grassroots Ecosystem Management] also relies extensively or exclusively on collaborative decision processes, consensus, and active citizen participation, which means that private citizens and stakeholders often take on leadership roles and are involved directly in deliberative decision-making, implementation, and enforcement processes along with government officials, especially when it comes to how goals are to be achieved."

Weber (2003, 67) concisely captures the accountability problem: "Can the new governance arrangements known as grassroots ecosystem management produce positive-sum, or broad, simultaneous accountability without detracting from obligations and duties to state and national interests? Or does improved accountability to local interests have to come at the expense of accountability to broader public interests, whether it is state and national interests, or future generations?" In a very careful and in-depth examination of accountability mechanisms present in local collaborative watershed efforts, he argues that accountability occurs at different levels and along multiple dimensions. Local collaborative efforts, even if they do consist of unelected volunteers, are accountable in numerous ways to the citizens of the communities and localities in which they are organized. Collaborative efforts are open to all who wish to participate, and collaboratives often engage in considerable outreach and education in their local communities. Furthermore, consensus decision making encourages deliberation, discussion, and the exchange of ideas. Thus, open meetings and consensus decision making mean that it is virtually impossible for a narrow set of interests to dominate and drive the process. Rather, a wide variety of people, representing a variety of interests and values, participate.

Weber argues that watershed collaboratives are accountable to regional and national interests and values as well. Such broad-based accountability occurs through several mechanisms. Most importantly, watershed collaborative efforts are strictly advisory bodies that "rely on negotiation, broad-based representation of interests, self-generated information regarding watershed conditions, and persuasion (rather than mandates and coercion) to shape policymaking and problem solving" (Weber 2003, 62). Since collaboratives are advisory, they cannot develop enforceable rules and regulations. In addition, the federal agencies that participate in collaborative efforts remain accountable for faithfully abiding by and implementing the federal laws over which they have jurisdiction. Thus, according to Weber (2003), local watershed initiatives are fully accountable both to the local communities within which they operate and to national interests and values as reflected in environmental laws.

To others it remains uncertain how collaborative nongovernmental efforts relate to the administration of existing environmental laws, and how citizens can challenge decisions made through collaborative efforts (Tarlock 2000a, 195; Coggins 2001, 165). Wester and Warner (2002, 68) concur: "Serious thought needs to be given to how hard-won democratic rights in conventional social and political domains are [to be] assured in the river basin domain." Thus, the very attractiveness of watershed initiatives to their supporters—that they may operate "free from the constraints of inflexible mandates or program requirements" (Gregg et al. 1998)—is their primary vulnerability in the view of their detractors.

THE PLATTE RIVER COOPERATIVE AGREEMENT

Boundaries, decision making, and accountability are regularly contested, challenged, and changed in the Platte River Basin of Colorado, Wyoming, and Nebraska. Historically, the states controlled the allocation and use of water within their boundaries. Numerous times they engaged in cooperative agreements with the U.S. Bureau of Reclamation to develop and store their water through the building of large surface water projects. Thus, they began to share decision-making authority over water with the federal government. On occasion, the states fought over shared water resources and they called upon federal entities to help them solve their conflicts. In 1923, Colorado and Nebraska turned to the compacting process and devised the South Platte River Compact. In the 1940s, Nebraska filed suit against Wyoming over the North Platte River, asking the U.S. Supreme Court to equitably divide the waters of the river between the two states. The Supreme Court responded by issuing a North Platte River water decree, which Nebraska has repeatedly attempted to enforce through lawsuits before the Supreme Court.

River allocations, either through compacts or decrees, required states to take each other into account in their administration of water. All of these actions involved conflict, but also cooperation, and all were aimed at a single purpose—withdrawing as much water as possible from the river and putting it to beneficial use. The passage of the Endangered Species Act (ESA) eventually called into question the single-minded focus of drawing water from the river and spurred another round of changes in boundaries, decision making, and accountability. To understand these changes requires some background.

Background

The Platte River begins high in the Rocky Mountains of Colorado. The North Platte River rises in North Park, Colorado; flows north into Wyoming; and eventually turns east and south into the panhandle of Nebraska. The

The Platte River Basin.

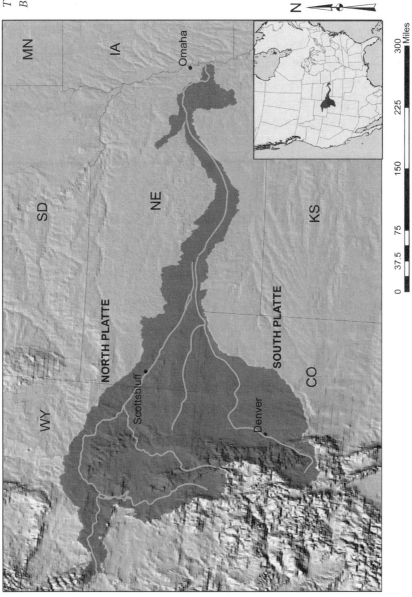

N

MN

IA

Omaha

SD

NE

WY

NORTH PLATTE

Scottsbluff

KS

SOUTH PLATTE

Denver

CO

0   37.5   75   150   225   300

Miles

South Platte River begins southwest of Denver, in South Park, Colorado, where for a brief stretch it flows south before twisting to the northeast, through Denver and Greeley, and then turning more to the east where it eventually flows into southwestern Nebraska. At the town of North Platte in south central Nebraska, the two rivers join to form the Platte River. Flowing east from there, the Platte begins a big bend, southeast and then northeast, before emptying into the Missouri River near Omaha. The Big Bend section in south central Nebraska is a major bird feeding area in the central flyway of North America (Platte River Whooping Crane Maintenance Trust 2004).

Between 1900 and 1940, large dams and reservoirs were built to provide flood protection, irrigation water, and hydropower. Multiple dams and reservoirs—Pathfinder, Seminoe, and Guernsey, in Wyoming; the Antero, Elevenmile Canyon, and Cheeseman, in Colorado; and Kingsley Dam and its reservoir, Lake McConaughy, in Nebraska—have tamed the river (Draft Environmental Impact Statement 2003, 2–14). Habitat for migratory birds—cranes, piping plovers, and least terns—disappeared rapidly as the river was rebuilt to serve human uses. Annually, it generates 300 megawatts of power, irrigates over a million acres of farmland, and provides water to 3.5 million people (Supalla 2000, 253). Between surface water diversions and groundwater pumping, river flows have been substantially depleted. Prior to the reengineering of the river, it is estimated that the average annual flow at Grand Island, Nebraska, right in the middle of the Big Bend region, was 2.6 million acre-feet. Today that flow has been roughly halved (Platte River Draft Programmatic Environmental Impact Statement 2003, 2–21). It should come as no surprise that in 1978, the U.S. Fish and Wildlife Service (FWS), under the auspices of the ESA, declared the whooping crane, the interior least tern, the piping plover, and the pallid sturgeon threatened or endangered (Draft Environmental Impact Statement 2003). Thus began the struggle to reclaim habitat and to allow more water to remain in the river.

Federal courts have interpreted the ESA as providing the FWS with broad grants of power to recover endangered species. As Aiken (1999) notes, federal courts have handed down decisions concerning water and the ESA in three cases, and "[i]n all three of these cases the interests of endangered species were placed above the interests of appropriators. . . . *If the FWS determines that appropriated water is needed in order to accomplish the recovery of endangered species, the endangered species get first claim.* In negotiations regarding the recovery of endangered species, the FWS negotiates from a very strong legal position" (Aiken 1999, 127; emphasis added). With the listing of endangered species on the Platte River, the FWS designated critical habitat for species in the Big Bend area of the river in Nebraska and began working with the state to protect and enhance the habitat.

Initially, the FWS and the State of Nebraska were the two primary participants engaged in endangered species recovery efforts on a rich but limited segment of the river. However, recovery and protection efforts around the Big Bend area reverberated throughout the entire basin, eventually resulting in a basin-wide recovery effort involving many participants. Between 1978 and 1998, *all* proposed water projects in the Platte Basin were stopped, deferred, or substantially modified, engendering considerable conflict, particularly in Colorado and Nebraska, that sometimes flared up to the highest levels of the national government (Aiken 1999).[4] For instance, the Two Forks reservoir that was to supply water to the Denver metropolitan region was killed when the EPA, after close consultation with the White House, denied permits for the project. What captured people's attention, though, was a high-profile case that significantly affected the operation of an existing water project. Two Nebraska power and irrigation districts operated Kingsley Dam and Lake McConaughy, just upstream of the Big Bend area. When their operating licenses came up for renewal, the Federal Energy Regulatory Commission (FERC), under pressure of a lawsuit, requested that the districts dedicate up to half of their stored water to habitat recovery. Although one district voluntarily complied, the other refused, challenging the FERC decision in court. Eventually, the State of Nebraska intervened, overrode the district, and began negotiations with FERC. The state proposed to create in the reservoir an environmental storage account, owned and operated by the two districts, to support habitat and to be controlled by the Nebraska Game and Parks Commission. The districts agreed to provide up to 100,000 acre-feet of water annually for the account, which FERC accepted (Aiken 1999).

Boundaries

Aiken (1999) argues that the re-licensing of the hydropower dam in Nebraska set in motion actions on the part of states and the federal government that eventually led to a basin-wide cooperative agreement. The Nebraska dam was the first existing water project subjected to the ESA in the Platte River Basin. Nebraska public officials came to realize that species recovery efforts in the Big Bend region were becoming increasingly onerous, and that those efforts depended not only on what occurred downstream in Nebraska but what occurred upstream in Colorado and Wyoming. Officials in the two upstream states came to understand that it was simply a matter of time before existing water uses in their states would come under federal scrutiny. At the urging of Nebraska, and with the support and cooperation of the U.S. Department of the Interior (which contains the FWS and the Bureau of Reclamation), Wyoming and Colorado agreed to cooperate to address endangered species issues (Draft Environmental Impact Statement 2003).

Thus, the boundaries determining who directly participates in endangered species conflicts and their resolution dramatically changed. No longer would participation be confined to the owners and operators of local water projects, the federal agency licensing the projects, and the FWS. Rather, it would broaden to a negotiating group of higher-level authorities—state governors, the secretary of the interior, the FWS, and the Bureau of Reclamation, which had built major federal water projects in each state. These officials represented entities that together exercise considerable authority over water allocation and use across the entire river basin.

From 1994 to 1997, the Department of the Interior and the three states devised the Platte River Cooperative Agreement. The three states agreed that by 2010 to 2013 they would provide 130,000 to 150,000 acre-feet of water for habitat recovery, mitigate new water uses, and monitor species response to improved habitat conditions (Cooperative Agreement 1997). The increment of water is intended to substantially reduce the impact of existing water uses on the river. In addition, all new uses must also mitigate their effects. If the states abide by the agreement and provide the promised water, they will be deemed in compliance with the ESA and can avoid consultations on new and existing water uses. In other words, if new or existing water projects are in compliance with the agreement, they cannot have their licenses refused or revoked over endangered species. If, however, even one state fails to abide by its commitment, the entire agreement fails and endangered species consultations will be resumed. Furthermore, if after the agreement is in place for thirteen years and if the research suggests that the increment of water is insufficient to adequately protect the endangered species, the three states and the Department of the Interior will negotiate over an additional increment of water (Cooperative Agreement 1997).

Even though the Platte River Cooperative Agreement signaled a dramatic redrawing of boundaries and of who was allowed to directly participate in decision making, local entities and projects were not excluded, as we will see. Owners and developers of local water projects could opt out of the cooperative agreement and attempt to obtain licenses through the regular permitting process, and that would include endangered species consultations. Given the precedent set by the Nebraska hydropower dam, with the FERC demanding and receiving over half of the water of one of the power districts, local districts were unlikely to pursue this option. Rather, the participation of local entities was redirected to the state level. Local water users and project owners and operators had to abide by state requirements in order to have their projects covered by the cooperative agreement. Furthermore, local entities had to cooperate with state agencies and abide by state laws if the states were to realize the commitments they made in the cooperative agreement.

The boundary shift achieved some goals of Nebraska officials but also placed new challenges upon them. First, Nebraska is required to ensure that new water uses do not affect the Platte River. Second, it must ensure that the additional amounts of water that Colorado and Wyoming deliver to its borders are safely shepherded to the Big Bend region. The two issues are closely linked: if new water uses within the state are not effectively mitigated, they could easily consume the water that the other states make available for restoration of the river.

The major use of water in Nebraska is for agriculture. The major source of water for agriculture is groundwater that is hydrologically connected to the Platte River. Consequently, groundwater pumping must be carefully regulated if Nebraska is to meet its commitments under the cooperative agreement. Until very recently, Nebraska water law placed very few restrictions on groundwater use. Groundwater is governed by local natural resource districts. Districts, by law, have the authority to develop and administer groundwater management plans; however, no district straddling the Platte River has chosen to do so. In effect, then, overlying landowners may pump as much groundwater as they can put to beneficial use on their lands. The only requirement is that they obtain state well permits and do not violate well spacing rules (Mossman 1996).

Agricultural interests have actively and effectively resisted state-level efforts to require natural resource districts to develop and implement groundwater management plans that would limit the effects of pumping on surface water flows (Mossman 1996). Farmers believe they are being asked to bear a disproportionate share of the burden of protecting endangered species and that in so doing their livelihoods will be undermined. Furthermore, they resist granting the state additional powers to regulate groundwater, a resource that historically has been under local control. Agricultural interests have attempted to avoid becoming participants in protecting endangered species. By all these means, they have worked to opt out of the process and to prevent the boundaries of water conservation and habitat protection from being drawn around them.

As a result of this strong opposition from agricultural groups, it took the Nebraska legislature, governor, and several citizen task forces almost a decade to develop and adopt legislation requiring integrated water resources management by natural resource districts and the Department of Natural Resources in over-appropriated basins. Natural resource districts, which have authority over groundwater, now must adopt regulations to limit the effects of groundwater pumping on surface water flows, and the Nebraska Department of Natural Resources, which has authority over surface water, must adopt conservation and best management practices for surface water users (Mossman 1996; Aiken 2004). Following the passage of legislation in 2004 granting the Department of Natural Resources the authority to declare over-appropriated basins, the department declared the Platte River upstream of the Big Bend region as over-appropriated. The immediate effect was to forbid the development of new wells until a management plan for the area was adopted (Nemec 2005).

The Platte River watershed consists of nested sets of overlapping boundaries with different groups of participants central to each. States and federal agencies are the primary participants in providing for endangered species recovery; however, such efforts rest on the intricate relations between states and local water users. The ability of states to deliver the first increment of water and to protect river flows from new uses depends centrally on their ability to persuade, cajole, entice, and coerce local water users to change how they acquire and use water. Although local water users and environmental groups have seats at the Platte River governing table, as discussed below, their authority relative to state and federal representatives is highly circumscribed. Rather than being full and active participants at the watershed level, they are full and active participants at the state level, where they participate in legislative hearings, agency rule makings, blue ribbon panels, and court cases, and where as citizens they vote.

The reluctance of agricultural interests in Nebraska to embrace close regulation of groundwater pumping and the cause of endangered species certainly appears to vindicate a healthy suspicion of local, place-based interests. As argued earlier in the chapter, local interests may focus on economic activities to the exclusion of a variety of other legitimate values. That, however, would be too simple a reading of this case. At various times, actors at a variety of scales—including federal agencies, state governments, and interest groups—supported, were indifferent to, and opposed addressing endangered species issues. FERC, for example, a federal agency charged with abiding by the ESA, only reluctantly addressed endangered species issues after it lost a court case brought by the Whooping Crane Trust, a small nonprofit organization located in the Big Bend region of Nebraska (Aiken 1999). The Whooping Crane Trust was created when Nebraska sued two federal agencies for funding and licensing a large surface water project in Wyoming that would have siphoned off a large volume of water from the North Platte, negatively affecting crane habitat. Nebraska successfully claimed that the agencies neglected the consultation requirements of the ESA (Aiken 1999). Federal, state, and local entities often represent a variety of interests and values—interests and values that change over time.

Ultimately, the question of boundaries is not so much either/or—either everyone who takes an interest in a watershed participates or only local and directly affected interests participate. Nor is it safe to assume which values will be best realized by governments or groups organized at which scales. Instead, as we see in the Platte River Basin, the question of boundaries is primarily a question of how: how to accommodate the many, varied, and conflicting interests present in a watershed. Most often, in the United States, it has been a process of defining multiple decision-making arenas that overlap one another and that at varying times complement and at other times conflict with one another.

Decision-Making Processes

The decision-making processes established by the cooperative agreement are also varied and contingent: they depend on who is making the decision and the level of conflict involved. The agreement creates a governance committee that reviews, directs, and provides oversight to the activities undertaken as part of the cooperative agreement. The governance committee consists of a representative from each state, an FWS representative, a Bureau of Reclamation (BOR) representative, two environmental representatives, and three members representing specific water interests, for a total of ten representatives. A quorum is met with the representatives of the FWS, BOR, each state, and two of the other representatives. Thus, although a quorum is possible without a majority of the water and environmental interests present, a quorum is impossible without all of the federal and state representatives present.

Informal consensus is the preferred decision-making mechanism, although a voting process may be used if consensus cannot be reached (Cooperative Agreement 1997, 9–10). The governance committee's bylaws state: "The Governance Committee will attempt to operate by informal consensus. Votes will be taken when appropriate" (Draft Platte River Recovery Implementation Program, 2003, Attachment 6, 3). Yet, even voting must achieve near-unanimity: nine of the ten representatives, including all of the federal and state representatives, must vote in the affirmative for the governance committee to act.

Furthermore, the governance committee is allowed to establish specialized committees to carry out specific duties. For instance, a financial management committee provides oversight for funds provided to the governance committee, contracts engaged in by the governance committee, and the payment of expenses. It consists of seven representatives, one for each state and federal agency, one for water interests, and one for environmental interests. A quorum consists of the representatives from the states and federal agencies. Consensus is the only decision rule. If consensus on an issue is not reached, the issue is passed along to the governance committee with a complete report outlining the different viewpoints on unresolved issues (Cooperative Agreement, 1997, 2–4, Milestones).

These decision-making rules appear designed to encourage the participants to identify and process differences and conflicts before coming to a collective decision. Action by a minority is avoided, but the federal agencies and states can ensure through their veto capabilities that they do not have to take actions that would violate laws that they are bound to uphold.

Accountability

Earlier we asked how, and how should, new forms of watershed governance fit within the existing political system and all of its familiar accountability mechanisms. The Platte River Cooperative Agreement demonstrates the relevance of this question. The agreement exemplifies the new forms of watershed governance that do not easily or readily fit within familiar accountability mechanisms.

Often when states engage in cooperative undertakings to address shared problems, they develop compacts, which are enforceable agreements recognized and protected under the U.S. Constitution. For states to engage in a compact, they must first receive permission from Congress. Once a compact is negotiated, each participating state's legislature must ratify it, as must Congress (Zimmerman 2002). States may enforce compacts by bringing their grievances before the U.S. Supreme Court—the court of original jurisdiction in addressing conflicts among states. Compacts are thus buttressed by familiar accountability mechanisms—multiple legislative approval points and judicial oversight.

The Platte River Cooperative Agreement, however, is not a compact. It is a purely voluntary arrangement among the states. Any party to it may withdraw at any point. The legislatures of the three states do not have to ratify the agreement, nor does Congress. Yet the states have promised considerable sums of water and money, have committed to future projects and activities that will provide additional volumes of water for the river, and have committed themselves to working for new state water laws and codes that will allow the realization of their commitments. Furthermore, the governance committee and its specialized committees that oversee the agreement and that have the authority to commit states and federal agencies to engage in various activities are populated by appointed officials and citizens. Although the appointed officials are at least accountable to elected officials who appoint them, citizen appointees are accountable to no one save the interest groups they represent. At first glance, all of the familiar accountability mechanisms appear to be missing. Is it possible to hold the parties to the agreement accountable?

If we view the agreement through the lens of Weber's (2003) argument that accountability occurs at different levels and along multiple dimensions through a variety of mechanisms, and not just through the lens of traditional forms of accountability, then we see an arrangement laced with accountability mechanisms. The parties to the agreement—federal agencies and states—utilize multiple methods for holding one another to commitments made. Furthermore, the water users, citizens, and taxpayers subject to the agreement and to paying for it have access to multiple accountability mechanisms, some familiar, some not.

First, the parties to the agreement bound themselves tightly together. If the states abide by the agreement and if they provide the promised water, they will be deemed in compliance with the ESA and they can avoid consultations on new and existing water uses, which to this point have resulted in new uses that require federal permits disallowed and existing uses threatened. Thus, the states and the major water users in the states have much to gain from abiding by the agreement. If, however, the agreement is not followed, if even one state fails to abide by its commitment, the entire agreement fails and endangered species consultations will be resumed. The parties to the agreement either succeed or fail together.

Second, the states established readily measured goals tied to specific time lines in order to track their overall progress and to detect whether a state was failing in its commitment. In addition, to ensure that the water committed by the states does not simply get absorbed through new uses, each state is required to mitigate the effects on the river of all new surface and groundwater projects. Wyoming and Colorado argue that their state laws require new users to cover their impacts. And they agreed to ensure that outcome. If it were discovered that new uses were not adequately covered, the states committed to providing additional amounts of water that they have under their control (Draft Recovery Implementation Program 2003). Nebraska, with the passage of major water legislation in 2004, can make the same commitment. Its water laws require that all new water uses are mitigated.

In an environment with such high stakes and with an appreciable level of uncertainty, monitoring water users' actions and the natural system becomes critical. The cooperative agreement contains four major monitoring provisions. First, each state is required to provide data on water use to the governance committee several times per year. The data are to include baseline flows of the river, existing water uses, new water uses, and how new uses were covered. Each state also provides a final year-end water accounting. Second, an employee of the FWS acts as a water accounting manager.

The accounting manager, working with each of the states and water project operators, monitors river flows and directs the release of water at times and places to best assist in the protection and recovery of species. The accounting manager is also required to report to the governance committee multiple times throughout the year. Third, the implementation plan establishes a relatively sophisticated biological response monitoring program targeted at the Big Bend region of the Platte River. Its purpose is to monitor the response of endangered species to determine whether the program is achieving its goals of protecting and recovering the species. Information from the biological monitoring program is provided to the water accounts manager to inform his water release decisions. Fourth, the information is supplied to the governance committee to be used to modify implementation plans. Overall, the implementation plan envisions a relatively sophisticated monitoring system that requires the participation of all participants. The states monitor their own water users, an accounting manager monitors the states, a group of scientists monitors the biological responses of the species, and the governance committee monitors each of the individual monitoring mechanisms. The monitoring plan holds the potential to provide participants with sufficient information to determine whether all are following through with their commitments.

Furthermore, the parties to the agreement hold one another accountable through the decision process, much as Weber (2003) argued concerning small-scale watershed collaboratives. The preferred decision rule is consensus, which requires discussion, deliberation, and the exchange of ideas. If consensus cannot be reached, then voting is allowed, but it requires that all of the state and federal representatives, and most of the water and environmental representatives, vote in the affirmative in order to reach a binding decision. These decision rules prevent bare majorities and single holdouts from dominating the process. The combination of decision rules allows the participants to hold one another to account without holding one another hostage.

The participants to the agreement may hold one another accountable for decisions and actions, but what about larger forms of democratic accountability? Can those who are not direct parties to the agreement exercise some forms of accountability? The answer is yes, although these forms tend to be weighted more heavily toward legal mechanisms and less toward political, hierarchical, or professional mechanisms. The federal agencies and states remain bound by federal and state laws. If the governance committee makes decisions that appear to violate those laws, citizens may invoke judicial review. Also, at the behest of local water users, the governance committee agreed to limit its powers. The agreement specifically forbids the exercise of certain types of authorities that the states, under other circumstances, are allowed to exercise. For instance, states are not allowed to exercise their powers of eminent domain in order to condemn private property or water rights. All acquisitions of private property and water rights are to be from voluntary sellers. Thus, for citizens, water users, taxpayers, and property owners, their first and most prominent forms of accountability are legal.[5]

The creation of the Platte River Cooperative Agreement and its implementing governance structure provides an enlightening glimpse of the many and difficult political decisions that must be made in devising workable and accountable institutional arrangements for governing watersheds. At no time did the authors of the agreement and governance structure engage in "either/or crafting," that is, either consensus or majority rule, either all interests or local interests, either political accountability or legal accountability, and so forth. Rather, the authors of the agreement developed multiple ways of addressing boundaries, decision making, and accountability, typically with a primary approach buttressed by secondary approaches.

No doubt, there is plenty to criticize concerning the Platte River Cooperative Agreement. It is complex in its governing structure and its science, it is incremental and effects only gradual change, it is slow to make decisions, it provides state governments and federal agencies with disproportionate influence, it does not provide for a single decision maker, and it fails to take advantage of some traditional political accountability mechanisms, such as allowing citizens or state legislatures to vote on the agreement.

It is certainly all of those things, but all of those things must be understood in context. Before the agreement, all new water projects were shelved or substantially modified. Before the agreement, existing water projects were subject to substantial revision as they came up for re-licensing. If the agreement fails, endangered species protection in the Platte River Basin will revert to business as usual: a project-by-project battle to protect endangered species. Given that context, it is understandable that its designers view it as a more effective, efficient, equitable, and adaptive approach than what preceded it and what is likely to occur if it fails.

CONCLUSION

By now, it should be apparent that there are multiple ways of defining who matters in decision making, how collective decisions should be made, and how decision makers should be held accountable. Furthermore, there is no one best way to define who should matter or how decision making or accountability should be realized. As is so often the case in politics, it depends. It depends on the issues, their causes, their impacts, and possible solutions, and how those things are distributed across space, time, and people. In practice as well as in theory, multiple answers are available to these issues, and many different choices have been made.

The answers are invariably imperfect. They involve trade-offs. Using a more expansive notion of who matters risks undervaluing local interests; privileging local interests may neglect broader values. Consequently, the choices people make in watersheds are contested and challenged.

Furthermore, watershed settings are dynamic—economic activity, demography, culture values, and understandings of human-nature interactions change, and at least some of today's choices will not make sense in future circumstances and will be contested and challenged anew. Watershed settings in the real world also have histories. In choosing among the imperfect institutional alternatives available, people do not begin from scratch. Ordinarily, they try to accommodate new circumstances, and realize more pressing values, by adding to existing arrangements and then figuring out how to make it all work in terms of efficiency, effectiveness, and fairness.

These arguments are pragmatic, but they are not merely pragmatic inductions derived from numerous watershed case studies. They are also analytical, deducible from some basic considerations of governance and management in a watershed or other setting. The next chapter presents such an analysis.

NOTES

1. See Milon, Kiker, and Lee 1998 for an account of consensus results in the Everglades Restoration Project; and see Coglianese 1999 for an evaluation of consensus decision making used by the EPA to develop the report on Enterprise for the Environment.

2. As Kagan (1997, 873) states, "The contemporary search for collaboration often springs from a desperate effort to hold at bay the costly and alienating delays

and deadlocks that spring from litigation—litigation that in turn springs from the complexity of our legal system."

3. As Scharpf (1997, 174) notes, proponents of integrated watershed management are not the only ones enamored with hierarchical direction: "[S]ubstantive policy research . . . is characterized by a strong elective affinity to hierarchical coordination. Policy recommendations are characteristically addressed to an idealized 'policymaker' with the assumed capacity to overrule the preferences of other actors, regardless of any conflicting interests and perceptions. . . . [E]conomic theorists following Pigou who were impressed with the inefficiency of market failures have opted for hierarchical state intervention in the economy to correct negative externalities; and transaction-cost economists following Coase who were impressed with the difficulties of negotiated agreements have opted for vertical integration in hierarchically organized firms to avoid the high costs of contracting under conditions of uncertainty and opportunism. From all of these perspectives, the focus is on the social benefits that can in principle be achieved through hierarchical coordination rather than on the contextual preconditions for the effective exercise of hierarchical authority."

4. In Wyoming, the Grayrocks Dam and reservoir were substantially modified and the owners of the proposed Deer Creek reservoir were required to purchase and manage critical habitat as a condition of building it; in Colorado, the Wildcat and Narrows irrigation projects have been deferred, the Two Forks reservoir that was to supply water to the Denver metropolitan area was stopped, and numerous special-use permits issued by the U.S. Forest Service that allowed communities to impound and divert water on Forest Service land were modified; in Nebraska, the Little Blue/Catherland irrigation project, the Perkins County Canal, the Enders irrigation project, the Prairie Bend I and II irrigation projects, and the Landmark irrigation project were all stopped (Aikens 1999, 128–137).

5. Legal mechanisms are not the only ones that may be exercised. At the request of numerous citizens and interest groups, the governance committee, in cooperation with the Department of the Interior, commissioned a review by the National Research Council of the science used to develop the agreement. The National Research Council review supported the science developed thus far and urged that it be more broadly developed. Thus, professional review of data and modeling was exercised.

4

Imaginary Watersheds and Political Realities

Salmon are important not merely for those who harvest them, but also
are the ultimate barometer of the health of aquatic ecosystems. Salmon
also have deep cultural, historic, and religious significance, particularly
to Northwest Indian tribes. For these reasons it is not an exaggeration to
suggest that salmon are the spiritual soul of the Pacific Northwest.

MICHAEL BLUMM (1997, 655)

INTRODUCTION

As discussed in Chapter 2, for more than a century, the U.S. government,
at various times, has attempted to organize large-scale river basin entities
to coordinate and manage the activities of federal and state agencies. Many
of these efforts, especially of a national scope, such as the Title II river basin
commissions, have failed for a variety of political reasons—turf wars among
federal agencies, conflicts between states and federal agencies over control of
commissions, demands by local governments and citizens for greater roles

in planning and decision making, and conflicts over the proper role of the federal government in water development, protection, and management (Derthick 1974; Allee et al. 1981).[1] Nevertheless, urgent calls for comprehensive, integrated watershed management continue to be made (Reisler 1981; Stakhiv 2003).

Derthick (1974) labels regional governments (including the Title II river basin commissions and the Delaware River Compact Commission, discussed in Chapter 6) political accidents. For Derthick (1974, 226), political accidents occur "only in very special circumstances, when there is a fortuitous coming together of opportunity, leadership, and political backing, so that it becomes possible to go against the institutional grain and create a genuinely new form." The term "political accidents" suggests two points: (1) comprehensive, integrated management is rare; and (2) if the political stars align properly, it is possible. In this chapter, we explore the second point. Assuming a highly favorable political environment, is it possible to devise a strong form of comprehensive integrated watershed management?

This question is important to ask and answer because it strikes at the thesis of this book—politics matters. Politics matters because as people cooperate, bargain, negotiate, make trade-offs, and fight over how to govern a watershed, they devise many overlapping institutional arrangements. Suppose, however, that a "political accident" occurs, where people agree on watershed goals and how to accomplish them. Would comprehensive integrated watershed management emerge then?

Admittedly, this is a difficult question to answer, because such positive political settings do not exist. Consequently, to explore it requires an experiment—a thought experiment. We engage in a thought experiment for two reasons. One, there are no watersheds in the United States that are free of institutions. Thus, to examine whether it is possible to construct integrated, comprehensive watershed management that will not be undermined by existing institutional arrangements, it is necessary to begin with a thought experiment that allows for a clean institutional slate. Two, a clean institutional slate provides every advantage to the designers of an integrated comprehensive system. If it is possible to design such a system from scratch, then comprehensive, integrated watershed management remains a promising policy alternative. If, however, it is impossible to design such a system, even in a highly supportive environment, then comprehensive, integrated management must be set aside for more feasible options.

We rest our analysis on the cornerstones of bounded rationality and transaction costs. They capture two essential and unavoidable aspects of social settings: human decision making has well-known and well-understood limitations, and the creation and operation of institutional arrangements is costly. It may seem unusual to emphasize two such elemental features, but often people advocate policies without regard for the cognitive demands of such policies or the costs of their creation and operation (Jones 2001). If we are interested in understanding what institutional designs are possible, we must make reasonable assumptions about how people make choices, including choices about designing institutions, and the costs they must bear in so doing.

We proceed in this chapter by first introducing the key theoretical concepts of bounded rationality, the different forms of transaction costs, and how transaction costs are linked. Second, we develop a thought experiment in which we assume a watershed that is free of politics, at least initially, where we can explore the challenges of developing a comprehensive integrated management system in a world of transaction costs. In the final section of the chapter, we examine the effort to realize a more comprehensive and integrated form of watershed governance in the Columbia River Basin. Congress created an overarching organization to bring together the different governments, interest groups, and citizens to protect and enhance salmon stocks while maintaining dynamic economies founded on inexpensive hydropower. The Northwest Power Planning Council is statutorily created with specific mandates and authorities. It has a dedicated source of funding and its own staff to support plan development, technical analyses, and monitoring. At least on paper it appears to come close to comprehensive integrated management under a watershed-wide authority, and, in fact, it can boast of many positive accomplishments, such as closer working relations between state and tribal fish and wildlife agencies, the development of many watershed collaboratives and watershed plans, and a greater understanding of adaptive management in practice, among others. But the two most sought-after goals—salmon recovery and comprehensive integrated management—have remained terribly elusive. Those goals remain elusive not simply because of politics but because of boundedly rational people struggling to achieve collective goals in the face of transaction costs.

BOUNDED RATIONALITY

Bounded rationality is best understood in relation to perfect rationality, which is the neoclassical microeconomics model of the individual. The perfectly rational person makes choices so as to maximize his or her utility. Individuals are quite capable of maximizing their utility because they exhibit perfect and boundless computational abilities and possess perfect and complete information. For analytical purposes, such individuals possess well-defined utility functions, complete and well-defined sets of alternatives from which to choose, and probability distributions over all possible states of the world. Armed with such information and computational power, individuals, when confronted with a choice, select the alternative that maximizes utility. As Simon (1983, 34) suggests, the model better describes the mind of God than of man.

A boundedly rational individual possesses limited cognitive processing capabilities and information. Such an individual is intendedly rational in the pursuit of instrumental goals but is limited in that pursuit by her cognitive and information resources (Simon 1957). Boundedly rational people systematically and predictably violate the tenets of perfect rationality. For instance, people are influenced by how a decision is framed. If a decision is framed in terms of the gains that a person may realize, people make choices as if they are risk seeking. If the same decision is framed in terms of the losses a person may experience, people make choices as if they are risk averse—same decision, differently framed, leads to different choices (Markman and Medin 2002). A perfectly rational individual would not be affected by framing. That individual would always choose the alternative that maximizes utility, no matter how the alternatives are framed. Furthermore, people are satisficers and not optimizers. They select alternatives that are good enough rather than expending inordinate amounts of time gathering information and making careful and systematic comparisons among alternatives. Finally, how people process information and make choices is influenced by goals, motivations, beliefs, and emotions. People who are more cooperative and altruistic tend to be more concerned with collective outcomes than are people who are more individualistic and competitive (Kopelman et al. 2002, 119). Both cooperators and competitors, however, tend to attribute greater intelligence to their more preferred strategy than to the opposite strategy. That is, cooperators view other cooperators as more intelligent than competitors and vice versa (Kopelman et al. 2002, 121).[2]

None of this should be read to imply that instead of being perfectly rational, people are perfectly irrational. People are goal-oriented and purposive, but limited in their cognitive competence (Simon 1957). Boundedly rational individuals can learn and adapt to their immediate environment and, over time, learn and adapt to changing environments; however, learning and adaptation will be episodic and disjointed because of the structure and operation of their cognitive architecture (Jones and Baumgartner 2005).

At this point, supporters of comprehensive, integrated watershed management may object and claim that they do not expect individuals to make comprehensive, integrated decisions; rather, they expect institutional arrangements to support and guide people's choices so that choices are more nearly comprehensive and integrated. Although institutional arrangements allow people to collectively accomplish what they could not as individuals, institutions are created by boundedly rational people and they must be understood in terms of the goals and capabilities of their designers (Williamson 1985). As Jones (2001, 14) notes, "the institutions that exist as a product of human culture seem to work best when the limits and potentialities of human nature are taken into consideration." Assuming decision makers are boundedly rational is critical for understanding institutional design and performance.

TRANSACTION COSTS

Boundedly rational people act in a costly world. They must expend resources—time, money, expertise, social capital, and so forth—in developing, implementing, monitoring, enforcing, and revising institutional arrangements. Those costs shape and constrain the types of institutional arrangements that people devise (Williamson 1985).

The most common types of transaction costs are decision making, agency, and commitment (Moe 1989; Horn 1995). Making a collective decision involves information costs in identifying the problem or opportunity, identifying and developing alternative courses of action, and bargaining and negotiating over selecting a single course of action. Furthermore, in many instances the process of decision making will not occur in such a rational sequence (Kingdon 1995). Some people will prefer a particular policy alternative no matter the problem. Also, problems may be poorly defined and their underlying causes unidentified, but policy decisions are made anyway, even if they may not address the problem.

Decision-making costs are partly a function of characteristics of decision makers and partly a function of context. Decision makers with diverse values, preferences, and goals are much more likely to experience higher decision-making costs than decision makers with similar values, preferences, and goals. Diverse decision makers will have to spend more time discussing, bargaining, and negotiating in order to reach a decision. Of course, the ability to reach a collective decision is also a function of decision rules. A unanimity rule imposes very high decision-making costs, as each person must agree to a course of action, compared to simple majority rules. Finally, the larger social and physical context affects decision-making costs. Well-defined problems with clear causal mechanisms are likely to present clearer courses of action and consequently lower decision-making costs.

Most decision makers do not implement their decisions. Rather, policies are turned over to others to carry out. Agency costs involve ensuring that policy implementers, the agents of the policy makers, put the policies into place in ways intended by decision makers. Some slippage always occurs between what policy makers intended and what implementers of the policies do. Agency costs arise from a variety of sources. Agents may not have the expertise or experience to competently carry out the tasks. Or they may pursue courses of action that are more aligned with their own values or interests and not those of policy makers or key constituents.[3] In a number of instances, detecting agency problems is difficult. Government programs often bear multiple and conflicting mandates (the residue of high decision-making costs), providing implementers with considerable discretion in carrying out their duties. Thus, it may be difficult to distinguish between purposeful undermining of policies and the legitimate exercise of discretion.

Finally, commitment problems arise because sometimes people are tempted to act in ways that run counter to what they promised.[4] Commitments support cooperative endeavors as parties to a project are assured that at some later date they will not be taken advantage of. For instance, a common rule used to allocate resources among miners, ranchers, and irrigators during the nineteenth century in the western United States was "first in time, first in right." Those first to exploit a resource were granted rights protecting their uses from newcomers who sought access to the resources. Secure rights encouraged people to invest in economically productive activities. With rights in water, farmers could make long-term investments in irrigation systems, knowing that their systems would not be rendered useless by others taking their water.

Commitments are made credible through mechanisms that limit the opportunities and the value of breaking an agreement.[5] For instance, water-use rights based on first in time, first in right are recognized and protected in the constitutions of most western states. For a state government to change to different rules of water allocation and use, the state's constitution would have to be amended as opposed to simply passing a piece of legislation. Constitutional amendments are difficult and costly, so writing a property right into a constitution limits the opportunities for dismantling the right and therefore strengthens the credibility of commitments by individuals based on those assignments of rights.

The commitment coin has two sides. Credible commitments allow citizens, organizations, and communities to cooperate to solve shared problems or realize common goals, but at the same time, it is difficult to change or transform credible commitments. That is, after all, what makes them credible. Over time, as circumstances change and new interests seek to participate in policy making and have their goals credibly committed to, existing institutional arrangements representing commitments to different interests act as barriers to change. For instance, urban and environmental interests are frustrated that agriculture controls significant portions of water in most western states, even though agriculture no longer dominates western states' economies. Urban and environmental interests want to draw water out of agriculture but find it very difficult to overcome the credible commitments made to agriculture in an earlier time.[6]

These different types of transaction costs are not independent of one another—they are interactive. One type of transaction cost may be reduced, but often at the expense of increasing another type of transaction cost. People have to attend to these trade-offs among transaction costs to develop institutional arrangements. One approach to reduce decision-making costs is to adopt relatively vague directives. Instead of spending time and resources agreeing on all details of a policy, decision makers may leave portions of the policy vague, with the expectation that policy implementers will imbue them with greater content and specificity. Vague directives granting implementers more discretion, however, increase agency costs. Agency costs may be reduced, but usually through increased decision-making costs as policy makers design more specific policies to limit the discretion of implementers.

Commitment problems and agency costs also interact. Credible commitments are costly to undo, opening the possibility of higher agency costs. For instance, decision makers could commit to pursuing environmental goals by hiring a group of professional experts with impeccable environmental credentials and granting them civil service protection, making it very difficult and costly to fire them. Such a credible commitment raises agency costs. Policy makers will find it difficult to hold implementers protected by civil service accountable. Policy makers could anticipate these agency problems and insert a sunset clause into the environmental policy requiring policy makers to reconsider and review the policy and either renew it or let it expire. Reopening the policy to address agency problems, however, allows commitment problems to reemerge. In revising the policy, policy makers can just as easily undo their commitments to various aspects of the policy as they can address agency problems. Trade-offs among transaction costs are as ubiquitous as transaction costs themselves.

Transaction costs influence and condition the institutional choices people make. People are not free to design any type of institution or policy they desire: they must settle on a tolerable mix of transaction costs. Different types of institutional arrangements represent different mixes of transaction costs and trade-offs among them. Are decision makers willing to bear greater agency costs in order to avoid commitment problems? Are they willing to take on greater decision-making costs in order to reduce agency costs? Answers to these questions are heavily influenced by the values and goals of the decision makers as well as the types of problems they are attempting to address.

A THOUGHT EXPERIMENT

We begin our thought experiment with an ideal situation for an advocate of watershed-level integrated and comprehensive management. A like-minded group of boundedly rational people are committed to the broad goal of integrated watershed management and possess comprehensive authority to make governing decisions on all aspects of a watershed. These watershed decision makers are faced with two types of choices. First, they will have to choose policies for governing the watershed. Second, they will have to choose how to best organize and direct the people implementing the policies.

Choosing Policies

Decision costs of like-minded policy makers may be lower because they will mostly agree on what constitutes good policy. Comprehensive integrated decisions, however, present special challenges to boundedly rational people. Comprehensiveness requires consideration of the multiple components and dimensions of a watershed, not just one or two. Integration requires that the policies are ordered and sensible, working together, not at cross-purposes, to realize a shared vision of the watershed. Making comprehensive, integrated decisions about a complex adaptive system requires a considerable level of information about the structure and functioning of the watershed and mechanisms to continuously update the information. Thus, information costs to support comprehensive, integrated decision making will be high.

Even more challenging for decision makers is choosing among incommensurate alternatives. Incommensurate alternatives are things, people, or policies that possess multiple attributes in different combinations and degrees. They do not correspond in degree or extent in their attributes and consequences and no common metric exists to ease the choices among them.[7] The epigraph for this chapter notes such a choice involving watersheds—water development versus fish, and not just fish but aquatic life, riparian habitat, and, in the case of the Pacific Northwest, human cultures.

Almost by definition, comprehensive, integrated watershed decision making means that policy makers will confront choices among incommensurate alternatives. As Jones (2001) notes, boundedly rational individuals struggle mightily with incommensurate choices. Are there mechanisms or decision-making processes that would ease the burden?[8]

One approach is to identify each attribute of each alternative, assign a weight to each attribute, use the weighted attributes to develop an overall score for each alternative, and then compare the scores of the alternatives and select the one with the best score.[9] The decision-making costs of such a process for each decision that policy makers must make would be quite high, even for a like-minded group of policy makers.[10] Other ways of addressing the high decision-making costs associated with choosing among incommensurate alternatives involve simplifying the alternatives and their attributes so the burden of comprehensive integration is reduced (Jones 2001).

Derthick (1974), in examining the decision-making processes of the TVA, noted the struggle of the three commissioners in choosing among incommensurate alternatives. They handled sharp differences among themselves over how the major activities of the organization should be integrated and coordinated by specialization (Derthick 1974, 205). Each commissioner took control of a major activity, with little attempt to engage in close coordination. Eventually, the board hired an executive director to handle the day-to-day operations and decisions, but the divisions among functions remained (Derthick 1974, 205). As Derthick (1974, 206) argues: "There was nothing here to suggest the incomparable superiority of the autonomous regional corporation as an integrative instrument. Eventually, electric power operations came to predominate overwhelmingly, although an ideal of coordination would probably have called for harmonization of a wide range of related activities."

Besides simplifying decisions, policy makers could turn to professional experts to develop more comprehensive analyses of alternatives and score them. Doing so would lower their decision-making costs but increase agency costs. Policy makers would have to take steps to ensure that the professionals who developed and evaluated the alternatives did so in a way that was responsive to their values.

Decision-making tools may relieve decision makers of developing copious amounts of information, but they are only useful to the extent decision makers rely on them. Invariably, decision makers will confront situations in which they prefer an alternative different from the one the decision tool suggests is best. Such situations occur for a variety of reasons—an alternative may impose costs on a well-defined group of citizens that can least afford to bear them, for instance, or an alternative may require that a particular habitat or species receive greater protection than people's livelihoods. The reasons are likely to be innumerable.

In order to commit to a decision-making tool, policy makers must in some way tie their hands so that they cannot discard the tool when it serves their purposes to do so. This may be accomplished in different ways. Decision makers may write into legislation that the tool must be used in making decisions or can be disregarded only if an extraordinary majority agrees to use a different process. That is, they can avoid their commitment only through increased decision-making costs.

Decision makers may instead direct professional experts to use the decision-making tool and only forward to them the alternatives with the best scores. This, however, invites agency costs. If the experts have a stake in the options selected or strong preferences for particular alternatives, they may manipulate the decision tool to realize their preferences. A classic case of decision makers and professional experts grappling with decision-making tools concerns the relationship between Congress and the Army Corps of Engineers. Since at least 1936, with the passage of the Flood Control Act, Congress has required the Corps of Engineers to use cost-benefit analyses to select viable projects (Committee to Assess 1999). Over time, Congress has required the Corps of Engineers to engage in more sophisticated analyses and consider additional dimensions of projects, but cost-benefit analyses remain as the foundational decision tool. Congress and the Corps have struggled with such analyses. The budget, prestige, and political support of the Corps hinge on building projects, even projects with marginal or poor cost-benefit ratios. Members of Congress benefit from having a project in their districts or states, even if the project cannot be justified in cost-benefit terms, since the benefits are concentrated in specific districts and states and at least a portion of the costs is spread across all U.S. taxpayers. Consequently, the Army Corps of Engineers has exercised its discretion in ways that have made some projects more attractive, and members of Congress have not objected.

Over the past two decades, increasing pressure has been brought to bear from a variety of sources—reform-minded members of Congress, environmental groups, taxpayer groups, National Academy of Sciences committees, to name a few—to revise the process by which the Corps recommends projects to Congress (Committee to Assess 1999; Coordinating Committee 2004; New York Times 2006). The reform that has been repeatedly pursued, but that has not yet received congressional approval, is independent review of any project costing more than $40 million (New York Times 2006). Such independent oversight is intended to encourage Congress and the Corps to renew their commitment to selecting and funding projects in a more objective fashion.

Advocates of integrated watershed management rarely assume that integrating and coordinating various complex and difficult aspects of human uses of watersheds will be easy, but they do assume that it can be done reasonably well. With sufficient information, resources, and authority, difficult comparisons and trade-offs can be made and comprehensive, integrated choices can be achieved. The above analysis suggests, however, that comprehensive, integrated decision making will rapidly overwhelm people's cognitive capabilities. Boundedly rational people will seek to cope with such complexity by using a variety of simplifying mechanisms that they hope will reduce their decision-making costs. As transaction cost theory suggests, reducing decision-making costs inevitably creates opportunities for agency problems and/or commitment problems to emerge. People confront cognitive and cost limitations in developing and selecting policies, limitations that push them away from comprehensive integrated decisions.

Implementing Policies

Agency costs accrue as boundedly rational policy makers try to ensure that the policies they have selected are implemented appropriately. Policy makers usually do not implement policies but turn the policies over to others to implement. How do decision makers ensure that their agents implement policies as the decision makers would want? Once again, we return to the now-familiar transaction costs trade-off story, but we add a time dimension.

Agency problems may be anticipated and addressed in a number of ways, none of them costless. One approach is to select implementers from a profession whose values, norms, and preferences are most closely aligned with those of the policy makers. Policy makers may then rest assured that as implementers make choices, even in uncertain or unique situations unanticipated by policy makers, they will do so in ways that the policy makers would themselves have done (Moe 1990). Another approach is for policy makers to define specifically and concretely the actions they want the implementers to follow. Providing specific instructions, guidelines, and even time lines limits the discretion of implementers and lowers agency costs.[11]

Relying on appropriate professionals or detailed instructions and guidelines will work as long as the values, norms, and preferences of policy makers do not change. Inevitably they will. At the very least, current policy makers can readily anticipate that they will be replaced and that their replacements may have different values, norms, and preferences. Current policy makers are then confronted with another set of choices: how to ensure the policies they adopt, which they believe are best for the watershed, remain in place even after they are no longer in positions of authority and no longer able to protect their programs. In other words, how can current policy makers commit future policy makers to particular courses of action?

One answer is to use mechanisms to insulate agencies, programs, and their employees from the reach of policy makers. Civil service systems, preventing policy makers from removing employees at will, are widely viewed as a means of insulating public employees from politics (Frant 1993; Horn 1995). Other examples include commission forms of agencies, in which commissioner terms are staggered and are for longer periods than elected officials; making it difficult for any particular coalition of decision makers to remove commissioners. Another mechanism is to adopt long periods between reauthorization dates, allowing a policy or program to become firmly established before policy makers have the opportunity to substantially revise or eliminate it (Moe 1990; Horn 1995). Or policy makers may provide individuals with property rights in the benefits of a program. If such property rights are recognized and protected in the larger legal system, they will be very difficult to substantially alter or eliminate.

Committing to an agency or program by insulating it from future policy change raises the probability of higher agency costs. Programs and employees may be more difficult to terminate, not just for future policy makers but for current ones. The ability of policy makers, present and future, to adjust programs to better fit changing circumstances, or to hold employees readily accountable, becomes increasingly constrained.

Consequently, future policy makers come into office confronting policies, organizations, and employees, put in place by their predecessors, that reflect values, norms, and preferences not of their own choosing. Even if these new policy makers are like-minded so that they may make decisions readily, they are now making decisions in a context with a history, and that history is difficult to back out of, just as their predecessors intended. They must attempt to realize their preferences in a context that will make it costly to do so. They may proceed along several avenues, none of which are mutually exclusive. They may attempt to roll back or eliminate programs and agencies created by their predecessors, which is the most costly and difficult approach to take. Employees will attempt to save their programs and their jobs, as will citizens who benefit from the programs. Policy makers will have to spend some of their limited time and resources overcoming such opposition. Although they may eliminate undesirable programs, they will still face the task of creating new ones better suited to their preferences.

A more attractive alternative than eliminating programs is creating additional programs that better suit their preferences and assign their implementation to existing organizations. Or create new organizations to implement the new programs and hire individuals whose professional values are aligned with those of the policy makers. In the former case, organizations evolve whose goals, missions, and programs may conflict. In the latter case, multiple organizations work in the same issue or problem area but with different authorities, activities, and missions. No matter which approach is selected, overall watershed management will begin to appear fragmented, piecemeal, limited, and myopic. Such appearances are amplified as boundedly rational policy makers struggle with incommensurate choices by simplifying decisions and pursuing less comprehensive and less integrated alternatives.

ADDITIONAL COMPLICATING FACTORS

Thus far, we have explored the choices made by like-minded, boundedly rational policy makers. Let us now assume that the policy makers are no longer like-minded. Instead, they hold different values, norms, and preferences. The most immediate effect is on decision-making costs. Policy makers with diverse preferences will experience increased levels of conflict and disagreement, leading to higher bargaining and negotiation costs as they search for common ground. Furthermore, incommensurate choices become that much more difficult and thus that much more important to minimize as policy makers contest over which attributes of a given policy are vital and which can be safely ignored, and which weights should be given to important attributes.

Policy makers with diverse preferences can attempt to lower decision-making costs in a variety of ways so that choices can be made and actions taken. One approach is logrolling, which should not be confused with comprehensive, integrated policies. Logrolling gives each policy maker some of what he or she wants, but the policies do not fit together in a comprehensive meaningful fashion. Another approach is to adopt vague policy, allowing each decision maker to interpret the policy as he or she prefers. The implementers bear the decision-making costs and the conflict of turning the vague policy into a better-defined and specified policy that could be implemented. Vague policies may lower decision-making costs but at the expense of increased agency problems. Also, commitment problems become more acute among policy makers with diverse preferences. Policy makers want to protect their hard-won policies not just from future policy makers with different preferences but from current policy makers as well. Addressing commitment problems by insulating them from politics ensures their durability, but at the price of agency problems. Agency problems could be reduced, but at the expense of commitment.

Another complicating factor is that watersheds are complex adaptive systems, as discussed in Chapter 1. It is just such an environment that has led to the call for comprehensive, integrated management. However, such an environment works against comprehensive, integrated management. Appropriate types of flood control, water quality, habitat protection or restoration, stream flows, and so forth are a function of time and place information. Water quality, threats to it, and approaches to recovering and/or maintaining it depend on a variety of factors, such as the type and location of the water sources and the types and locations of human activities that are impacting the sources. The transaction costs of making and implementing comprehensive, integrated policies that appropriately account for the wide variety of circumstances within a watershed simply explode. Decision-making costs escalate as policy makers struggle to obtain critical time and place information and address the distributional consequences of the policies under consideration. Commitment problems become more acute, as locking in one policy for one set of interests adversely affects other interests or limits policy makers' ability to act in other areas. Agency costs escalate as implementers struggle to apply uniform policies across a diverse and highly differentiated watershed.

As boundedly rational policy makers struggle to make choices among incommensurate alternatives in a world characterized by complexity and transaction costs, the choices they make and the means by which those choices are implemented are likely to appear fragmented, duplicative, and narrow. We do not end up in a world of watersheds advocated by proponents of comprehensive, integrated watershed management, even though that was our point of departure. Comprehensive, integrated management at the watershed level taxes the cognitive abilities of people and generates burdensome levels of transaction costs.

Should we abandon the goal of comprehensive, integrated watershed management? The previous analysis suggests that there are hard limits to accomplishing such a goal. Instead of ignoring those hard limits and continuing to press for such a goal, it may be more appropriate to design watershed governance systems that take bounded rationality and transaction costs into account. Paraphrasing Jones (2001), watershed management is more likely to be successful if it accounts for the limits and potentialities of human nature.

Our discussion of bounded rationality and transaction costs has been relatively abstract to this point, so we now turn to a specific watershed—the Columbia River Basin. It provides a rich setting for exploring the effects of bounded rationality and transaction costs. In 1980, Congress engaged in an experiment by superimposing the Northwest Power Planning Council on the many governments within the watershed. The council was to integrate fish and wildlife goals with power goals across the basin. The council has experienced limited success for a variety of reasons, including bounded rationality and transaction costs.

THE COLUMBIA RIVER BASIN

The human uses of the Columbia River Basin are diverse, stretching across the entire basin and at multiple scales. Thousands of acres have been transformed into irrigated agriculture. Irrigation districts and companies, large and small, divert millions of acre-feet of water from the river and its tributaries each year. Compared with the volume of water that passes through the river annually, such diversions appear modest. Compared with the water diverted for municipal and industrial use, they are significant, and not merely because of their magnitude. Irrigated agriculture absorbs much of its water roughly at the same times that anadromous fish need it, in the spring for smolt to traverse to the ocean and in the late summer for adults to travel upstream to spawn.

Mining and timber harvesting have also sustained generations of people in the Columbia River Basin. The impacts of both activities have reverberated throughout the basin. Extensive cutting of old-growth forests has imperiled several species of wildlife. Mining and timber harvesting together have polluted the region's streams and rivers with silt and toxic chemicals.

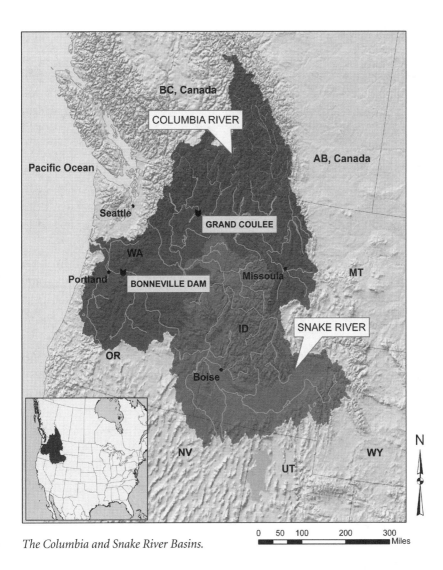

The Columbia and Snake River Basins.

Agriculture, mining, and timber harvesting dot the landscape, but what has led to the most extensive and tightly intertwined human use in the basin is harnessing the power of the Columbia River and its largest tributary, the Snake River, for electricity generation. Over fifty major dams and twelve major storage projects, built by the Army Corps of Engineers and the Bureau of Reclamation, capture and control the flow of the Columbia (Wandschneider 1984). Furthermore, under the Treaty Related to the

Cooperative Development of the Water Resources of the Columbia River Basin, signed by Canada and the United States in 1961, Canada built a series of dams and reservoirs, capturing much of the spring runoff that had, until that point, served to propel smolt to the ocean (Wandschneider 1984; Blumm and Simrin 1991). The system of dams and powerhouses in an average water year generates 16,000 average megawatts of power, fueling a large and robust economy (Northwest Power and Conservation Planning Council 2005). The dams have also had a profound effect on what many consider the touchstone species of the Columbia River Basin—salmon and steelhead trout. In recent years, about 1 million adult fish return to the basin each year to spawn. Prior to dam and hydroelectric power development, spawning fish numbered 10 to 16 million annually (Northwest Power Planning Council 2000).

These many uses of the Columbia River Basin are governed by many different and overlapping institutional arrangements.[12] Water allocation and use are governed by each of the states within the basin. Although all use the prior appropriation doctrine to govern water allocation and use, each state has its own distinct system of administration and rules. Furthermore, states do not coordinate or consult with each other concerning overall water allocations, nor do they have a mechanism, such as an interstate river compact, that provides a means of coordinating off-channel water uses. In addition to the states, the federal water agencies, especially the Bureau of Reclamation, are notable water allocation actors. Although federal projects, in developing water, must abide by state water laws, once the water is captured, it is governed by a different set of rules. Federal project water is typically not governed by prior appropriation; rather its allocation and use are governed by a series of contracts that the federal water agency enters into with water users, particularly irrigation districts.

A similar institutional description holds for many other uses of the Columbia River Basin's resources. State and federal laws and agencies govern forests on state and federal land, respectively. Fishing, even for salmon, is governed by states, Indian tribes, the federal government, and a treaty between the U.S. and Canadian governments. Compared with water and forestry, fishing is more closely coordinated, with a variety of governing bodies at different scales allocating fish and devising harvesting rules (Wandschneider 1984, 1049).

The institutional arrangements that govern hydropower are striking for their limited diversity and high degree of coordination, unlike the institutional arrangements governing the other resources of the Columbia River Basin. Even though there are many dams and reservoirs and many electric utilities, the hydropower system is dominated by several large agencies and a coordinating agreement that tightly ties the utilities and agencies together. The Army Corps of Engineers and the Bureau of Reclamation by far generate the most power. The Bonneville Power Administration (BPA), a regional organization created by Congress, markets the power of the two federal water agencies. The Federal Energy Regulatory Commission licenses and monitors private hydropower plants.

The Pacific Northwest Coordination Agreement of 1964 established detailed operating criteria and power exchange principles. It also established an annual system-wide planning process to maximize power production (Blumm and Simrin 1991, 705–707). Wandschneider (1984, 1051) argues that the coordination agreement acts to manage hydropower as if there were a single, centralized utility. The physical effect of operating the river for hydropower production is to shift peak streamflow from spring to winter when demand for electricity is greatest (Wandschneider 1984, 1050).

Human uses and institutional arrangements governing those uses have had a profound effect on the ecosystems of the Columbia River Basin, but by far the most direct and negative effect has been on salmon. Concern over the fate of salmon has been expressed repeatedly over the past century, but not until Congress adopted the Fish and Wildlife Coordination Act in 1976 was there a concerted effort to coax the federal water and power agencies to address the effects of their actions on salmon. Although the act was well intentioned, it failed to accomplish its goal of providing equal consideration for fish and wildlife in project planning and development. The act created a consultation process between federal and state fisheries agencies and federal water and power agencies. In the consulting process, projects could be altered to reduce their effects on fish and wildlife, mitigation measures could be adopted to compensate for negative effects, and studies of project impacts on fish and wildlife could be conducted. However, the federal water and power agencies were given implicit veto power. They could reject project alterations or mitigation efforts if they deemed them to be unjustifiable in maximizing overall project benefits. Even if alterations or mitigation efforts were adopted, they often were inadequate because it was difficult to estimate the impact of the project on fish and wildlife. Attempting to incorporate additional alterations and mitigation measures after project completion was challenging, especially with regard to developing additional financing (Blumm 1982, 110–112).

The Northwest Power Act

Treating fish and wildlife as an afterthought in water projects changed dramatically within four years of the adoption of the Fish and Wildlife Coordination Act. During the 1970s, a series of events set the stage for congressional adoption of the Pacific Northwest Electric Power Planning and Conservation Act of 1980. Tribes successfully sued to have their treaty fishing rights recognized and enforced. The U.S. National Marine Fisheries Service and U.S. Fish and Wildlife Service initiated a review to determine whether various salmon stocks should be listed as threatened or endangered (Blumm and Simrin 1991, 690). The recognition of tribal treaty rights and the listing process coincided with a national energy crisis and the fear of a regional crisis in the Northwest. Congress's attention turned to energy policy, including the expansion of electric generation capacity in the Northwest. Congress adopted the Pacific Northwest Electric Power Planning and Conservation Act of 1980 (often referred to as the Northwest Power Act), addressing both hydropower and fish and wildlife issues. As a result, the National Marine Fisheries Service and the Fish and Wildlife Service suspended the endangered species listing process in lieu of the development and implementation of what appeared to be an innovative and comprehensive approach to protecting and restoring salmon stocks (Blumm 1986).

The Northwest Power Act, in its structure and directives, signaled that its congressional creators understood that placing fish and wildlife on an equal footing with hydropower would be challenging. The act moved well beyond what was required of federal water and power agencies under the Fish and Wildlife Coordination Act, which largely required the agencies to take into account anadromous fish on a project-by-project basis. In contrast, the Northwest Power Act encompassed the entire Columbia River Basin, and planning and implementation activities were to be undertaken with the entire basin in mind (Blumm 1984).

The also act created a regional council consisting of two representatives from each of the basin states (Washington, Oregon, Idaho, and Montana). The Northwest Power Planning Council was charged with developing a basin-wide power plan and a basin-wide fish and wildlife recovery plan. The plans would guide the actions of the various federal, state, and local governments and public and private power producers. Council decision rules required a high level of agreement among members to adopt and amend the plans. Plan adoption and revision required a majority of members appointed to the council, including a member from each state or, alternatively, six members of the council. The former rule required only five affirmative votes, although each state had to vote in the affirmative; whereas the latter rule required any state combination that yielded six affirmative votes. No single state exercised veto power, but states' interests had to be adequately addressed for plan approval. In contrast, non-plan decisions simply required a majority vote of a quorum of members. A quorum consisted of five representatives; thus, only three votes were necessary to conduct day-to-day business.

Congress granted the council greater discretion in devising the power plan, which was to coordinate the development of additional power supplies among producers, than in devising the fish and wildlife plan. Congress constrained the council's discretion in a variety of ways. First, the council was given strict time lines for developing and adopting a fish and wildlife plan. The council was to adopt a fish and wildlife plan within a year of receiving recommendations from the region's fish and wildlife agencies, whereas the council was given two years to develop a power plan. Furthermore, the council was directed to develop a power plan that was fully consistent with the fish and wildlife plan (Public Law 96-501, section [h][9]).

Second, Congress directed the council to rely heavily on the expertise of the federal, state, and tribal fish and wildlife agencies in developing and revising a plan. The council was required to solicit in writing recommendations from these agencies for measures that would recover and protect fish and wildlife. Federal and state water and power agencies could also submit recommendations; however, the council was not required to solicit recommendations from them and the recommendations from the fish and wildlife agencies were to be given greater consideration. This was to be accomplished in several ways. If recommendations were inconsistent with each other, the council was directed to resolve the inconsistency, giving due weight to the expertise of the fish and wildlife agencies. Moreover, if the council declined to adopt recommendations from fish and wildlife agencies, it had to justify its action in writing by explaining how the recommendation violated the purposes of the act or how the council chose to adopt a measure that provided greater protection than the recommendation that was rejected (Public Law

96-501, section [h][7]).

Third, Congress directed the council to use several criteria in developing and revising the fish and wildlife plan. The plan should (1) complement
existing and future activities of federal, state, and tribal fish and wildlife
agencies; (2) be based on best available scientific knowledge; (3) use the
alternative that is least costly among equally effective measures for achieving biological objectives; (4) be consistent with tribal rights; and (5) in the
case of anadromous fish, provide improved survival at hydroelectric facilities and provide flows of sufficient quantity and quality between such facilities to improve production, migration, and survival of such fish (Public Law
96-501, section [h][6]).

Fourth, Congress created a dedicated funding source for developing and
implementing the plan. Consumers of electricity were to pay for the effects
of the hydropower system on fish and wildlife through the creation of a
Bonneville Power Administration fund. Fifth, BPA and the federal water and
power agencies were directed to abide by the plan. In particular, they were to
exercise their responsibilities "in a manner that provides equitable treatment
for such fish and wildlife with the other purposes for which such system and
facilities are managed and operated" (Public Law 96-501, section [h][11]).

For its time, the 1980 Pacific Northwest Electric Power Planning and
Conservation Act was innovative and creative. It was greeted warmly by organizations, agencies, and individuals who were actively attempting to protect
the salmon of the Columbia River Basin. Viewed as the "most ambitious
salmon recovery plan ever undertaken" (Blumm 1986, 464), the act broke
with previous protection efforts in its scope, authority, diversity of recovery measures, and funding. By creating a single entity whose jurisdiction
spanned the basin, a more holistic and coordinated approach to the recovery and protection of fish and wildlife could be realized. No longer would
mitigation efforts occur on a piecemeal, project-by-project basis. Instead,
a variety of critical measures could be adopted that worked together to
recover salmon, such as simultaneously improving river flows, dam passage,
and habitat restoration. True, the act did not address the myriad assaults on
salmon, such as water diversions and fishing, but it did focus on a dimension
over which the federal government held considerable leverage, the federal
hydropower system. Furthermore, the act was more proactive than previous
attempts at saving salmon. Best available science, not certainty in science,
was to be the foundation of the measures and projects undertaken (Blumm

1984). The act envisioned changes in the operation of hydropower projects in order to improve production, migration, and survival of fish. Finally, recovery efforts would not compete for funding with hundreds of other programs in the annual congressional budget process, because funding for the recovery program was ensured by the consumers of electricity.

The Northwest Power Act's congressional authors paid careful attention to transaction costs, providing it with independence from other well-established organizations and programs that it challenged, while imposing structure and direction to try to ensure that it achieved congressional goals. The balance was delicate, and it was at the trade-off points among transaction costs that the act was most vulnerable. Rather than relying only on existing organizations to carry out innovative programs, Congress created an independent organization that afforded each basin state equal representation. A new and independent organization holds the promise of more faithfully realizing its creators' goals and intentions than does housing new and possibly threatening programs in existing agencies with their well-developed operating procedures and well-organized supporters. In terms of electric power, the new organization provided states with a much greater role in regional planning and development, a role that they actively sought, rather than being marginalized in the BPA power planning process (Blumm 1983, 229). In terms of fish and wildlife, avoiding the ESA listing process required housing recovery efforts in an organization independent of the federal water and power agencies, which had demonstrated little interest in protecting fish and wildlife.

So that the council could move forward in a relatively timely manner and avoid becoming bogged down in making immediate and direct trade-offs between fish and wildlife and electricity generation, Congress directed it to develop two plans—plans that took account of each other, but two plans nonetheless. Congress steered the council clear of some very difficult choices among incommensurate alternatives. Furthermore, in developing each plan separately, the council was to rely on two very different sets of experts and professionals. The power plan required the council to work closely with state regulatory agencies and utilities. The fish and wildlife plan required the council to work closely with tribal, state, and federal fish and wildlife agencies. In both cases, Congress attempted to address potential agency problems by selecting experts whose professional values and skills were most closely aligned with the goals of Congress to actively engage in plan development.

Finally, as noted, Congress demonstrated its commitment to fish and wildlife recovery by creating a dedicated source of funding for plan development and implementation.

As discussed earlier, resolving commitment problems often comes at the risk of agency problems. The Northwest Power Act anticipated some of the agency problems that could arise. In the legislation, Congress took steps to ensure that the council acted in intended ways by constraining its discretion. For instance, the fish and wildlife plan was to mitigate only the hydropower system's effects on fish stocks, not other human activities that harm fish. In addition, the plan was to be consistent with other criteria important to Congress, such as protecting tribal rights and not working at cross-purposes with existing recovery efforts. Finally, to ensure that the dedicated source of funding (which was beyond annual congressional control) was used appropriately, the act directed the administrator of the BPA, who controlled the source of dedicated funding, to use the revenues to protect, mitigate, and enhance fish and wildlife to the extent affected by hydroelectric projects on the Columbia. Furthermore, the administrator was specifically advised that the expenditures are in addition to, not in lieu of, expenditures required of other entities; the administrator was not to undercut funding by paying for other recovery efforts out of the fund or by reducing fund expenditures by counting other recovery efforts against it (Public Law 96-501, section [h][10][A]).

Limiting agency costs is often accomplished at the expense of decision-making costs. Certainly, Congress expended additional effort devising the various criteria that the council was to realize in developing a fish and wildlife plan, but the increase in decision-making costs was largely borne by the council rather than by Congress. To limit the council's ability to evade congressional intent, Congress increased its decision-making costs by requiring the council to put in writing its reasons for rejecting measures proposed by the fish and wildlife agencies. Congress placed the burden of proof on the council to publicly justify its decisions. Limiting agency problems was further addressed through extensive public participation requirements. Rather than Congress expending decision-making resources to closely monitor the activities of the council, Congress invited the public to take on those costs by providing for a variety of participation mechanisms—submitting comments, attending public meetings, and participating in hearings.

Congress demonstrated a credible commitment to the recovery of fish and wildlife by creating an independent organization and charging it to rely heavily on fish and wildlife experts in devising a recovery plan. It further demonstrated its commitment by imposing a strict time line on the adoption of a plan to discourage the process from becoming bogged down. However, it also imposed decision rules that required a high level of agreement among council members in order for a plan to be adopted, but once adopted, a plan would be hard to unravel or water down. The other notable commitment mechanism was a dedicated source of funding.

The Northwest Power Planning Council

Somewhat surprisingly, given tight deadlines, super-majority decision rules, and hundreds of submissions of measures to be included in the fish and wildlife plan, the council did adopt a plan on schedule that largely followed the directives of Congress. The plan reflected the major substantive measures proposed by the fish and wildlife agencies. The centerpiece was a water budget, controlled not by the federal water agencies that operated the dams but by two water budget managers who were fisheries experts. The more than 4.6 million acre-feet of water was to be used during the spring and early summer to support the migration of juvenile salmon downriver (Blumm and Simrin 1991, 696). The water budget managers could call for the water from federal water agencies at times and in places that they judged would be most beneficial.

The council, perhaps anticipating agency problems, placed constraints on both federal water agencies and the water budget managers. The water budget could easily be undercut by federal water agencies as they released water to generate power.[13] For instance, they might release less "power" water in order to compensate for "fish" water. In an attempt to avoid that possibility, the council adopted a fixed schedule of "firm power flows" that provided for at least a certain level of spring flows to which the water budget would be added (Blumm 1984, 314–315). The council also recommended that the water budget take priority over reservoir fill and secondary power generation. That is, the federal water agencies were not granted the discretion to trade the water budget for goals that they found more desirable. The water budget managers, in turn, were not allowed to release water that would have the effect of increasing river flows above a recommended maximum.

The second major component of the plan addressed dam bypass measures for migrating juveniles. Not only is it important to speed the passage of juveniles down the river, but it is also important to protect them from passing through the power turbines. The plan adopted spill requirements on the middle section of the Columbia and ordered studies and eventual incorporation of mechanical bypass devices on dams throughout the basin. Both requirements were controversial, with fish and wildlife managers arguing that the measures were inadequate and dam operators arguing that less expensive alternatives, such as barging and trucking of juvenile salmon around the dams, should be used more widely (Blumm 1984).

The third major substantive component of the plan focused on rebuilding fish stocks. In addition to funding a number of specific projects, the council created the Fish Propagation Panel to develop a coordinated, system-wide plan for recovering wild stocks, improving hatchery operations, and identifying potential hatchery sites and to coordinate the propagation plan with existing efforts (Blumm 1984, 314–315). Overall, the council adopted an initial plan that was comprehensive in scope, addressing the major hydroelectric impacts on fish and wildlife, from river flows to dam bypass systems to habitat restoration.

Separate and apart from substantive components, the council also addressed a number of issues involving coordination and funding in order to ensure that the federal agencies abided by the plan. The council anticipated agency problems by attempting to limit the discretion of federal agencies. In the plan, the council requested that the BPA expeditiously act to develop funding for the plan's measures. Such funding would largely come through BPA's rate-setting process. In addition, the council reminded the federal water and power agencies that according to the statute, they were to implement the plan to the fullest extent practicable. Consequently, the council directed the agencies to indicate in writing that they would implement the various measures or, if they were unable to implement the measures, to provide an explanation with supporting documentation (Blumm and Simrin 1991, 679–680). Finally, the council requested that FERC assess the cumulative impacts of hydroelectric proposals instead of assessing impacts on a project-by-project basis. The council also directed the BPA to ensure that all power sales and power scheduling were in accordance with the plan (Blumm 1986, 475).

The fish and wildlife agencies had suggested a more aggressive approach to implementation. They requested a series of studies to examine how federal water and power agencies engaged in decision making and to identify appropriate mechanisms for inserting fish and wildlife considerations into the decision-making processes. In other words, the fish and wildlife agencies wanted the council to design and adopt mechanisms that would commit the federal water and power agencies to implementing the plan. The council viewed implementation as an agency problem; the fish and wildlife agencies viewed it as primarily a commitment problem. In 1987, frustrated with the slow progress made by federal water and power agencies, the fish and wildlife agencies once again pressed the council to address the issue. This time, the fish and wildlife agencies viewed the issue as an agency problem and requested that the council adopt a conflict resolution mechanism whereby the council would investigate and make a written report in response to any allegation that a program item was not being implemented. The council refused to adopt the conflict resolution mechanism, claiming that existing procedures were adequate (Blumm and Simrin 1991, 692–693).

Federal Water and Power Agencies' Responses

The council and the fish and wildlife agencies were disappointed in the implementation response of the federal water and power agencies. The substantive portions of the plan became embroiled immediately in a variety of agency problems. First, the water budget was inadequately implemented. The firm power flows were often not provided, and the water and power agencies gave priority to reservoir fill and to the sale of electricity on the secondary power market. These activities acted to undermine the value of the water budget (Blumm and Simrin 1991, 676–677).[14] Second, federal agencies were also slow to request funding for dam bypass mechanisms, delaying their implementation. Dam bypass mechanisms competed with funding for other projects that the agencies valued more highly. Third, hatchery and habitat restoration projects and a variety of studies became entangled in funding disputes between the council and the BPA. For instance, the BPA refused to fund a study requested by the council to measure the effects of the hydropower system on fish and wildlife so that overall program goals could be established. After all, consumers of electricity were to pay only for the effects of the hydropower system and no more. The BPA stated that the study plan developed by the fish and wildlife agencies was unacceptable to BPA management and in violation of ratepayers' interests (Blumm and Simrin 1991, 675). Much the same occurred with hatchery and habitat restoration projects in the Umatilla Basin, a tributary of the Columbia River (Chaney 1986).[15] Conversely, the council feared that the BPA would use program monies to fund studies that the council had not requested. Eventually, the council and the BPA came to an understanding over the studies that would be funded.

The Council's Response to the Federal Agencies

Given the earlier discussion of transaction costs and trade-offs, the council's response to the agency problems encountered was predictable. The primary response was to increase the decision-making costs of the council and of the federal water and power agencies. The council's decision-making costs increased as the council engaged in almost annual amendments to the plan. Although some amendments were substantive in nature, such as declaring hundreds of miles of streams off limits to hydropower development and adopting spill requirements for the Snake River dams to allow smolt to bypass power turbines, many of the amendments were directed at implementation problems. The agencies' decision-making costs were increased as the council subjected them to stricter time lines and directed them to follow more detailed and transparent decision-making processes.

In 1984, the council adopted a series of deadlines for various projects and activities. For instance, deadlines were established for the installation of bypass systems at several main-stem dams (Blumm and Simrin 1991, 681). In addition, time lines were established for a variety of habitat improvement and fish propagation projects (Blumm and Simrin 1991, 683). Also, the council adopted a five-year action plan that set priorities for various program measures. As part of the action plan, federal water and power agencies were to develop work plans and budgets for program measures and to make annual progress reports (Blumm 1986, 477–478).

Over the course of the 1980s, the council spent a considerable portion of its time attempting to cajole the federal water and power agencies into implementing the fish and wildlife plan. Although progress was not as rapid as desired, the council, nevertheless, could point to a number of accomplishments, from developing a solid foundation of research on a variety of dimensions of the Columbia River Basin, to protecting hundreds of miles of streams from hydropower development, to adopting a water budget, to funding dozens of habitat restoration projects, to adopting spill programs at dams on the Columbia and the Snake, to placing the term "adaptive management" into the popular lexicon through its insistence on study designs that maximized learning opportunities, and so on. By the end of the 1980s, the council could point to a number of substantive changes. These accomplishments, however, were overshadowed by one disturbing fact: salmon stocks continued to dramatically decline.

The Rest of the Story

Beginning in the 1990s, the Northwest Power Planning Council was slowly displaced as the central actor in recovering salmon stocks. By 1990, Indian tribes and fish and wildlife agencies were increasingly restless and dissatisfied with the limited progress of the council and its fish and wildlife plan. The Columbia Fish and Wildlife Authority, a coalition of state and tribal fish and wildlife agencies, released a report calling for specified flows on the Columbia and Snake Rivers. The council's water budget did not provide sufficient flows to mitigate the effects of the hydroelectric system on fish runs. Consequently, the authority wanted river flows established (Blumm et al. 1997). At roughly the same time, tribes and environmental groups petitioned to have various Snake River salmon runs listed as endangered under the Endangered Species Act. In 1991, the National Marine Fishery Service (NMFS) listed some Snake River salmon runs as either endangered or threatened. In response, the council amended the fish and wildlife plan by establishing specified flows on the Snake River. NMFS relied on the amended plan to issue a "no jeopardy" ruling, which specified that the operation of hydroelectric projects was not to jeopardize the continued survival of the salmon in light of the revised fish and wildlife plan. Both the council plan and the NMFS biological opinion were challenged in court, with environmental and state fish and wildlife agencies charging that the plans were inadequate and industry groups charging that they were too aggressive and costly. The courts largely ruled in favor of the environmental groups and chided the council and the NMFS for adherence to an incremental approach that favored the status quo (Blumm 1995).

The results of the court cases were three plans by three different organizations for the recovery of salmon (Blumm et al. 1997). In 1994, the council adopted a new fish and wildlife plan that established specified river flows, largely through reservoir drawdowns. It also established spill requirements for dams throughout the basin and it relied less heavily on trucking and barging of smolt. Furthermore, to supplement flows in the Snake River it called for the leasing of up to 1 million acre-feet of water. The plan was largely ignored by federal water and power agencies, which focused more on the NMFS plan. The NMFS adopted an approach heavier on studies and lighter on changes in system operations than the council plan. It too established flow targets, albeit lower than those established by the council; it deferred reservoir drawdown and instead called for drawdown studies; it adopted a much more limited spill program; and it relied heavily on trucking and barging smolt (Blumm et al. 1997). A third plan, which was unenforceable against federal water and power agencies, was proposed by a coalition of tribes. It was closer in content to the council plan, although it contained more rigorous drawdown, spill, and hatchery components (Blumm et al. 1997). The council recognized the confusion engendered by three plans and called for the reconciliation of the plans, ideally under the stewardship of the council. Little progress was made toward plan reconciliation, and over time, the NMFS, under its ESA authority, became the principal leader in salmon restoration efforts (Blumm et al. 1997).

In the meantime, the council has added a layer of complexity to its planning approach. Historically, its fish and wildlife program focused on the basin level. The water budget was devised at the basin level as was the dam bypass and passage plan. Only the rehabilitation of salmon habitat was concentrated in promising sub-basin areas. Initially, the council refused to engage in sub-basin planning. By the close of the 1980s, however, the council realized that the sub-basins of the Columbia Basin were diverse, with different habitats, different salmon species, different economies, and different threats and challenges to salmon recovery (Blumm and Simrin 1991, 688). It instituted a sub-basin planning process that it recently completed. Using community participation processes, sub-basin plans were developed that conformed to the council's basin-wide framework but addressed the unique problems and community goals of each area. The plans will continue to guide the council's funding decisions as it seeks to recover, enhance, and protect salmon habitat.

Prospects remain rather discouraging. In 2002, Oregon State University and the Environmental Protection Agency formed Salmon 2100. The coalition drew together thirty-three fisheries scientists and policy analysts to determine the likely future of wild salmon in 2100. The consensus was that under current policies only remnant populations of salmon would be present throughout the Pacific Northwest and California.

CONCLUSION

The shape and form of fish and wildlife recovery efforts in the Columbia River Basin have changed dramatically over the last three decades. In the 1970s, the federal water and power agencies were required to consult with fish and wildlife agencies only on a project-by-project basis. In the 1980s, a new basin-wide organization, the Northwest Power Planning Council, developed and administered a basin-wide fish and wildlife recovery plan. The 1990s saw three basin-wide plans: one by the council, one by NMFS in response to the listing of salmon as endangered, and one by a coalition of tribes frustrated with the other two organizations' plans. By the end of the 1990s, the council was actively overseeing the development of sub-basin plans as a primary mechanism for implementing its basin-wide plan.

Comprehensive, integrated watershed management remains elusive in the Columbia River Basin for a variety of reasons, including bounded rationality and transaction costs. The many choices among incommensurate alternatives, diverse agencies with missions that conflict with the overall goal of recovering fish and wildlife, and the complexity of the watershed all work against comprehensive management. Bounded rationality and transaction costs, however, are not the only reasons why multiple, overlapping governments and organizations are likely to emerge in a watershed. They are also likely to emerge because of the different values and uses people pursue in a watershed, as we will discuss in the next chapter.

NOTES

1. As Derthick (1974, 4) colorfully summarizes the politics of river basin management, "Regional organizations are excrescences on the constitutional system, unusual things that must be superimposed on the universe of functionally specialized federal and state agencies. The odds are against their being formed and, if formed, against their flourishing."

2. See Markman and Medin (2002) for an excellent survey of the psychology and social psychology literature on decision making. See Kopelman et al. (2002) for an excellent survey of the psychology literature that applies decision making to environmental settings.

3. For instance, it has become increasingly common for elected officials or key constituencies to complain that government employees are not using the best available science in carrying out their duties. For elected officials who desire less regulation, there is often the assumption that government employees are pursuing extreme environmental values that scientific evidence simply fails to support. For elected officials who desire more regulation, there is the assumption that government employees are purposely failing to act as they await more certain scientific results.

4. North and Weingast (1989) used this concept to explore the relations between the Stuart kings and the British parliament during the seventeenth century. Kings increasingly turned to manipulating and seizing private property to acquire sufficient resources to fight wars. In response, parliament refused to provide kings with a regular source of revenue. Both sides would have been better off if kings had committed to protect private property and parliament had made a reliable stream of revenue available to the king. However, a simple promise by the king to stop seizing private property hardly would have constituted a credible commitment, since he easily could, and had, gone back on his word. Only after several decades of conflict did the king and parliament devise institutional arrangements, such as a judiciary and a parliament independent of the crown, that acted as checks against the crown, making such a commitment on the part of the king credible. See David Weimer (1997) for numerous case studies that apply to the concept of credible commitment to explain the economic reforms occurring in Russia, the Czech and Slovak republics, Poland, Hungary, and East Germany. Also see Gary Miller (1992) as he explores the problems managers experience in making credible commitments to share the gains realized from efficiency-enhancing activities adopted by employees.

5. Williamson (1985) calls such mechanisms "hostages."

6. On the other hand, the security of senior water rights, which in western states are held mostly by agricultural users, is what makes those rights especially valuable, and those rights tend to command high prices in locations where transfers of water rights are feasible.

7. For instance, regulatory agencies make choices among incommensurate alternatives in devising and adopting rules. An ozone standard set by the EPA affects not only businesses and industries but also citizens who have chronic and severe respiratory ailments. Regulatory agencies are regularly criticized for the incommensurate choices each makes, and for the differences in choices across agencies. Some agencies impose quite strict rules that limit human exposures to risk; others adopt less strict rules, exposing people to greater risks, but there is little consistency among agencies. Not all choices among incommensurate alternatives involve human life-and-death matters, but they are difficult to make nevertheless.

8. As Jones (2001, 47) notes, "Of all the limitations cited in people's ability to put rational choice theory into practice, the most important is probably the difficul-

ties people have in handling incommensurate attributes."

9. For instance, if decision makers wanted to establish a surface water quality standard, they would first identify the different attributes of each standard they were considering, such as the effects on different types of aquatic plants and animals, the functioning of wetlands, the different uses of water and wetlands made by humans, groundwater quality, economic development, and so forth. They would then place a weight on each of the attributes—they may give functioning wetlands greater weight than groundwater quality, for instance. Once they have assigned weights to each of the attributes, they would then develop a score for each water quality standard and they would select the one with the best score.

10. The Water Resources Council attempted to develop a multi-objective planning process to be used by each of the river basin commissions that would allow the commissions to prioritize different projects and programs with the goal of optimal use of the watershed (Holmes 1979).

11. Both approaches for limiting agency costs come at the expense of other types of transaction costs. For instance, providing specific instructions increases decision-making costs. Decision makers must expend additional time and resources attempting to anticipate the variety of circumstances implementers are likely to encounter and then devise appropriate decision rules. Such actions may ultimately work against the larger goals of decision makers. Weighing down implementers with a multitude of rules and time lines may promote policy failure and not policy success (Moe 1990).

12. Wandschneider (1984) provides a detailed description of the various institutional arrangements governing the numerous natural resources of the Columbia River Basin.

13. The BPA attempted to convince the council to adopt a smaller water budget and to adopt alternatives to a water budget (Blumm 1984).

14. As Blumm (1986, 495) noted, "the program's clear elevation of Water Budget flows over reservoir refill and secondary power sale considerations has been frequently ignored or evaded by the federal operating agencies."

15. The BPA also refused to fund projects that it anticipated Congress would appropriate funding for (Blumm 1984, 347).

5

Multiple Goals, Communities, and Organizations

As we have mentioned in previous chapters, the popularity of watershed management has grown as other values and goals have emerged alongside more traditional ones, such as water supply development and flood control. In this chapter, we draw together those goals and values for a closer look and focus on some organizational issues associated with the effort to pursue multiple goals and values simultaneously.

Managing a watershed conveys an incorporation of several considerations, including those shown in Box 5.1 and described below. The relative significance of each will vary according to location characteristics and residents' values.

Box 5.1. Watershed Management Goals
Water supply reliability
Drought protection
Flood hazard reduction and flood response
Water conservation and reuse
Sustainable economies
Water quality protection
Water-based recreation
Instream flows
Habitat protection and species recovery
River restoration

Water supply reliability involves reducing risks of interruption or loss of supplies currently relied upon for human activities and other uses in the watershed. Distinguishable from the earlier water management goal of supply development (bringing more water to a location to provide for growing consumptive demands), the emphasis of water supply reliability is securing a supply and distribution infrastructure that is likely to be able to sustain current or foreseeable demand levels with reduced risk of significant economic losses and/or health risks associated with supply interruptions. In addition to traditional practices, such as storing water to guard against seasonal shortages, this goal encompasses activities such as guarding against the failure of facilities like treatment plants and distribution pipelines, acquiring option contracts for supplemental supplies to use in the event of emergencies, cooperative agreements with neighboring jurisdictions for emergency water transfers, and so forth.

Drought protection is distinct enough to treat as a separate goal, although it is obviously related to the goal of water supply reliability. Depending on the climatologic and hydrologic characteristics of a particular location, drought protection may include measures such as construction and maintenance of larger-scale water storage facilities, long-term underground storage of recoverable water, a plan for informing water users about escalating drought conditions, and a plan for reducing usage based on some assigned priorities among categories of use.

Flood hazard reduction and flood response are distinguishable components of flood protection. Flood hazard reduction is not exactly the same as flood prevention, which traditionally connotes the construction and maintenance of barriers such as dams and levees. Flood hazard reduction may include such structures, of course, but also land-use policies that locate interruptible land uses (parks and outdoor recreation facilities, for example) in floodplains for the purpose of accommodating some seasonal flooding. As the name implies, flood hazard reduction focuses primarily on minimizing the risks of significant losses of life and property from flooding rather than on trying to prevent any flooding from occurring within a watershed. In a similar vein, flood response conveys something distinguishable from the older flood control, with an emphasis on emergency preparedness, rescue and recovery, temporary relocation of people or property, and restoration.[1]

Water conservation and reuse are terms with multiple meanings and applications. They relate to the broader notion of squeezing the greatest amount of beneficial use out of a given water supply. Rather than taking existing uses and disposal of water as given, the goal of water conservation and reuse is to examine current practices of use and disposal and pursue opportunities for reducing or redirecting them. The activities falling under this heading include pricing practices intended to curb lower-valued uses, recirculating water for cooling or landscape irrigation, and even advanced wastewater treatment to supplement supplies for potable use. Although it may also seem to be an aspect of traditional water management, water conservation and reuse in the contemporary watershed context are often related to the search for ways to accommodate emerging demands for limited water supplies.

Sustainable economies are among the purposes to which the above goals are linked. Traditional water development programs sometimes bore slogans such as "water for people," and watershed management concepts of sustainability are still directed largely at the communities and residents within the watershed. Preserving ranchlands or timber operations in locations pressured by urbanization, keeping small towns and businesses viable, and promoting economic prosperity while forestalling certain kinds of economic transformation all have been touted as potential accomplishments of integrated watershed management and as incentives for stakeholders to participate.

Water quality protection in the watershed management context has several applications, which include pollution prevention, runoff reduction and treatment, remediation of contamination, and salinity management. The goal has expanded from ensuring adequate treatment of drinking water supplies to protection of the source waters themselves by reducing threats to water quality.

Water-based recreation has been enjoyed by people for all recorded history, but its relative importance as a value for water resource management has risen lately. These non-consumptive uses of water are not only valued individually by the participants but can be important components of local economies and community identities. Fishing, rafting, boating, and skiing have claimed places at the watershed management table alongside irrigation and municipal and industrial uses.

Instream flows are important for other reasons in addition to water-based recreation. Support of aquatic species and the aesthetic values of flowing water for communities in a watershed make instream flow protection an independent goal of watershed management in the contemporary scene. Also, although not often highlighted in the watershed management literature, navigation depends on instream flow protection.

Habitat protection and species recovery are of course related to instream flows but not identical. These goals include protection of riparian and off-channel habitat (for example, keeping wetlands and vernal pools from being eliminated by surface water diversions or groundwater withdrawals). Furthermore, just maintaining a certain level of instream flow—to support recreation, for example—may not suffice for recovery of a valued aquatic or riparian species that has become threatened or endangered. Thus, habitat protection and species recovery constitute a distinct goal of watershed management not subsumed by instream flow protection or water-based recreation.

River restoration may also seem to be covered by other goals already identified, yet it has its own dimensions. River restoration efforts are not only in the service of instream flow preservation, species recovery, or recreation; they may entail the removal of concrete channels, dams and weirs, abandoned bridge pilings, and the like purely for purposes of restoring the natural appearance and ecological health of a river itself. In many communities in the United States in the late twentieth and early twenty-first centuries, river restoration has an economic development component: recapturing (or, in some locations, discovering) the value of a riverfront or a lakefront as a community attraction.

Two other points are important in regard to this overall topic of multiple goals. First and perhaps more obviously, the multiple goals of watershed management may conflict in certain respects and under some conditions. Diverting surface water flows into storage facilities, for instance, may serve the goal of drought protection but not the goal of water-based recreation or the maintenance of instream flows. Flood hazard reduction means maintaining unused storage capacity in reservoirs and emptying them when they are full, whereas drought protection indicates maintaining maximum water in storage, and instream flow protection suggests steady releases of stored water. Goal conflict is not fatal or even tragic, since reasonable trade-offs are usually feasible, but it is important to be mindful of the fact that the multiple goals of watershed management are not inherently complementary.

The other important point is that although all of the goals listed above are relevant to the scale of a watershed, the goals themselves can be pertinent to, or most effectively achieved at, alternative scales within the watershed or across watersheds. Recreational opportunities and demands may be focused within a particular portion of the watershed. Depending on the physical and social circumstances, organizing flood hazard reduction or drought protection measures or supporting sustainable economies might be more effective across multiple related and/or neighboring watersheds. The fact that the various goals of watershed management are all present or relevant within a particular watershed does not mean that they are necessarily best pursued or organized at the watershed scale.

Although these may appear to be obvious or commonplace observations, the fact that watershed management involves the simultaneous pursuit of multiple (but not necessarily complementary) goals at multiple scales is a statement worth contemplating. Its implications for the design, performance, and modification of institutions for governing and managing the watershed are so extensive they would be difficult to overstate. One of those implications is that people trying to achieve a variety of goals within a watershed could quite rationally opt to organize several overlapping institutional arrangements. Thus, in addition to the transaction cost considerations discussed in the preceding chapter, people create multiple organizations within a watershed because of the multiplicity of relevant goals and scales.

Beyond raising the prospect of multi-organizational, polycentric institutions within a watershed as a theoretical possibility, we can and should explore why and how such arrangements might emerge and how they might function. Equally if not more useful is to present and discuss empirical examples of such settings and how they work. In this chapter, we do both as we explore how multi-organizational arrangements can work and present an example of a watershed governed and managed through a polycentric structure that has been modified on several occasions to adapt to the emergence of new goals and previously unrecognized problems, as well as to take advantage of functional specialization and diversity of scale among the various organizations. The example in this chapter—the San Gabriel River watershed, located in Southern California—is a substate watershed where coordination is at the scale of municipalities and special districts. In Chapter 6, we will use an interstate example to illustrate polycentric arrangements at a larger regional scale.

AN INTEGRATED ORGANIZATION OR MULTIPLE ORGANIZATIONS?

In light of the introductory discussion, perhaps the question that begs hardest to be asked is why not just establish a watershed-scale governing body to prioritize, balance, and pursue these multiple goals? With so many interrelated goals, and with pursuit of one often conflicting with the achievement of others, it is understandable that some watershed management proponents are inclined to advocate an organizational umbrella under which all stakeholders gather to discuss and plan and implement an integrated strategy.

A related question, raised also in Chapter 1, is why have water users and communities within watersheds rarely created such governing bodies? What explanation can be given of the motivations and choices of individuals in crafting instead the complicated and multi-layered arrangements found in most (if not all) American watersheds? In Chapter 4, we provided an initial answer to both questions. Boundedly rational people, crafting governing arrangements in light of transaction costs, devise a variety of arrangements as a means of limiting cognitive demands and easing transaction costs.

Building on that initial answer, this chapter adds that the varied arrangements crafted by boundedly rational people reflect also the diverse character of problems and the different and sometimes conflicting values that people attempt to realize in the context of a watershed. People indeed seek to realize a variety of values and goals in a watershed, but they line up differently in relation to those values and goals. Some people want less of x and more of y. They line up differently also because of when and where they reside in the watershed, the types of livelihoods they are pursuing, and other factors. As Lebel, Garden, and Imamura (2005) have wisely pointed out, in addition to the politics of scale (e.g., watershed vs. river basin vs. other area), there are the politics of position (related to the specific location within a given area) and the politics of place (related to the stakeholder's identity, status, and resources). Handling such diversity is difficult within a single governing structure. People often choose instead to create a variety of different types of governments and organizations.

One way of making sense of the complicated and multi-layered arrangements found in most American watersheds is to use the theory of public economies, which was developed over the past fifty years to explain complex polycentric systems, such as the governance of metropolitan areas in the absence of a metropolitan government (Ostrom, Tiebout, and Warren 1961; Bish and Ostrom 1973; U.S. ACIR 1987; Oakerson 1999). The application is particularly apt, since so many contemporary debates about how best to govern watersheds echo earlier debates among scholars and practitioners of metropolitan government (see King 2004 for a recent review). The most important components of such an explanation are the provision-production distinction, specialization, economies and diseconomies of scale, and coordination versus hierarchy.

In all social settings—from households to watersheds—decisions about provision of desired resources, goods, and services may be made without actually engaging in the production of those desired resources, goods, and services. Members of a household decide how (and how much) they will obtain of the necessities and conveniences of life—housing, food, schooling, entertainment—but they do not necessarily produce their own housing, their own food, their own schooling, or all of their own entertainment. Similarly, a community of individuals may organize a town, a water district, or a Web page and decide what services they want to receive, what forms and amounts of revenue they will contribute, what content they want to disseminate, and so forth. These are provision decisions. They do not imply that the individuals in the community will actually police the streets, construct wells or pipes, or make the Web page; they may choose to procure any or all of those services from other individuals or organizations that produce them (Oakerson 1999).

In a watershed, the provision-production distinction can help to explain some of the number and variety of organizations that exist when water users create those organizations themselves. As in the watersheds described in this book, there may be a few large organizations that produce water from large-scale projects but a larger number of smaller organizations that decide how much they want to receive and pay for relative to other water sources to which they may have access. A group of pumpers sharing the same groundwater basin may decide to establish a replenishment program, but they may choose to contract with an agency that operates flood control facilities to operate those facilities for water conservation rather than construct and operate their own. Many of the organizations found in a watershed are *providers* representing or organizing smaller communities of individuals and then entering into contractual or other arrangements with *producers* of water supplies, flood control, contamination remediation, and so forth. Classifying the organizations within a watershed into provider and producer categories can help to begin sorting out the arrangements among them, making a different kind of sense out of what may appear at first blush to be mere fragmentation.

Following this logic, provision decisions may be appropriately organized on a smaller scale than production decisions. Sub-watershed organizations, for instance, often are organizations of water users with something in common (e.g., the same basin or the same part of the watershed, the kinds of characteristics Lebel, Garden, and Imamura [2005] call "position" or "place"). In these watersheds, inter-organizational and intergovernmental relationships often involve smaller service provision organizations contracting or otherwise arranging with larger service production organizations for the performance of desired functions. In the smaller provider organizations, water users or their representatives consider information about water supply conditions and decide, for example, how much project water to provide themselves with, how much to divert from a stream or pump from underground, how much water to purchase for replenishment or augmentation, how much to pay, and how to raise the money. In some cases, there are multiple producers, and the provider organizations act as buyers' cooperatives on behalf of water users, securing the combination of water supplies that nets the best deal for them.

In this light, the distinction between provision and production brings into view the concept of functional specialization. There may be, and often are, advantages in organizing activities by taking advantage of specialization. Operating physical facilities such as dams is a task that could be undertaken by the same agency that also contracts for water supplies, monitors water quality, and sets groundwater production targets for every basin within a watershed, but it certainly does not have to be. There may even be good reasons for having a separate organization perform that task—or, for that matter, a separate organization performing each of the tasks in that short list. Water users in the watersheds we have observed appear to have made deliberate choices in both directions—sometimes adding a new function to the portfolio of an existing organization (e.g., having the county flood control district operate the seawater barrier in the San Gabriel watershed described below) and other times creating a new organization (e.g., a joint-powers agency to organize and finance contamination remediation efforts in the main San Gabriel Basin or a conservancy to address riparian ecosystem restoration).

The choice about whether to add another organization or increase the responsibilities of an existing one will depend upon matters such as the skills required for the function, the resources available within existing organizations, the costs of coordination if a new organization is created, and the political issues of governance and control. There is not a single answer that fits all situations. Rather, it is to be expected that water users will create some single-function entities and other multiple-function ones based on considerations such as these. Their choices do not necessarily reflect hapless fragmentation or rampant duplication; indeed, when organizations truly specialize, they are not duplicates (Parks and Oakerson 1989). As Ingram and colleagues noted: "There are a variety of institutional structures through which decisions about water resources allocation and use occur. These structures are likely to have different policy orientations. They are also likely to vary in their accessibility and responsiveness to particular interests, their capacity to generate the appropriate flow of information, and their preference for certain problem solutions" (Ingram et al. 1984, 328).

Another concept that follows closely with those of specialization and the distinction between provision and production is that of scale. Some activities are less costly and more efficient if organized on a large scale. Others exhibit diseconomies of scale, becoming inefficient or cumbersome when too many people or too diverse a set of interests is involved.

We will illustrate using the Southern California region, the location of this chapter's case study. It might well represent wasteful duplication if each municipality in a watershed such as those in Southern California had built its own aqueduct to the Colorado River or to Northern California, because such a facility exhibits significant economies of scale. Instead, municipalities in Southern California chose either to join the regional Metropolitan Water District or to contract with the state for access to its State Water Project. These arrangements allowed local communities to take advantage of scale economies without merely subsuming their interests into a regional governance organization. Each of those smaller local districts retains the ability to determine how much imported water to purchase in a given year (if any) and how to pay for it, without having to build and operate enormous facilities. By the same token, the large producer organizations, such as the California Department of Water Resources and the Metropolitan Water District of Southern California, do not have to try to determine for each local community the desired mix of imported and local water supplies. This is one example of provider-producer arrangements in a public economy where the presence of multiple organizations at diverse scales holds the prospect of enhancing efficiency and responsiveness rather than diminishing them.

INTER-ORGANIZATIONAL COORDINATION

It is reasonable to ask, of course, whether all these organizations—provider organizations and producer organizations, specialized by function and created with some effort to capture scale economies and avoid diseconomies—create immense coordination costs. Do they overwhelm whatever advantages of scale and specialization may be gained? Why not just organize a single authority encompassing all these activities? These questions have motivated nearly a century of debate in public administration, public policy, and political science.

Inter-organizational coordination is costly, of course, but the alternatives are not costless either. Organizational integration has its own costs of internal coordination and communication, information distortion, control losses, and the like, described in the political economy literature on bureaucratic pathologies. Bureaucratic abilities to effectively and comprehensively engage in and coordinate a multitude of activities has suffered sustained criticism from public administration theorists and political scientists for more than five decades (e.g., Simon 1955; Knott and Miller 1987; Chisholm 1989; V. Ostrom 1989; Miller 1992).

Integration costs may be quite substantial even on the scale of a watershed, as suggested by Behrman (1993, 11–12):

> There was a study made some years ago . . . of the Columbia River basin, which is if anything even more complicated than the South Platte basin. The study looked for any empirical evidence (and there again, the control is very fractured) that a unified control system would produce superior results compared to the existing system, which is very similar to the South Platte. The conclusion was that there was no evidence that it would be

superior. The unified system, by bringing in bureaucratic control, creates unanticipated results that are not all that favorable.

Furthermore, Milon, Kiker, and Lee (1998) pointed out that the comprehensive watershed-scale approach to Everglades restoration produced an unintended bias toward engineering analyses and the construction of physical structures to alleviate problems rather than addressing institutional alternatives based on social science analyses.

Undoubtedly, Woolley and McGinnis (1999, 579) were correct in observing, "Watershed policymaking is particularly difficult when the decision making context includes a large number of relatively autonomous governmental and nongovernmental participants with dissimilar values." What remains unclear is how much easier watershed policy making would be if a large number of participants with dissimilar values were operating within a single organization or jurisdiction. On balance, whether organizational integration or inter-organizational coordination is more costly is an empirical question, and the answer will vary from one situation to another.

In an earlier study of conjunctive water management in Arizona, California, and Colorado (Blomquist, Schlager, and Heikkila 2004), we uncovered no instances of comprehensive organizations with extensive authority to manage and engage in a wide variety of activities on a watershed or river basin scale. To the contrary, time after time and place after place, water users apparently chose *not* to center all water-related activities in a single agency. In Arizona, which is the most nearly centralized of the three states, specific limitations were placed on the authority that the Arizona Department of Water Resources (ADWR) could exercise when it was first created in 1980. ADWR was granted authority only to manage and limit demand for groundwater, not to engage in groundwater supply development or in surface water management. In Colorado, water users have repeatedly declined to extend the authority of the state engineer and division engineers. Water users vigorously and successfully opposed a proposal to grant division engineers the authority to act as water referees within water courts, insisting instead on referees who were independent of the state and division engineers and employees of the courts. And after water users brought repeated litigation over the state engineer's actions in integrating well pumpers into the state's water rights system, the state legislature, state engineers, and water user organizations worked out a decision-making process that vets proposed rules through the water courts before they take effect—again opting for polycentricity over integration in the design of institutions for policy making in the state's watersheds.

COMMUNITIES OF INTEREST AND COMMUNITIES OF IDENTITY

Of course, there are more considerations than economic efficiency at stake in the watershed. The creation and preservation of institutional arrangements constructed around interests in a watershed is not just an effort to construct a local public economy and reap efficiency advantages. It also reflects real distinctions among groups within a watershed.

A watershed may be a single, interrelated physical system, but it places people in distinctly different positions. Some will be downstream, others up. Some may overlie a capacious and easily replenished groundwater basin, others will not. Some may reside adjacent to wetlands or riparian habitat that others wish to see preserved. Some may be at risk from contamination whereas others enjoy relatively pristine water. Such differently positioned groups may well wish to work toward watershed-scale management actions but through organizations that reflect their sub-watershed distinctions.

As we have observed in a number of places, within the physical system of the watershed is a complex social one. Overlaid upon the differences in people's physical situations within a watershed are the myriad other distinctions that come from the broader social, economic, and cultural settings within which the watershed is found. Topography is not destiny, as Woolley and McGinnis noted: "As one moves from the science of geography and biology to culture, definitions become increasingly subjective. A cultural 'map' of a watershed includes political, economic, and social conventions. Participants in watershed policymaking may well think of themselves in terms of political affiliations rather than biogeographical identification with an entire watershed" (1999, 579–580). Distinctions of wealth, ethnicity, religion, occupation, social status, and the like will also exist among and between watershed residents and the groups or communities with which they identify (Lebel, Garden, and Imamura 2005).

Thus, in addition to the opportunities to take advantage of scale efficiencies, institutional arrangements can be designed to enhance responsiveness and equity. There is certainly no guarantee that polycentric organizations will be more responsive or fairer than centralized ones, but neither is the opposite necessarily true (Rockloff and Moore 2006). As with efficiency questions, the responsiveness and equity of a polycentric system versus a unitary one are empirical questions and the answers can differ from one circumstance to another. Where a particular problem affects one portion of a watershed more than others, organizational diversity can allow for a more equitable matching of costs to benefits than can a central organization. Where multiple communities of interest or identity exist, organizational diversity can allow for more effective representation of communities than can combining them into a single constituency or expecting a single set of decision makers to take all interests into account. As always in political situations, the questions of who gets to decide and how are as important as, and often more important than, the question of what shall be done.

When water users create water resources management institutions, they tend to organize at least some of those entities around communities of interest and communities of identity. Their communities may be defined by their physical position in the watershed, by their identity in the larger social system, or (most likely) a mixture of both. People draw multiple boundaries that reflect their differing positions and their differing communities. Merely to observe or repeat that a watershed is a single community hydrologically or ecologically will not overcome this social reality.

Furthermore, polycentric arrangements allow decision-making processes to vary within and among different organizational arrangements. Consensus building, super-majority voting rules, simple majority voting rules, and judicial decisions are combined and nested, allowing multiple opportunities for conflict articulation, conflict resolution, and the taking of decisions. Nested decision-making entities are a characteristic of federal political systems, which are the focus of the next chapter. First let us consider the topics of diverse interests, functions, and values in the watershed through a case study from Southern California.

MULTIPLE GOALS, MULTIPLE COMMUNITIES, AND MULTIPLE ORGANIZATIONS: THE SAN GABRIEL RIVER WATERSHED

The San Gabriel River watershed is a complex physical system situated in one of the largest metropolitan accumulations of people and commerce in the world. The watershed includes most of coastal Los Angeles County, from the San Gabriel Mountains to the Pacific Ocean. It contains two rivers—the

San Gabriel and the Rio Hondo—several creeks and washes, and four major groundwater basins. The lower area of the watershed is adjacent to the lower area of the Santa Ana River watershed described in Chapter 1.

Toward the midpoint of the San Gabriel River's course from the mountains to the sea, the Whittier Narrows divide the watershed's upper area from its lower area. The upper area includes the Main San Gabriel and Raymond groundwater basins. The lower area contains the Central and West groundwater basins. These are coastal basins, in hydrologic contact with the Pacific Ocean, and vulnerable to saltwater intrusion.

Three of the groundwater basins in the San Gabriel River watershed form an interconnected chain. Most of the Central Basin and all of the West Basin are confined by a surface layer of relatively impermeable clay-like soils, so only the northeastern portion of the Central Basin is susceptible to direct replenishment from the land surface. All of the natural freshwater replenishment to West Basin comes from subsurface inflow from Central Basin, and most of the natural freshwater supply to Central Basin comes through Whittier Narrows from the Main San Gabriel Basin.

Virtually the entire area is urbanized; all or parts of 100 municipalities are found within the watershed. Urbanization brought the paving over of soils through which rainfall used to percolate into the underground water supply, the collection and export to the ocean of storm and wastewater that used to return underground, and the lining of miles of surface water channels for flood control purposes.

Several water resources management problems have arisen in the San Gabriel River watershed, owing to the combined effects of the region's limited water supplies, its extensive agricultural and then urban development, and the hydrogeology of the watershed itself. Each of these problems has been multi-jurisdictional in scope. Water users responded to each by developing new institutional arrangements. Those arrangements are fitted together through a system of inter-organizational and intergovernmental relationships.

Securing Supplemental Water Supplies to Support Urban Development

As the Los Angeles area began to urbanize at the beginning of this century, municipal water departments (some of which contracted with private water companies) became the principal water suppliers for urban resi-

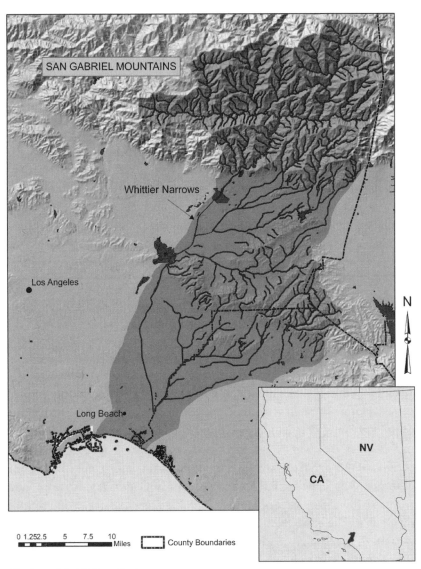

The San Gabriel River Basin.

dences and businesses. Local surface water supplies were scarce, unreliable, and already committed to agricultural uses. Several municipalities turned to groundwater production for a more reliable local supply. A subset also pursued more ambitious schemes of importing water from near or distant sources.[2]

In the 1920s, a group of thirteen cities decided to form a partnership to pursue water importation from the Colorado River and organized the Metropolitan Water District of Southern California (MWD). Nearly half of the original member cities were within the San Gabriel River watershed, including Los Angeles, Pasadena, Compton, Long Beach, San Marino, and Torrance.

After MWD's aqueduct from the Colorado River was completed and began deliveries in the 1940s, MWD was interested in expanding its service areas, and other communities were interested in joining MWD. The original member cities thought that allowing other communities to join one at a time would be administratively and financially tedious, and might ultimately expand the size of MWD's board of directors to more than 100 members. Therefore, MWD adopted a policy of requiring the formation of water districts covering multiple communities prior to annexation and membership in MWD.

This policy, and the desire of the remaining communities within the San Gabriel River watershed to annex to MWD for reasons described later, led to the formation of five municipal water districts within the watershed over the period 1948 through 1960. The West Basin Municipal Water District brought a dozen coastal communities mostly overlying that groundwater basin into MWD. The Central Basin Municipal Water District encompassed another thirty-seven municipalities on the coastal plain. The Foothill Municipal Water District gathered four of Pasadena's immediate neighbors in the upper area. The Upper San Gabriel Valley Municipal Water District (USGVMWD) covered twenty-two communities overlying most of the Main San Gabriel Basin. The Pomona Valley Municipal Water District (now renamed the Three Valleys Municipal Water District) straddled the hilly divide from the eastern edge of the San Gabriel watershed to the western portion of the Santa Ana River watershed, taking in some communities on the boundaries of each.

A few municipalities in the upper area of the watershed had chosen not to join any of these districts and come into MWD's service area. By the 1950s, the State of California was planning the State Water Project to bring Northern California water to the central and southern regions of the state. The state was establishing its own contracts for Northern California water, including one with MWD that brought all of MWD's member cities and districts potentially within reach of State Project water. But the option also existed to contract directly with the state without joining MWD, and a handful of municipalities in the upper area of the watershed chose to do so. Those four cities (Alhambra, Azusa, Monterey Park, and Sierra Madre) formed the watershed's sixth municipal water district—the San Gabriel Valley Municipal Water District—which has its own contract and facilities for delivery of State Project water.

Managing Groundwater Use

By the time imported supplies from the Colorado River and Northern California reached the San Gabriel River watershed in the late 1940s and early 1970s, respectively, the watershed had become home to millions of residents and an immense industrial economy. During that period of development, the public and private water suppliers had intensified their groundwater production, significantly exceeding the rate of natural replenishment and creating overdraft conditions in each of the watershed's four major groundwater basins.

The arrival of imported water supplies relieved some of the pressure on the local groundwater supplies but also triggered a new debate. Since imported water was much more expensive than water pumped from underground, the pressing questions became who should curtail groundwater production, in what amounts, and how would any such arrangement be reached and enforced. Every water producer had a significant incentive to keep using groundwater in preference to imported water, but for each to do so would bring the detriment of all.

In this atmosphere, new organizations emerged. Water production in each basin was dominated by a mix of public and private organizations—municipalities, water districts, water companies, and industrial and other commercial entities that pumped their own water. Nongovernmental water-user associations were formed in three of the four groundwater basins to bring these diverse organizations together for discussions of the condition of the water supply and of their common and conflicting interests therein. The West Basin Water Association was formed in the 1940s, the Central Basin Water Association in 1950, and the Upper San Gabriel Valley Water Association in 1955.[3]

From the 1930s through the 1970s, groundwater production rights were defined and limited in each of the groundwater basins through a series of adjudications. The adjudications were adversarial, but once the issues had been brought to court, the devices of civil discovery were used to develop a shared information base from which the parties began negotiations. In each of the four basins, stipulated judgments were reached by the parties, presented to the court, and approved.

The adjudications occurred in a series rather than all at once because the circumstances of each basin were different. Overdraft problems had become acute first in the smaller Raymond Basin of the upper area and in the coastal West Basin, which was exposed to saltwater intrusion from the ocean once underground water levels fell below sea level. The Raymond Basin litigation began in the late 1930s and concluded in the mid-1940s. The West Basin litigation began in the late 1940s and ended in the early 1960s.

Since West Basin receives its entire freshwater inflow from Central Basin, West Basin could not be brought back into balance once overdraft in Central Basin began choking off the underground flow from there. West Basin water users encouraged the Central Basin Water Association and the Central Basin Municipal Water District to adjudicate and limit pumping in that basin, too, which was done during the 1960s.

Finally, overdraft in the Main San Gabriel Basin was perceived to be a threat not only to pumpers there but to the supply of water coming across the Whittier Narrows from the upper area to the lower area. After the downstream interests had sued the upstream interests to guarantee an average annual flow (described in the next section), upper area pumpers used the leadership of the Upper San Gabriel Valley Water Association and the Upper San Gabriel Valley Municipal Water District to initiate and complete an adjudication and limitation of pumping rights in the Main San Gabriel Basin.

By the mid-1970s, groundwater use in each basin of the watershed was limited by a court judgment that was potentially enforceable by each pumper against all others. Pumpers were required by the terms of the judgment they had negotiated to report their groundwater production monthly so compliance with the judgment could be monitored.

In each basin, the court appointed a "watermaster" to collect data on pumping and groundwater conditions and report annually to the court. In the first three basins to be adjudicated (Raymond, West, and Central), the court appointed the Southern District office of the California Department of Water Resources (DWR) as the watermaster, since DWR had produced several reports on water conditions in these basins already and had a base of data with which future conditions could be compared. Using DWR as watermaster also avoided creating a new organization with its own staff for each basin.

By the time the Main San Gabriel Basin adjudication was completed in 1973, however, new ideas had emerged about how to manage groundwater basins, resulting in a different watermaster arrangement there, as described later. And in 1984, watermaster duties in Raymond Basin were transferred by the court from DWR to the new Raymond Basin Management Board. DWR continues to serve as watermaster for the West and Central Basin judgments.

Upstream-Downstream Division of the River

In addition to the groundwater supplies provided by the four basins, the San Gabriel River itself represented a significant local water supply source. Like the local groundwater, water carried by the river was less expensive to use than imported water. Continued growth in total water use in the upper area in the 1950s threatened to leave almost no San Gabriel River water crossing over to the lower area at Whittier Narrows, costing the lower area a valuable resource and leaving the downstream communities even more dependent on imported water.

Once the Upper San Gabriel Valley Water Association and the upper area municipal water districts had been formed, the Central Basin Municipal Water District and the cities of Compton and Long Beach, on behalf of lower area water users, took the major upper area water producers to court for a determination of the lower area's right to the waters of the San Gabriel River. The litigation began in 1959 but quickly turned into a negotiation that achieved a common statement of "Principles of Settlement" by 1961 and a stipulated judgment approved by the court in 1965.

The settlement guaranteed the lower area an annual average of 98,415 acre-feet of usable water through Whittier Narrows. The court appointed a three-member San Gabriel River watermaster, composed of representatives of the upper area and lower area chosen by the water users, to monitor compliance with the judgment. The data on river flow at the narrows are provided to the San Gabriel River watermaster by the Los Angeles County Department of Public Works, which operates a flood control facility there. Accordingly, the San Gabriel River watermaster needs and has no staff, providing purely a governance function.

Groundwater Contamination Remediation

Some of the greatest challenges in the San Gabriel River watershed have come from water quality problems. In 1972, amendments to the California Administrative Code required water suppliers serving domestic consumers to institute adequate water quality monitoring programs. The California Department of Health Services suggested that producers within common hydrologic units avoid unnecessary duplication of effort by forming programs to monitor water quality on a regional basis. In the upper area of the watershed, the Upper San Gabriel Valley Municipal Water District and the San Gabriel Valley Municipal Water District proposed to undertake the Area-Wide Water Quality Monitoring Program. The first Area Water Quality Monitoring Report for the Main San Gabriel Basin, filed on September 1, 1974, revealed excessive concentrations of nitrates in drinking water, especially in the easterly portion of the basin. Subsequently, the Main San Gabriel Basin watermaster assumed responsibility for the basin's Area-Wide Water Quality Monitoring Program, which quickly became the largest item in the watermaster's administrative fund budget as discoveries of water quality problems in the watershed's upper area multiplied.

Another concern emerging in the 1970s was the siting of municipal waste landfills on lands overlying the upper area's groundwater supplies. The Main San Gabriel Basin watermaster published conditions for conditional use permits for landfills, more stringent than those imposed by existing regulatory agencies, and began a program of inspection of all active landfills within the Main San Gabriel Basin. The watermaster's inspections augment the inspection programs of the Regional Water Quality Control Board and the county Department of Health Services.

In 1979, water quality monitoring discovered relatively high concentrations of trichloroethylene (TCE), a volatile organic chemical, in a Valley County Water District well in the Main San Gabriel Basin. Several nearby wells were tested and found to have varying concentrations of TCE and other volatile organics, predominantly tetrachloroethylene (PCE) and carbon tetrachloride (CCl_4), all suspected carcinogens. California Department of Health Services and Regional Water Quality Control Board preliminary investigations concluded that basin groundwater supplies were potentially in jeopardy (Stetson 1986, 13). A threat to the upper area's groundwater supplies was also worrisome for the lower area's Central and West Basins, since groundwater migrates through the Whittier Narrows from the upper area to the lower.

In January 1980, the affected water producers met in the USGVMWD offices with representatives of the state and county health departments, the Regional Water Quality Control Board, and the county Flood Control District. State and county health officials announced that they had closed four wells because of high TCE concentrations and would begin an intensive well-testing program to determine the areal extent and size of TCE concentrations. The Flood Control District would provide groundwater contour maps with which to plot the movement of TCE concentrations. The Regional Water Quality Control Board would attempt to identify the source or sources of the TCE and recommend steps to prevent further contamination. Possible remedial measures were discussed, such as aeration, water blending, and replacement of groundwater use via direct connections to imported water supplies. The Main San Gabriel Basin watermaster held a special meeting a few days later, where the watermaster's attorney reviewed the situation for the watermaster board and staff.

Monitoring programs continued, and wells with concentrations of TCE, PCE, CCl_4, or other hazardous organic chemicals were closed, or water from them was treated or blended with clean water to reduce contaminant concentrations to below state action levels. By 1985, eighty-eight wells operated by thirty-three different producers in the Main San Gabriel Basin and representing one-fourth of the basin's total groundwater production had been found to have concentrations of these chemicals in excess of state action limits. The number of active producing wells in the basin dropped from an average of 333 at the time of the late 1970s judgment to 237 at the end of the 1980s.

Four large areas of groundwater contamination in the Main San Gabriel Basin became Environmental Protection Agency (EPA) Superfund sites in 1984, making cleanup activities eligible for funding under the federal Superfund program. EPA officials characterized the San Gabriel site as one of the worst in the western United States and estimated that full implementation of basin cleanup could take up to fifty years and cost up to $1 billion.

Discussions among the Main San Gabriel watermaster, the California Department of Health Services, and the EPA arrived at a planned approach to basin remediation. The remediation program would be directed by the Department of Health Services, financed with Superfund monies, and assisted by the Main San Gabriel Basin watermaster as the water users' representative, with the Upper San Gabriel Valley Municipal Water District as the principal provider of staff support. A technical committee and a management committee were established to coordinate aspects of the remediation effort.

In the late 1980s, the EPA shifted its focus from the long-term cleanup effort within the Main San Gabriel Basin to short-term efforts to treat the worst areas and intercept contamination plumes before they passed through Whittier Narrows and hit Central Basin in the watershed's lower area. Also, the EPA wanted to focus on identifying the polluters so they can be forced to pay the long-term cleanup operation's costs, whereas state and local officials and valley residents wanted to press ahead with full basin cleanup. The political question arose regarding what entity should have principal responsibility for the cleanup operation.

A report released by the Regional Water Quality Control Board in spring 1990 recommended that the cleanup program be supervised locally by the Main San Gabriel Basin watermaster. The MWD, local water producers, the overlying municipal water districts, and the watermaster agreed with that recommendation. However, two prominent local public figures, U.S. representative Esteban Torres (D–La Puente) and California state senator Art Torres (D–Los Angeles) opposed expanding the watermaster's powers and, along with the Sierra Club and a local group called the East Valleys Organization, have called for the creation of a new "super-agency" to organize and perform the cleanup. Senator Torres sponsored legislation in December 1990 to create such an agency, and his bill passed the California State Senate in April 1991.

In August 1990, the Main San Gabriel Basin watermaster returned to Superior Court, seeking an amendment of the judgment to expand its authority to oversee the cleanup and to control pumping patterns within the basin in order to arrest the migration of contamination plumes. The watermaster's motion was supported by the MWD, the Regional Water Quality Control Board, and the three overlying municipal water districts. The motion was opposed by the Sierra Club, the East Valleys Organization, and the office of Los Angeles County district attorney Ira Reiner. Those opposing the motion alleged a conflict of interest of the water producers who are represented by the Main San Gabriel Basin watermaster, and the lack of public accountability of the watermaster. Maxine Leichter, speaking for the Sierra Club's Angeles Chapter, said, "The Watermaster cannot protect both the private interests of water companies and the public's interests." A brief by the county district attorney's office emphasized that the cleanup operation vitally affects all valley residents and water consumers, but the watermaster is accountable for its actions only to the court and the roughly 100 water producers in the basin. There is no provision for participation by the general public in watermaster selection or decision making.

A negotiated result produced a new element in the watershed's governance system. In August 1990, the Main San Gabriel Basin watermaster, the Upper San Gabriel Valley Municipal Water District, the San Gabriel Valley Municipal Water District, and the Three Valleys Municipal Water District formed a joint-powers agency, the Main San Gabriel Basin Water Quality Authority, to develop financing for the cleanup operation. The Water Quality Authority represented neither an independent "super-agency" nor the mere addition of cleanup responsibilities to an existing body; it lies somewhere between those alternatives. Although its form may be somewhat difficult to classify in traditional public administration categories, the Water Quality Authority has provided an organizational means for pursuing state and federal funding of the cleanup operation and supervising its ongoing progress. Contaminated groundwater has been pumped and treated in several locations, the contaminant plumes have been intercepted, and the impact on the lower area of the watershed has been limited. In the meantime, EPA has pursued the polluters through a series of investigations and trials, securing monetary judgments against some of the largest ones.

River Restoration

During the first half of the twentieth century, the lower reach of the San Gabriel River was converted into a concrete channel for flood control purposes. The same was done with other Southern California streams, most famously the neighboring Los Angeles River. It was not inevitable: in the late 1920s, a committee from the Los Angeles Chamber of Commerce hired the famed design firms of the Olmsted Brothers and Harland Bartholomew and Associates to plan regional recreation areas in the rapidly urbanizing Los Angeles Basin. The 1930 plan produced by the designers envisioned the San Gabriel River as a ribbon of parkland running through the metropolis, with construction kept back at least 1,000 feet from the water and natural banks providing a buffer for flood flows. A variety of concerns—the expense of implementing the plan, the difficulties of establishing a governmental body with the territory and authority to do so, the foregone construction opportunities, and whether flood protection for communities along the lower reaches of the river would be adequate, to name a few—led to another choice, lining the channel and confining the river.

Since by mid-century most of the natural flows into the San Gabriel River were captured and impounded by dams in the upper area and at Whittier Narrows, with controlled releases diverted and spread for ground-water replenishment, the concrete-lined portions of the channel conveyed little or no natural flow except during significant flood events. Municipalities throughout the upper and lower areas of the San Gabriel watershed discharge treated wastewater into the river channel, and these discharges have made up most of the flow in the channel since the mid-twentieth century.

In the 1970s, the Los Angeles County Department of Public Works paved a bicycle trail along the banks of the San Gabriel River from Azusa (at the base of the mountains) to Long Beach. The primary purpose of the 37-mile bike trail was to facilitate alternative transportation, but over the ensuing two decades it became increasingly popular for recreational riders. Municipalities along the river constructed access points at numerous inter-sections and increased patrols and lighting in higher-crime areas along the trail, and the county public works department made further improvements to the trail itself. As many as fifteen small parks and recreation areas were established or restored along the trail, and the California Department of Fish and Game stocks catfish and trout at the Santa Fe Dam Recreation Area, the Whittier Narrows Recreation Area, and other sites.

As the river course gained popularity as a recreation site, public attention to the condition of the river increased. Community organizations began weekend river cleanups, removing trash and other debris from the channel and banks and covering graffiti on the concrete surfaces. Birds flourished along the cleaned-up sections of the river, drawing more attention and visi-tors. A network among members of community organizations located along the river developed into a group called Friends of the San Gabriel River. In the 1990s, the Los Angeles and San Gabriel Rivers Watershed Council formed to advocate restoration efforts for both rivers. By the end of the decade, the San Gabriel River Master Plan Committee, composed of repre-sentatives from thirty-five conservation groups, municipalities, and government agencies, was meeting monthly to compose a blueprint for restoration and protection of the river ecosystem.

In 1999, the California legislature approved the creation of the San Gabriel and Lower Los Angeles Rivers and Mountains Conservancy, with $15 million in capital to acquire land and continue restoration efforts along the rivers. A single conservancy was created for both rivers for a number of reasons, including the fact that they are connected via the Rio Hondo Channel, itself a target for restoration efforts. In a political concession to the state's funding of the conservancy, Sacramento was given the power to appoint most of the board members. On the other hand, the conservancy lacks eminent domain powers, so it must work closely with municipalities along the length of each river to ensure agreement on parcels of land to acquire. In 2000, the Los Angeles County Department of Public Works established a watershed management division to work with the watershed council and the conservancy on projects to improve and restore the rivers.

The conservancy is an example of an additional governmental body established to overlap numerous other jurisdictions, but with a limited mission and authority. The conservancy cannot displace the functions of other local governments, but it can perform functions they cannot achieve together or independently. It adds to the number of governmental bodies at work on water resources in the San Gabriel River watershed, but it is not an addition that necessarily comes at the expense of the authority of other bodies. It increases coordination costs, but if the same authority to acquire land for river restoration projects had been distributed among existing jurisdictions, it is doubtful the coordination costs would have been smaller. What a body such as the conservancy can do is specialize and focus on watershed-wide restoration activities that would have been difficult for other existing bodies to accomplish. Whether its accomplishments in this regard warrant the expense and effort of establishing another water resource organization in the watershed remains to be seen, of course, but its creation in 1999 was consistent with the logic presented in this chapter and book.

CONCLUSION: POLYCENTRICITY AND THE PURSUIT OF MULTIPLE VALUES IN THE POLITICAL WATERSHED

The San Gabriel River watershed exists as a physical phenomenon, and it can certainly be said that all resources and problems within the watershed are interrelated to some degree. On the other hand, different portions of the watershed confront different problems and are home to distinguishable communities. Furthermore, watershed management within the San Gabriel River case clearly exemplifies the presence of a multiplicity of goals, some of which have been present since the earliest organization of water management activity within the watershed and others of which have emerged over time in connection with newly recognized problems or developing social values.

Under these circumstances, individuals and organizations within the watershed have established institutional arrangements and operated a number of resource management efforts at several scales. Groundwater supplies were allocated among pumpers within each of the watershed's four major basins through largely (although not entirely) separate processes over four decades, rather than for the watershed as a whole through a single process. The flows of the San Gabriel River were divided between upper and lower watershed areas by another process. The representative body that monitors the river agreement is not the same as the bodies that monitor the four groundwater basin judgments. More recently, new organizations (one a joint-powers agency, the other a nonprofit conservancy) have been established to focus, respectively, on groundwater cleanup in the Main San Gabriel Basin and on river restoration throughout the watershed and beyond.

The resulting institutional array is complex but does not necessarily fit characterizations such as "fragmented," "piecemeal," or "myopic." Although unquestionably imperfect (as any institutions created by human beings are), the institutions of the San Gabriel River watershed are comprehensible and do display a logic. The complexity of the institutional arrangements in the San Gabriel River watershed results from the combined effects of differences among the interests of individuals and organizations within the watershed, changes over time in the understanding of problems and in values for water, the need to pursue multiple resource management goals, distinctions in the efficient scale of operation of organizations performing diverse functions, and the importance of finding distributions of benefits and costs that are perceived as fair by those who bear them.

Taking the multiple problems and goals apart and pursuing them through diverse organizations therefore represents a plausible alternative, and one might even conclude represents a reasonable approach. Although control of groundwater pumping in each of the four major groundwater basins mattered to some degree to everyone in the watershed, it plainly mattered most to the collections of pumpers within each basin, and the adjudications of pumping rights in each basin took place through negotiations and litigation between and among those pumpers. With respect to the division of San Gabriel River flows, the most relevant interests were the interests of lower area communities on the one hand and all upper area communities on the other. Groundwater contamination in the Main San Gabriel Basin certainly threatened Central Basin and even potentially West Basin, but its most direct and costly consequence was the shutdown of wells within the Main San Gabriel Basin. And its causes were traceable to polluters within the Main San Gabriel Basin, so it could be argued that establishing a water quality authority for that basin rather than the entire watershed exhibited some political and economic logic. The river restoration programs undertaken more recently affect people not only within the physical watershed but in adjacent communities, and the conservancy is organized over that broader area.

Diverse management functions within the watershed also exhibit different efficiency scales, as the public economies literature would predict. The agency that imports water to the San Gabriel River watershed from the Colorado River and from Northern California is not the same as the entities managing local supplies or the various sub-watershed local governments that decide on behalf of their residents how much imported water to purchase each year. The importing organization, the Metropolitan Water District of Southern California, is enormous and encompasses several watersheds besides the San Gabriel, but the choices of what to purchase and what to supply are made at a much smaller scale through municipalities and municipal water districts.

In some ways, the San Gabriel River watershed is pretty typical. Previously existing jurisdictions—cities and the county, for example—did not match the contours of the watershed, and within that watershed, natural resources are interrelated. Merely observing that previously existing political jurisdictions did not match watershed boundaries, however, fails to take into account the possibilities of institutional design. Individuals and organizations within the watershed created institutional arrangements over several decades to fit, if not the watershed's topographic boundaries, then at least its principal problems and its principal communities of interest, and to provide means of pursuing multiple goals simultaneously. In those processes of establishing institutions, individuals faced numerous institutional design choices and debated at length (sometimes contentiously) over what to do—whether contamination remediation should be undertaken by an existing agency or a new one (in the end, they created a hybrid, a joint-powers authority of existing agencies), whether separate conservancies should be established for the San Gabriel and Los Angeles Rivers (and for the Rio Hondo that runs between them) or a combined one, and so forth. The choices they made reflected questions of hydrology but also of society, of scale efficiencies and transaction costs, of values, interests, power, and accountability—political questions.

As with the other case studies in this book, the San Gabriel River watershed does not represent an ideal. It represents a possibility. It is possible to manage a complex watershed facing significant problems, and to do so without a central watershed agency or authority. The patterns of organization in the San Gabriel River watershed are non-centralized, or polycentric. As a political watershed, the San Gabriel case represents the possibilities that may be available through a sort of watershed federalism, an idea to which we now turn.

NOTES

1. One could argue there is only a semantic difference between these terms and the older terms "flood control" and "flood prevention." It appears to us, though, that the shift of language is more than merely new labels on old bottles.

2. Los Angeles's efforts to bring water from the Sierras are legendary (or infamous) in this regard, but other municipalities such as Pasadena also explored water importation possibilities.

3. Water users in the smaller Raymond Basin did not form a water association, but there were far fewer major pumpers there and they embarked upon an adjudication and limitation of pumping more than a decade earlier than in any of the other basins.

6

Federalism and Watershed Governance

There also is the serious problem of "thinking federal," that is, of approaching the problem of organizing political relationships from a federalist rather than a monist or centralist perspective.

DANIEL ELAZAR (1987, 12)

As described in Chapter 1, many natural scientists and policy analysts accept that most natural systems, such as watersheds, are complex adaptive systems. These systems do not need to be simplified and managed for one or two values, their complexity is to be recognized, protected, and respected. The same thinking, however, has not pervaded the social sciences concerning watershed governance. Political complexity is viewed as a barrier to the sustainable use of natural systems and something to be corrected. As illustrated in Chapter 2, policy reforms are sought that simplify, integrate, and centralize so the externalities, spillover effects, commons dilemmas, and public goods that emerge from the human uses of a watershed may be traded off and balanced against each other.

The previous chapters offered an alternative view, namely, that social complexity is neither a barrier to sustainability nor something that is readily dispensed with. It arises from human decision-making capabilities, the many different conflicting values and goals people hold, the attempts to collectively achieve those many values and goals by designing multiple institutional arrangements in a world of transaction costs, and in so doing having to inevitably and unavoidably make difficult and challenging political decisions. All of this social complexity cannot be quieted by relying on science or nature to define boundaries or by forcing diversity into the well-designed box of hierarchy.

Building on Chapter 5, this chapter focuses on an approach for structuring complementary, cooperative, competitive, and conflicting relations among citizens, organizations, and governments at interstate watershed scales.[1] Citizens, public officials, and elected representatives in the United States have considerable experience developing working relations among organizations and governments at different levels and scales, because that is the essence of federalism, a fundamental principle of American politics. Federal systems of government exhibit both diversity and unity: diversity through many governments organized at different scales and for different purposes, and unity through coordination and cohesion among those governments. As such, federalism represents an important and powerful alternative to calls for more centralized governing forms. In this chapter, we explore federalism and how it structures watershed-level governance.

The chapter begins by distinguishing federalism from other forms of coordination and cooperation—federalism has particular defining features that differentiate it from other forms of governance. There follows a discussion of coordination, cooperation, and conflict resolution among governments and organizations in a federal system: that is, how unity or integration is achieved in a federal system. From there we sketch out a form of policy analysis appropriate for identifying and diagnosing the weaknesses and shortcomings likely to appear in a federal form of governance. The chapter closes with a case study of the creation and operation of the Delaware River Basin Compact and Commission, the first federal-interstate compact in the United States. For forty-five years, the participating states and the federal government, through the compact commission and its advisory committees, have addressed problems and provided benefits that the compact was intended for, failed to realize other benefits, created policy innovations to address unanticipated challenges, and resolved conflicts among themselves without recourse to the U.S. Supreme Court. The Delaware River Basin illustrates the strengths, challenges, and shortcomings of watershed federalism.

THE BASICS OF FEDERALISM

The United States has a long and rich history of contesting over and experimenting with watershed-level governance. That experimentation occurs in the context of federalism. Federalism encourages innovation and experimentation because of the dynamic tension between self-rule and shared rule. Federalism combines self-rule with shared rule. Federal systems are composed of equals, citizens and governments, who come together to form a common enterprise while maintaining their separate identities, rights, and authorities (Elazar 1987, 4). Achieving a workable combination of self-rule and shared rule depends on relationships among participants that protect the integrity of each while supporting and encouraging "the energetic pursuit" of common ends (Elazar 1987, 5).

In federal systems, citizens are constantly challenged to attend to issues of both political power (who gets what, when, and how) and justice (how power is to be exercised so good governance is realized) (Lasswell 1958; Elazar 1987).[2] Watershed collaboratives, and the literature they have spawned, for instance, explicitly encompass this tension between power and justice (Weber 2003). Collaboratives are formed to address specific problems in watersheds by gaining the commitment of collaborative members to engage in specific projects and activities. The process that is used to gain that commitment represents a particular form of justice—the deliberate coming together of equals whose free consent is required for the collaborative to act. The collaborative literature pays at least as much attention to the justice dimension (the relationships formed, the trust developed) as it does to the political dimension (the projects and plans adopted, the outcomes realized) (Sabatier et al. 2005).[3]

The focus on achieving self-rule and shared rule simultaneously is a critical feature that distinguishes federalism from other forms of governance. All forms of governance, no matter how centralized, are typically divided into subunits that are based on function, territory, or both for the many reasons outlined in Chapters 3, 4, and 5. Consequently, all forms of governance are faced with challenges of achieving integration and cohesion. Hierarchical forms of governance depend on institutional mechanisms that tie the subunits more tightly to the central decision maker, giving the central decision maker greater control and direction over the subunits. The mechanisms may be blatantly coercive, based on command and control, or they may be incentive based, appealing to the interest of the subunit. Either way, the integrity, independence, and discretion of the subunits are controlled by the center. Issues of power and justice are conflated within the central decision maker. The focus rests on how the central decision maker can best exercise power in order to achieve desired ends. Justice becomes a consideration only to the extent that it helps the central decision maker more effectively exercise power.[4]

Relationships among governments in a federal system are qualitatively different. They are not hierarchical but polycentric (Ostrom 1973), or non-centralized (Elazar 1987). Noncentralization refers to multiple centers of power, each with its own authorities and capabilities, and with no one center dominating or commanding the others.

Noncentralization, particularly in the U.S. federal system, is achieved and protected through constitutions. Constitutions define the *capabilities* and, just as importantly, *limitations* of governments (Lutz 1988). Governments' capabilities, such as making and enforcing laws, are limited by circumscribing the substantive areas in which governments may act and/or by structurally dividing authority through a separation of powers. Constitutions define relationships among governments, among branches within governments, and between citizens and governments.[5]

It would be a mistake, however, to consider the U.S. Constitution and the fifty state constitutions as the only constitutions that matter in the United States, particularly in relation to water. Hundreds of additional constitutions have been devised and adopted that create "water governments." For instance, interstate river compacts are constitutions devised and adopted by states that spell out the types of water and water-related issues the compact will govern, a formula for allocating water, a governing body to oversee the operation of the compact and to establish policy, and perhaps a conflict resolution mechanism for settling differences among the states before, or instead of, calling upon the U.S. Supreme Court.

For instance, Nebraska and Kansas entered into the Big Blue River Compact in 1971, which governs the Big Blue River and its major tributary, the Little Blue River, from its headwaters in Nebraska to its confluence with the Kansas River near Manhattan, Kansas (Kansas Revised Statutes, Chapter 82a, Article 5). The compact governs water allocation and quality of surface and groundwater. From May through September of each year, Nebraska must ensure agreed-upon minimum daily flows at the state line for both rivers. If minimum daily flows drop below compact-specified levels, Kansas may request that Nebraska shut down water diversions, both ground and surface, so as to restore the required minimum flows.[6] The compact recognizes water-quality issues, although it lacks regulatory authority. Nebraska and Kansas have developed a joint water-quality monitoring program and agricultural education and best practices programs (Big Blue Compact Administration, 29th annual report, 2002).

Interstate river compacts allow for a combination of self-rule and shared rule. States exercise their governing authority in ways and areas that they have historically used. Through compacts, however, they freely accede some of that control. Under the Big Blue Compact, for instance, Nebraska has had to regulate its citizens' water diversions not to meet the requirements of Nebraska water laws but to meet the requirements of the compact.

Compacts allow states to cooperate and coordinate their resource use. Most states have also provided enabling legislation that allows local water users to devise constitutions creating water organizations to govern intrastate water resources, as illustrated in the case studies in Chapters 1 and 5. For instance, most states allow for the creation of special districts that govern different aspects of water development and use. Among the most ubiquitous, at least in the western United States, are irrigation districts. State-enabling legislation typically spells out procedures for forming a district, such as who may participate in its creation and how, and once a district is created, its governing structure, powers (including taxing and spending authority), methods of reorganization and dissolution, and methods of electing and recalling board members.

Irrigation districts have allowed members to govern themselves, at least with respect to some aspects of resource use—arranging for water and its allocation, providing for system construction and maintenance, and allowing members to decide how and to what extent they wish to tax themselves. This self-governance occurs within a system of shared governance. Districts are governed by states' water laws, conflicts are addressed through state courts, and so forth. Conversely, the integrity and autonomy of a district are protected by the district's enabling legislation and constitution that spell out how the district may be reorganized or dissolved.

Given the centrality of constitutions in creating and sustaining noncentralized systems, amendment procedures are critical. The amending process must allow participants to revise constitutions to address new and changing circumstances while still protecting the integrity of the governing system. One way this is accomplished is by strictly limiting governments' ability to revise constitutions so one government does not become too powerful relative to the others and to its own citizens. A government cannot unilaterally change its own constitution, and member governments typically have greater powers to change the constitution of the general government than vice versa (Elazar 1987). For example, state governments have a constitutionally defined role in amending the U.S. Constitution, but the U.S. government does not have a constitutionally defined role in amending state constitutions.[7] Furthermore, the participation of elected officials in constitution-amending processes is limited. For nearly all states, either legislatures or citizens may place constitutional measures on the state ballot, but citizens must approve them.

COOPERATION AND COORDINATION IN A FEDERAL SYSTEM

Two important implications stem from a federal system of governance. First, in federal systems, joint action among members rests on mutual consent and building consensus rather than on threatening coercion or issuing commands. Mutual consent permeates federal systems. The multiple veto points sprinkled throughout the structure of a federal system, combined with the constitutional protections afforded governments and citizens, require participants to take one another into account in order to find mutual accommodation and agreement. Even if an actor has the authority to act unilaterally, often the initial tendency is to reach an understanding before acting. For instance, the U.S. Supreme Court has refused on a number of occasions to decree water allocations on an interstate river, although the court possesses the authority to do so at the request of one of the states. Instead, the court has urged the parties to devise their own water-allocation agreements through compacts. Elazar (1987, 67) refers to efforts to find mutual consent as an element of the federal process. As he explains, "The elements of a federal process include a sense of partnership among the parties to the federal compact, manifested through negotiated cooperation on issues and programs and based on a commitment to open bargaining between all parties to an issue in such a way as to strive for consensus or, failing that, an accommodation that protects the fundamental integrity of all the partners."

Second, strengthening and/or adapting a noncentralized, or polycentric, system is much different from doing so in a centralized system. Recall the earlier discussion in which centralized systems are strengthened by placing greater powers in the hands of the top-level decision maker. In contrast, a polycentric system becomes stronger by strengthening its constituent units, supporting their ability to communicate and coordinate, and providing means for resolving disputes among them.

Recently, several interstate river compacts have been before the Supreme Court to settle disputes and to revise operating rules and regulations to allow states to better coordinate their actions around shared rivers. The compacts include (1) the Arkansas River Compact between Colorado (upstream state) and Kansas (downstream state); (2) the Republican River Compact among Colorado (upstream state), Nebraska (downstream to Colorado but upstream to Kansas), and Kansas (downstream state); and (3) the North Platte Decree among Colorado (upstream state), Wyoming (downstream to Colorado but upstream to Nebraska), and Nebraska (downstream state). Conflicts centered initially on boundaries (what or who is covered by the agreement), as examined in Chapter 3. The downstream states claimed that the compacts governed groundwater, and consequently, groundwater use in the upstream states was to be counted against compact-defined water allotments. In each case, the text of the compact did not mention groundwater explicitly, and conflict over its inclusion simmered for decades as states attempted to resolve the issue through the compact commissions. However, because the commissions used unanimity rules, upstream states typically managed to block attempts to incorporate groundwater use in compact water allotments. Finally, the downstream states in each case filed lawsuits in the U.S. Supreme Court, and in each case, the court ruled that groundwater was within the bounds of the compacts.

With the boundary question resolved, the states, as part of the final settlements of each case, also adopted different institutional mechanisms to improve their ability to take joint action and to better realize their compact commitments. Adoption of a unanimity rule for all decisions, no matter how great or small, limited the compact commissions' competency to engage in governance. In each settlement, the states revised the commissions' decision rules, allowing for a rule other than unanimity to be used in at least some situations.[8] Also, in each of the settlements, the states devised a variety of conflict resolution mechanisms, providing the states with multiple opportunities to settle their differences before having to resort to the Supreme Court.[9]

In some of the cases, states better defined their own water rights laws and administrative practices so as to allow them to meet their compact commitments. For instance, the Supreme Court's ruling that groundwater pumping in the Colorado portion of the Arkansas River Basin caused harm to Kansas water users in violation of the compact required Colorado to limit and regulate groundwater pumping in the basin (*Kansas v. Colorado*, 514 U.S. 675 [1995]). Colorado water law recognizes the hydrologic connection between surface and groundwater and directs the state water engineer to incorporate wells into the prior appropriation system and to regulate them (Blomquist, Schlager, and Heikkila 2004). Although the state water engineer successfully adopted a set of well regulations for the South Platte River Basin, he was unable to do so for the Arkansas River Basin for a variety of reasons. Faced with the possibility of paying Kansas millions of dollars in damages for allowing its water users to take more than they were entitled to under the compact, the Colorado legislature allocated additional resources to the state engineer to adopt well regulations. Working with the major well associations in the Arkansas River Basin, the state engineer adopted rules within a matter of months that withstood a court challenge brought by a handful of well owners who adamantly opposed regulation.

In the Republican River case, Nebraska faced more difficult issues with the Supreme Court decision finding that groundwater was covered by the compact. Pumping would have to be regulated to prevent Nebraskans from taking more water than was allocated to them under the compact; however, as noted in connection with the Platte River case in Chapter 3, Nebraska law did not authorize the state to regulate groundwater pumping. After more than a decade of conflict among groundwater pumpers, surface-water users, and local and state officials, the Nebraska legislature passed LB 962, which allowed the state department of natural resources to declare watersheds overallocated. Once a watershed is determined to be overallocated, two things occur. A moratorium on new and replacement wells goes into effect and the natural resource districts overlying the watershed are required to engage in groundwater planning and adopt well regulations (LB 962, 98th Legis., 2nd sess., Nebraska Laws, 2004).

The strengthening of the three interstate river compacts most recently before the U.S. Supreme Court involved addressing relations among states and between states and citizens. It did not involve greater centralization. The rules governing the operation of the compacts were revised to allow states to better coordinate and cooperate with each other. Rather than being saddled with a unanimity rule for every decision, decision rules now vary depending on the issue, with the unanimity rule still in place for most major decisions. Furthermore, the compacts have conflict-resolution mechanisms that allow states to address disagreements without having to allow them to fester until they are severe enough for the U.S. Supreme Court to accept and resolve. Finally, states and citizens have wrestled with devising new laws and better implementing existing laws so that water providers and users abide by state laws and compact requirements.

Strengthening federal systems by tending to the ties among member governments, organizations, and citizens often involves the use of overlapping organizations. Overlapping organizations may take a variety of forms, from purely voluntary organizations serving as forums for discussion and consultation to formal governments possessing powers of rule making, enforcement, and taxation. As observed in the San Gabriel River case in Chapter 5, overlapping organizations may be highly specialized, addressing a single issue, or general, addressing a variety of issues.

Watershed collaboratives are a form of overlapping organization at the voluntary end of the spectrum. They are widely heralded for encouraging their members to recognize and act on a more general, comprehensive view of a segment of a watershed.[10] That is, in developing a watershed plan or designing a restoration project, multiple dimensions of the watershed are recognized and their interactions attended to, such as the interaction among land use, riparian areas, and the quality of water in the stream. As voluntary organizations, collaboratives rely heavily on persuasion and consensus to encourage members to exercise their discretionary authority in ways consistent with the mission and goals of the collaborative.

At the risk of stating the obvious, more authoritative forms of overlapping arrangements are qualitatively different from voluntary organizations.

These organizations are governments, either specialized (Type II, to use the language of Chapter 1) or general-purpose (Type I), with explicitly defined and delimited coercive powers. Interstate river compacts and commissions are examples of specialized (Type II) institutions grounded in enforceable laws. Compact commissions may adopt rules and regulations to carry out the purpose of the compact. They may monitor compliance with compact requirements, and member states may enforce compact commitments against one another and against their citizens. To be sure, persuasion, open bargaining, and accommodation among member states are vital if a compact is to work well; however, in the end if all else fails, members can resort to enforcement mechanisms to ensure that rules are followed and commitments carried out.[11]

Type II governments, because of their rule-making and enforcement authority and dedicated sources of funding, are often considered desirable mechanisms for accomplishing watershed management. Created through the design and adoption of a constitution, they are not easily dismantled or avoided. Rule-making and implementation powers allow them to request and command action. Dedicated sources of funding from taxes, fees, and bonds provide regular and dependable sources of capital. These authorities are significant when compared with voluntary organizations in which members must spend considerable time, effort, and resources toward encouraging and maintaining participation, gaining consensus, obtaining funding, and persuading members to follow through with their commitments of resources and action. Substantial energy is expended simply maintaining the existence of voluntary organization, energy that is not expended in maintaining governments. Instead, that energy can be devoted to operations, implementation, monitoring, and enforcement.

Although attractive in that sense, more authoritative overlapping organizations are more difficult and costly to create than are voluntary organizations. Given their coercive authorities, multiple veto points characterize the processes used to create them. Veto points are the means by which consent is solicited and obtained from those who are to be subject to and governed by the new government. For instance, in devising an interstate compact, the designated representatives of each state must adopt the compact they have devised unanimously before it is brought before the legislatures of each of the states for ratification. If each state ratifies the compact, then it is brought before Congress and the president for approval. Given the extensive consultation and review process, most interstate river compacts take more than a decade to devise and adopt, if they are devised at all.

The benefits from creating a new government must be significant to justify the high creation costs. Not only must the benefits be significant, but the allocation of benefits and costs of its creation and operation must be equitable among its members if it is to be formed. For instance, the South Platte Cooperative Agreement discussed in Chapter 3 took more than a decade to complete, even though the states initially believed that they would be able to finalize an agreement within three years. The benefits for each state were clear: avoid extensive endangered species consultations with the federal government and protect existing water users and uses. Adequately protecting and recovering endangered species, fairly allocating the costs of doing so, and devising acceptable and workable decision-making and monitoring arrangements were more difficult issues on which to agree.

The more comprehensive the government to be formed, both in scale and in scope, the more costly it will be to create. Creating a government at the scale of a watershed means that many governments and citizens within that watershed will have direct and indirect opportunities to support or inhibit its creation. Creating a government at the scale of a watershed that has a scope of authority encompassing many dimensions of the watershed will directly implicate and involve even more governments and citizens in its creation. The larger in scale and scope of the government being devised, the more costly and difficult it will be to gain the necessary consensus for its creation. As discussed in Chapter 4, Derthick (1974) labels these latter forms of governments "political accidents." Consequently, voluntary overlapping organizations will be easier to create than overlapping governments (Derthick 1974). And among governments, limited-purpose special districts will be easier to create than more encompassing and comprehensive general-purpose governments. Given the high costs of creation and adoption and the challenges of ensuring an equitable distribution of benefits and costs, in most watersheds, coercive forms of overlapping organizations are likely to emerge only after multiple attempts at creation. In many instances, voluntary forms of overlapping organizations will be all that participants are able to create; in other instances, voluntary forms will be created as stepping-stones to the creation of governments.

A FEDERALISM-BASED POLICY ANALYSIS OF WATERSHED GOVERNANCE

Most policy analyses of the management and governance of watersheds are based on methods of analysis not well suited for polycentric systems. Such analyses assume that centralized, hierarchical forms of government are or should be the norm. Diagnoses proceeding from such an assumption tend to center on the diversity of organizations, agencies, and governments; that is, watershed governance is fragmented, disjointed, and disorganized because there is no single controlling center. Policy prescriptions of reducing diversity, creating a centralized authority, and so forth readily follow.

A federal, or polycentric, policy analysis begins from a different starting point with a consideration of the major points of conflict within a watershed. Major points of conflict tend to encompass multiple actors and entail significant disagreement over the types and causes of problems or the failure, indifference, or inability of key actors to take steps to address the problems. From there, attention is paid to the types and qualities of the relations among the actors most directly involved in the conflicts. Policy solutions centering on creating, redefining, and restructuring relations among governments and organizations may then be considered.

Of course, this is easier said than done because in crafting policy solutions, the many political questions raised in previous chapters must be confronted. For instance, will a new government be created or will a new program and/or agency be incorporated within an existing government? Who will be included within the new program/agency/government? What will decision-making processes be like? To whom and how will the new program/agency/government be held accountable? Will the policy solutions likely reduce the overall magnitude of transaction costs among the key actors? Have the trade-offs among transaction costs made by the policy solutions been carefully attended to, and have the obvious points of weakness been identified?

Examples of policy makers, public managers, and citizens struggling to redefine relations in order to better address perceived watershed problems abound in the case studies included in previous chapters. One example from the Columbia Basin seems particularly apt. The incompatibility between the Northwest Power Planning Council's fish recovery plan and the laws governing the federal water and power agencies allowed agency costs to blossom, as the federal water and power agencies acted in ways that undermined the fishery plan. The council responded predictably. It increased its decision-making costs by defining more precisely specific actions that the federal water and power agencies were to engage in, such as developing and adhering to implementation plans and imposing timetables and deadlines on the completion of specific activities. In other words, the council attempted to limit the discretion of the agencies in order to reduce agency problems. The state and tribal fish and wildlife agencies that consulted and worked with the council on developing plans urged an additional approach. The state and tribal agencies understood that the federal water and power agencies would be reluctant partners. Consequently, the agencies requested that the council undertake a study on the federal water and power agencies' decision-making processes to identify appropriate points and procedures to directly insert consideration of the council's fish and wildlife plan, with the expectation that such a study would provide the information needed to revise the laws governing the federal agencies (Blumm 1984). For tribal and state wildlife officials, gaining the support of federal agencies required orienting their decision-making processes to include conservation goals; simply limiting their discretion in carrying out conservation activities was insufficient. In the end, the council's approach of limiting discretion met with only modest success, and it declined to engage in the study of federal agency decision-making processes.

Gaining the cooperation and commitment of semi-autonomous governments unfolds at different scales, as illustrated by the Platte River case study in Chapter 3. Colorado, Wyoming, and Nebraska together had to follow through on their commitments to provide additional water and to carefully regulate new water demands. If even one state failed to realize its water and regulatory commitments, the entire agreement failed, regardless of the actions of the other two states. Both Colorado and Wyoming believed that the weakest commitment was from Nebraska. Their state laws required the careful regulation of all new uses of both ground- and surface water so as to protect existing water rights, but Nebraska had no such laws, particularly in relation to groundwater. Nebraska could not credibly commit itself to regulate pumping so that its citizens would not pump the additional water that the three states made available in the river, other than to promise to actively pursue such legislation. Ultimately, the state was successful in realizing such legislation but an agency problem blossomed, undercutting the credibility of Nebraska's commitment to regulating new uses. Farmers, anticipating the adoption of new legislation strictly limiting wells, applied for and were granted new well permits by the natural resource districts. Once the legislation passed, the Nebraska Department of Natural Resources declared the Platte River Basin over-appropriated and a moratorium on new wells went into effect (Nebraska Department of Natural Resources 2004). Now the natural resource districts are required to develop groundwater management plans, but that task is more complicated because of the new well permits issued and new wells installed before the law took effect. Do the natural resource districts have sufficient expertise, resources, and social capital to develop groundwater management plans likely to realize the goal of protecting and enhancing river flows? The Nebraska Department of Natural Resources is likely to face challenging agency issues with the natural resource districts, issues that they will most likely attempt to address through increased decision-making costs for the department and for the districts.

One of the strengths of polycentricity is that the existence of independent, autonomous governments organized at different scales allows first attempts to address problems and conflicts to occur at smaller scales, among the citizens, organizations, and governments most immediately involved and affected. These actors have access to a variety of institutional mechanisms that they may call upon to address shared problems, including mechanisms that do not require them to appeal to or depend upon governments organized at a larger scale. These mechanisms extend from creating voluntary organizations through which participants may cooperate and coordinate their actions to giving up some of their autonomy and authority by creating overlapping special-purpose or general-purpose governments. At each step, actors have choices about how political they want the issues to become: the more participants that are invited into the conflict, or the broader and more comprehensive the solutions, the more difficult the political questions become.

On the other hand, federalism also rests on consensus, although at an organizational rather than an individual level. Whether it is the passage of legislation, the revision of an existing constitution and government, or the creation of a new constitution and government, citizens, branches of government, and governments must be supportive. That is, they must not exercise their veto authority. A consensus orientation makes achieving coordinated action challenging.

THE DELAWARE RIVER BASIN COMPACT: A FEDERAL EXPERIMENT

The Delaware River begins in the state of New York, just above the Catskill Mountains and zigzags, first to the southeast and then to the southwest, back and forth, creating the boundaries between New York and Pennsylvania, Pennsylvania and New Jersey, and New Jersey and Delaware, before finally flowing into the Atlantic Ocean through the Delaware Bay. It flows through and supports diverse habitats, from the wooded uplands of central New York and northwestern Pennsylvania, to the Philadelphia metropolitan area, to the tidal wetlands of Delaware.

In terms of the volume of water that passes through it, the Delaware is not a particularly notable river for the eastern United States. Its annual average discharge is less than 3 percent of that of the Mississippi, and just less than half of the Susquehanna, its neighbor to the west, yet it provides drinking water for almost 10 percent of the U.S. population (Albert 2005, 1). It supplies water for major cities that reside within its boundaries, like Philadelphia and Trenton, but also for New York City, which is located in the Hudson River Basin.

The Delaware Basin's physical complexity is readily matched by its institutional complexity. In 1783, Pennsylvania and New Jersey entered into a treaty to settle disputes over state ownership of islands in the Delaware River and to protect the river as a common highway by forbidding dams on the main stem (Albert 2005, 5). For the next 140 years the Delaware River was used largely for transportation purposes: its main stem was a major highway, and water from the main stem and tributaries fed transportation canals serving eastern cities.

Although the states bordering the Delaware River expressed interest in developing the river's hydropower potential, the 1783 treaty foreclosed the building of main-stem dams. Not until the 1920s, with the populations of New York City, Philadelphia, and north New Jersey rapidly outstripping water supplies, was serious attention paid to the Delaware River as something other than a common highway. With Pennsylvania, New York, and New Jersey considering water-supply projects on the Delaware River, the states began to discuss an interstate river compact that would allow them to coordinate their water-supply activities.

Creating a new overlapping government in the form of an interstate river compact proved difficult. The states could not agree upon a fair allocation of benefits. The initial compact negotiated by representatives of the three states established minimum flow requirements while allowing each state to develop three-fifths of its Delaware River drainage area (Albert 2005, 17). New York was the only state to ratify it. New York City intended to develop projects that would siphon off water from the Delaware and feed the water into its drinking water supply. Pennsylvania interests objected to New York City, located outside the watershed, taking water from the river and argued also that Pennsylvania deserved a larger portion of the river because the state contained the largest portion of the watershed (Albert 2005, 18). New Jersey suggested that the compact be revised and then submitted to the states as a second proposal for ratification. The revised compact allocated specific amounts of water to each state, with Pennsylvania receiving a third more water than New York and New Jersey. The minimum streamflow requirements were kept in place even though they were reduced. New York again ratified immediately, and New York City proceeded to work with the state to begin the development of reservoirs on the East and West Branches of the river. This time, however, New Jersey rejected the compact because its cities feared that the reduced minimum flow requirements would deprive them of drinking-water supplies during summers and drought years when river flows were already low.

The three states, representing the interests of their citizens, negotiated and renegotiated a compact to allocate the waters of the Delaware River. The states recognized that they needed to protect river flows while allowing for limited water diversions. The states also understood that they were more likely to gain federal assistance in the development of water projects if they were to first settle their differences over their uses of the river. New York ratified both compacts but the other two states rejected them, largely for distributional reasons. Lacking the required consensus to create an interstate river compact, New Jersey and Pennsylvania appealed to the U.S. Supreme Court to protect their interests in the river. New York City moved forward with its water development plans as if the compact had been adopted. New Jersey, joined later by Pennsylvania, filed suit before the U.S. Supreme Court against New York, seeking to prevent New York City from diverting water out of the watershed. The two states claimed that an out-of-basin diversion would violate the riparian doctrine that all three states used to govern the river, and that a diversion as large as the one planned by New York would harm New Jersey's waterpower potential, river recreation, potential water supply, and shad fish-

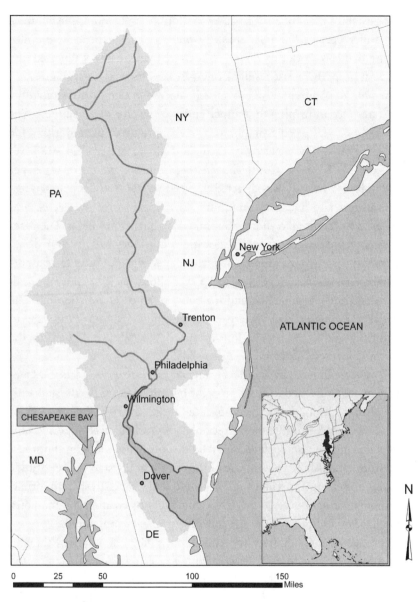

N

The Delaware River Basin.

eries, among other things. They argued that New York City should develop water within its own watershed (Albert 2005, 21).[12] Although joining New Jersey in the litigation, Pennsylvania sought only a decreed water allocation and the establishment of a river master to monitor and enforce the Supreme Court water decree. The river master would be an independent monitor ensuring that New York City did not take more than what was allocated to it and that it properly released water from its reservoirs in a timely manner.

In 1931 the Supreme Court issued its decree, which demonstrated the risks states face in turning to another entity to resolve their conflicts. The decree was a series of rules imposed by the Supreme Court governing the states' uses of the river. New York had the right to divert Delaware River water, and the Supreme Court allocated 440 million gallons of water per day to it. New York City was directed to release water from its planned reservoirs in order to maintain minimum flows specified in the decree, and New York was required to address several water-quality problems. The other two states would not receive water allocations until they had developed specific water projects. The Supreme Court retained the authority to reapportion the river, even to reduce New York City's allocation if considerations of equity demanded such action; and the court retained jurisdiction over the decree rather than establishing a river master. Thus, it was up to the states to monitor the decree and if violations occurred, the states could petition the Supreme Court for enforcement (Albert 2005, 24).

The decree differed in significant ways from the two compacts the states had negotiated but failed to ratify. First, the benefits allocated to the states differed substantially. Under both compacts all three states would have received water allocations, but under the decree only New York received a specific allocation. The decree also provided very little coordination among the states. Aside from establishing rules of use of the river that the states were to abide by, it did not create a mechanism that would allow states to share information, discuss, or fight over the river. The compacts, by creating commissions, would have established forums for coordination and cooperation.

The decree did not spell the end of interstate cooperation, though. Within five years, the three states created the Interstate Commission on the Delaware River Basin, or INCODEL. Delaware joined later. INCODEL was a voluntary organization with no enforceable authority. Nevertheless, the states embraced it and used it to coordinate joint efforts at water-pollution control. The commission worked closely with the four states to adopt water-pollution laws and construct wastewater treatment plants. By all accounts, these efforts were successful in improving the water quality of the river (Derthick 1974; Featherstone 1999; Albert 2005).

INCODEL's forays into water allocation and management, and project development, proved rockier. These were the issues that prevented the states from adopting an interstate compact, and the differences remained, as INCODEL was soon to discover. INCODEL's initial attempt to coordinate water allocation and use involved the development of a formula for overall diversions and flow releases. The commission intended the formula as a framework that would allow the states to coordinate their water-development activities while providing them with considerable flexibility in developing their own water-storage projects (Albert 2005, 33). The formula, however, was never adopted by the states.

INCODEL did not give up its efforts to coordinate the allocation and use of water. Rather, it switched approaches. Both Philadelphia and New York City were making preparations for water-supply projects, and New York was preparing to petition the Supreme Court to reopen the Delaware River decree and grant it a larger water allocation. Viewing the decree as an inadequate means of coordinating the states' uses of the river, INCODEL returned to the compact. It developed a comprehensive basin-development program that consisted of a series of water-supply projects to be built in a specified order that would supply billions of gallons of drinking water to all of the major metropolitan areas. It also proposed an interstate compact that would create a water-resources construction agency to implement the comprehensive basin-development plan. The compact agency would have no planning or regulatory authority, and it would issue bonds to pay for the construction of the dams and reservoirs (Albert 2005, 39).

This third effort at creating an interstate river compact and compact commission also failed, for many of the same distributional reasons that the first two efforts failed. Pennsylvania interests argued that the first water projects scheduled to be built would benefit New York and New Jersey, but Pennsylvania would have to help finance them. Projects designed to provide drinking water to Philadelphia would be built later. Furthermore, Philadelphia interests were not united behind the water-supply projects earmarked for them (Albert 2005).

Once again, having failed to settle their differences, the states returned to the Supreme Court. New York and New York City petitioned the court to reopen the original decree and increase New York's allocation to 800 million gallons of water per day, to recognize new water projects almost completed and another in the final planning stages. New Jersey, Pennsylvania, and eventually Delaware joined the lawsuit. The special master appointed by the Supreme Court worked with the parties to develop an acceptable settlement. In the final decree issued by the Supreme Court, which was the negotiated settlement devised by the states with the special master acting as facilitator, a number of changes were made to the original decree. First, New York's allocation was increased to 800 million gallons per day. Second, New York agreed to water-release requirements governing its reservoirs that would ensure minimum flows and prevent the holding of water that the New York City water system did not need for its customers. Third, New Jersey was allocated 100 million gallons of water per day and agreed to cooperate with Pennsylvania if that state undertook efforts to build a main-stem dam. New Jersey agreed to repeal the 1783 treaty provision prohibiting dams and agreed to exercise its powers of eminent domain on property in New Jersey that Pennsylvania would have to purchase if it were to build a dam. Fourth, Pennsylvania's request for a river master to administer and monitor flow releases was granted (Albert 2005, 47).

The second decree went well beyond simply allocating water; it laid the groundwork for the creation of an interstate river compact. It provided an independent river master and removed a number of obstacles that had prevented the building of a main-stem dam. Pennsylvania actively began planning such a dam, and to protect such an investment, it spearheaded efforts to revive interstate cooperation. Extensive flooding from two hurricanes brought the Army Corps of Engineers into the basin, leading to a comprehensive study and recommendations for multiple dams for flood control, water supply, and recreation purposes. Eventually, the Army Corps of Engineers requested congressional authorization and funding for eight water projects, one on the main stem of the Delaware River at Tocks Island and seven on the river's tributaries. In response, the states contracted with the Maxwell School at Syracuse University for an in-depth analysis of the economic, social, and political setting of the river basin and recommendations for interstate governance (Martin et al. 1960).

The Syracuse report cataloged the social, political, and economic diversity of the river basin, which included vastly different conceptions of water problems, from New York City residents' concerns over adequate supplies of drinking water to Catskills residents' desire to maintain the integrity of their mountain streams and Easton residents' apprehension about flooding. As the authors noted, "Water thus presents different faces to different places and people, and moreover the face it presents varies over time—indeed it varies with the seasons" (Martin et al. 1960, 5). The complexity of the river extended also to citizens' different uses and preferences for governments. After surveying dozens of organizations and associations actively involved in water issues, the authors concluded that what most people wanted were separate governmental agencies in charge of their issues and to whom they would have special access (Martin et al. 1960, 36). In response, the authors suggested that whatever type of government was created, it should be of general purpose in order to balance the many different particular demands and to accomplish some form of the public good (Martin et al. 1960, 55).

Creating the boundaries of a general-purpose water government, however, would not be straightforward. The activities of such a government would occur at different scales, some basin-wide and some not. Furthermore, the government would affect and be affected by forces beyond its boundaries: transportation networks, inter-basin water transfers, and other governments (Martin et al. 1960, 104). The last would be particularly challenging:

> [A]ny significant basin agency that may be devised at once becomes an orphan, with no strong parent government to look to for encouragement and support, no sister agencies with which to make common cause, no web of established procedure on which to lean, no body of precedent to serve as guide, and no articulate clientele to represent it in the public forum. . . . Few public bodies are likely to find much that is praiseworthy in a new regional program, and this is true especially of federal agencies in the field. (Martin et al. 1960, 104)

In the end, the authors proposed a two-phase approach to governance. They suggested the creation of a federal agency that would eventually be absorbed by a federal-state river compact. The agency would be vested with relatively broad water powers, including data collection and dissemination; comprehensive planning; building, owning, and operating all water-storage projects in the basin, including existing ones; governing all water allocations and diversions; and issuing standards and regulations for water-quality purposes. Their reasons for creating a federal agency first and transforming it into a compact later were several. First, they believed that a federal agency could be created relatively quickly, whereas a compact may take years to negotiate. Second, the federal government would likely be more generous in funding water projects of a federal agency than of a state-created government. Third, the initial activities of the agency would center on project construction, an activity at which the federal government is particularly adept; later activities such as water allocation and water-quality control are ones typically performed by states and could be done through the compact commission (Martin et al. 1960, 341–361). Such governing arrangements—transforming a federal agency into a federal-state government and having the federal government as an equal member of a river compact and compact commission—had not been tried before.

The states accepted only the second phase of the study's proposal. Within a year of the release of the Syracuse University study, the states had drafted a federal-state compact, and within another year, the four states and the federal government adopted it. The compact was unusual in two respects—its relatively comprehensive scope compared to other interstate river compacts and its federal member. Most interstate river compacts govern rivers in the western United States, and they only address water-allocation issues. Only a handful extend beyond allocation to include water quality. The Delaware River Basin Compact gives the compact commission the authority to engage in comprehensive planning, data gathering, and monitoring; water-supply development by partnering with the Army Corp of Engineers, who would build the projects; water allocations and diversions; water-quality standard setting; drought planning; and flood-control and floodplain planning (Featherstone 1999).

What nearly brought a presidential veto of the compact, however, was the inclusion of the federal government as an equal partner. Members of the executive branch, such as Interior Secretary Stewart Udall, questioned the constitutionality of subjecting the federal government to the compact. It would be possible for the state representatives, who outnumber the federal representative, to adopt programs, projects, and regulations to which the federal government would be committed even if it objected to them.[13] To allay such fears, two provisions were added to the compact. First, the federal government was committed only to those items that the federal representative voted to support. Second, the president was given the authority to suspend or delete any provision within the comprehensive plan out of considerations of the national interest (Derthick 1974, 53).

For their part, the states wanted the federal government as a partner in the compact. Federal interests in the river basin would expand rapidly as dozens of federally built and funded water projects were brought on line; also, national parks were planned that would be associated with some of the water projects; and, there was the continuing challenge of addressing water-quality concerns. Rather than working with multiple federal partners, the states wished to deal with a single federal partner who would represent all federal interests. The states believed that the increasingly important role of the federal government merited a seat at the table.

The first challenge the commission faced turned out to be one for which it was particularly well suited. The compact gave full recognition to the Supreme Court decree, granting the commission the authority to administer it but also the authority to override it by unanimous decision in cases of emergency, such as droughts or flooding. In 1961, just after the compact's creation, drought emerged in the basin. By 1965, New York announced that because of the drought it would not release water from its reservoirs in accordance with the decree. The commission declared an emergency and the representatives worked out an alternative water-allocation agreement acceptable to all. By 1967, the drought subsided, the emergency was rescinded, and the decree was once again followed (Derthick 1974, 54). The commission later developed a framework that established drought plans and operations, which the commission has called upon three times since the early 1980s, and each time the response has seen the states through the emergency (Featherstone 1999, 106–110; DRBC 2006a).

The commission has also experienced success around its water-quality activities, although not in the way it initially envisioned. Shortly after its creation, the commission sought to become the water-quality standard setter for the basin, as opposed to the states or the federal government. The commission's reasoning was that the states and the federal government are its members, thus standard setting should be centered in it. Neither the states nor the federal government were willing to concede direct regulatory authority to the commission, and it eventually changed its approach. Instead of seeking to become the standard setter for the basin, it worked with the states to develop water-quality standards and regulations that the states' legislatures or regulatory agencies could adopt as their own, and which they have largely done. Thus, there is considerable consistency in water-quality standards across the basin even though there is no single water-quality standard setter (Featherstone 1999, 137).

Many of the standards and regulations that the commission develops are adopted eventually by the states, or by municipalities, townships, and counties in the basin. For instance, the commission worked with each of the states to review drought plans and suggested numerous revisions to the plans, both to strengthen the plans and to make them more nearly uniform across the basin. The commission wanted to avoid a drought scenario where one state's water users were subject to strict conservation requirements while another state's users enjoyed the additional supplies of water made available by the other state's conservation efforts. All states revised their drought plans and regulations in accord with the commission's recommendations (Featherstone 1999, 111). The commission also adopted a set of conservation performance standards for fixtures such as toilets, faucets, and showerheads. All states except Pennsylvania adopted the standards, and most municipalities and water utilities within Pennsylvania adopted them independently (Featherstone 1999, 113).

In addition to working with the states to develop and adopt more uniform water rules and regulations, the commission coordinates the allocation and use of water across the basin through its licensing program.[14] All substantial new diversions, wastewater releases, floodplain encroachments, and streambed modifications must first be approved by the commission. The commission has defined substantial diversions as those involving more than 100,000 gallons per day for thirty days or longer (Featherstone 1999, 163). This allows all states and the federal representative to consider the impact of major projects on their interests and request modifications to projects even though they are located within a single basin state. Featherstone (1999) notes that before an organization or government formally requests a license, it works carefully with the staff of the commission. Considerable discussion, negotiation, and modification of projects occur before the commission issues a license. The licensing powers also apply to federal projects, and states have used the process to obtain modifications in federal activities. For instance, Delaware realized water-quality protections in relation to an Army Corps of Engineers dredging project in the lower Delaware River (Featherstone 1999, 166–167).

The commission has used its licensing powers to gain compliance with its standards and regulations. It regularly requires utilities to adopt water conservation plans and to install water meters as a condition of receiving a license. In turn, states have also used the commission's licensing powers to realize goals that they would not otherwise have been able to accomplish. By the 1970s, many municipalities in southeastern Pennsylvania relied almost exclusively on groundwater, and serious problems were emerging—water tables declining, wells drying up, reduced flows in streams and rivers, and water-quality problems. Furthermore, groundwater pumping in Pennsylvania was affecting the flow of the Delaware River. Pennsylvania law does not allow for the regulation of groundwater. At the request of the Pennsylvania representative, the commission undertook a study of the groundwater problems and developed a set of groundwater regulations and standards based on the study. In 1980, the commission declared a groundwater protected area in southeastern Pennsylvania and applied the groundwater regulations and standards to all new or expanded water diversions of 10,000 gallons a day for at least thirty days (Featherstone 1999, 118). In order to obtain a license for a new groundwater withdrawal, the applicant must demonstrate that the withdrawal will not adversely impact the aquifer or existing users, must meter all service connections, must adopt water conservation rules, and must develop a drought contingency plan (Featherstone 1999, 118). The commission has amended the reach of the protected area and the regulations several times. Most notably, the commission adopted numerical withdrawal limits in some reaches of the aquifer (Featherstone 1999, 119). Pennsylvania relies on the commission to actively regulate groundwater in its portion of the Delaware River Basin, and, in turn, it pays the costs for the operation of the program (Featherstone 1999, 119).

Compared with these successes in increasing coordination among the states and the progress that has been made with respect to river flows and water quality, the commission's efforts regarding water development and supply have not lived up to initial hopes and expectations for a variety of reasons, many outside the commission's control. One of the commission's first acts was to adopt a comprehensive plan. The initial plan largely consisted of the eight water-storage projects for which the Army Corps of Engineers had received congressional authorization. Of those eight, only two smaller projects were built, both on tributaries of the Delaware River.[15] The major project, a main-stem dam and reservoir at Tocks Island, and five other smaller reservoirs were not built. In some ways, the Tocks Island dam was a centerpiece of the compact, one of the primary reasons that the states entered into it. In fact, Pennsylvania was pursuing a similar main-stem project following the 1954 Supreme Court decree, which it put aside in favor of the compact and the Army Corps of Engineers constructing Tocks Island. Tocks Island was not built for a variety of reasons, mostly financial and environmental. As the planning and design of the project proceeded, its costs increased substantially. At the same time, the federal government began experiencing budget problems, and some members of Congress began to publicly question the value of the project. Financial problems delayed the project sufficiently that it was swept up in the environmental movement. Local and national environmental groups, such as the Sierra Club, raised a host of environmental issues, from eutrophication of the reservoir because of high phosphorus levels in the river, to the loss of fish and wildlife, to the loss of a free-flowing river (Albert 2005, 119). Eventually, opposition to the project among citizens of New York and New Jersey became so intense that by 1975, four years after the dam was originally scheduled for completion, the commission, over the strenuous protests of the Pennsylvania representative, voted against congressional appropriations for the project, effectively killing it (Featherstone 1999, 98).

The activities and performance of the federal representative also have not lived up to the hopes and intentions of the Delaware River Basin Compact. The expectation was that the federal representative would not only commit the federal government to particular courses of action but be able to forge a single unifying federal position among the numerous federal agencies active in the basin. Ideally, the representative would work with various agencies and develop a consensus position. Conflicts among federal agencies that the federal representative could not resolve would be turned over to the president (Featherstone 1999, 175). The federal representative, however, has no special power or authority in relation to federal agencies, no methods available to gain the cooperation and support of agency heads, and no more right to call upon the president than do cabinet secretaries. Consequently, the federal representative acts more as an ambassador than as a commissioner (Derthick 1974, 71; Featherstone 1999, 176). He conveys the interests of the different federal agencies to the commission and in turn reports to the agencies on the interests and activities of the commission.[16] Even that limited role has been threatened by actions of Congress. In 1995, Congress eliminated federal funding for the commission and replaced the federal representative with a representative from the Army Corps of Engineers, with the expectation that the Army Corps of Engineers would provide federal funding. It has not done so and the commission has experienced budget problems ever since (DRBC 2006b).

The federal representative has turned out to be a partner with few benefits but many costs. The primary benefit of having the federal government as a partner in the compact is that all federal projects must receive a license from the compact commission before they may be built, thus giving the states a greater say in federal projects than they otherwise would have. On the other hand, the federal representative has been unable to deliver federal cooperation and support for the commission's efforts, and the position has exposed the commission to national politics, both formally and informally. Formally, the commission is required to follow the federal Administrative Procedures Act and publish its rule makings and standard settings in the Federal Register (Albert 2005). Informally, powerful and well-organized interests have been able to derail commission activities by appealing to Congress or the president.[17]

Watershed-level governance in the Delaware River Basin is a federal form of governance, created and operated within a federal system. It consists of a variety of special-purpose and general-purpose governments and voluntary organizations organized at different scales. Over the last forty-five years, the basin states and the federal government have engaged in close cooperation and coordination of their uses of the basin by creating a special government of which they are members. They have used it to tightly coordinate their most important uses and policies concerning the river. The compact commission cannot impose water-quality standards on the states or the states' citizens; however, the legislatures have agreed to adopt the commission's standards. Also, the legislatures have agreed to adopt the commission's drought plans. In other areas, states have ceded more direct authority to the commission. The commission, not the states, licenses all types of water projects. Furthermore, the states have agreed to allow the commission to regulate in areas where they have chosen not to. For instance, Pennsylvania has allowed the commission to develop and implement groundwater rules and regulations for the southeastern portion of the state. As Derthick (1974, 72) notes, "A coordinating organization will work only to the extent that the participants share an interest in making it work." That is the hallmark of a federal system, political action through negotiation and consensus building.

CONCLUSION

In Chapter 1, we argued that complex adaptable systems of institutions are well suited for the management and protection of complex adaptive natural resource systems. In this chapter, we laid out a theory of federalism (which is a complex adaptable system), used the theory to develop a form of policy analysis appropriate for a federal system, and pointed out how a complex adaptable system of governance makes some of the political choices identified and analyzed in the previous chapters more manageable. Before leaving this topic, however, we believe that there are important normative dimensions to federal forms of watershed governance that should be pointed out.

In many watersheds, communities of interest have identified, defined, and organized themselves—albeit in a seemingly innumerable diversity of forms, from the most informal sorts of associations to the most formal incorporations of municipalities. As efforts to assemble sub-watershed or watershed-wide responses to problems get under way, these previously established communities of interest claim their place at the table. Having already organized, they are often in a position to either withhold their cooperation (the stick) or offer resources along with their cooperation (the carrot) in inter-organizational or intergovernmental water resources management arrangements. Their interests must be recognized and addressed. Communities of interest, communities that have invested in the watershed, are protected through federal arrangements.

Furthermore, Oakerson (1999, 5) argues that productive polycentric systems require committed and active citizens. The same theme is echoed in the ecosystem-management literature (Cortner and Moote 1999). However, supporters of ecosystem management and watershed-level management often fail to realize the connections between committed and active citizens and forms of governance. As de Tocqueville (1969) noted, American administrative decentralization (or as Elazar [1987] would say, noncentralization) has much to recommend it, even if it appears chaotic, and even if it moves forward in fits and starts. Noncentralization, which places problem-solving powers in the hands of citizens and communities, promotes liberty and freedom among citizens. Citizens view themselves as governors, capable of addressing shared problems and providing for shared benefits. Remove that problem-solving authority from citizens and place it in the hands of central administrators and, de Tocqueville (1969) argues, citizens become indifferent and passive, waiting for administrators to come to their aid. Thus, active citizens and communities, embedded in a federal system, engage in watershed management while at the same time preserving their liberty and their capacity for self-government.

NOTES

1. Earlier case studies examined interstate watersheds but for different purposes. Chapter 3 used the Platte River to illustrate fundamental political decisions involving boundary drawing, decision rules, and accountability mechanisms. Chapter 4 used the Columbia River to illustrate the unavoidable trade-offs among transaction costs. In this chapter, we explicitly focus on the ties and linkages among the many governments in a watershed through the lens of federalism.

2. As Elazar (1987, 84) explains, "One of the primary attributes of federalism is that it cannot, by its very nature, abandon the concern for either power or justice but must consider both in relationship to each other, thus forcing people to consider the hard realities of political life while at the same time maintaining their aspirations for the best polity."

3. Concerns with power and justice repeatedly emerge in the watershed governance literature. In a study of intergovernmental arrangements for deciding upon and implementing alternatives for wastewater treatment, O'Toole (1993) observed that the governance issue of community autonomy (a justice issue) was itself one of the values with which participants were concerned, along with the management issues of efficiency and regulatory compliance (a power issue).

4. How the central decision maker can utilize justice to more effectively exercise power is a central theme in the organization theory and behavior literature (Barnard 1938; Williamson 1985; Miller 1992).

5. For instance, the first ten amendments to the U.S. Constitution define relations between the federal government and citizens. Article I, Section 10, allows states to enter into compacts with one another, and Article IV governs relations among states through the full faith and credit clause and the privileges and immunities clause. Article VI establishes the supremacy of the national government and addresses the resolution of conflicts among the national and state governments. The designers of the U.S. Constitution anticipated the importance of coordination, cooperation, and conflict resolution among governments.

6. Over the history of the compact, Nebraska has met the minimum streamflow requirements except for brief periods during unusually dry years. In those periods, Kansas has requested that Nebraska actively regulate water diversions and Nebraska has done so, although on at least one occasion the minimum streamflow requirements were not met (Big Blue Compact Administration, 19th annual report, 1993).

7. The supremacy clause in the U.S. Constitution constrains and conditions state constitutions but does not give the U.S. government a role in amending them. The point at which the national government exercises the most immediate influence over state constitutions is in the adoption of enabling legislation that spells out the process and conditions for a territory to become a state. For instance, the enabling legislation for Arizona, the last of the lower forty-eight states to be admitted into

the Union, dictated specific items to be included in the state constitution. Congress imposed strict limits on the use and disposal of state trust land, the land the federal government granted to Arizona. In addition, the enabling legislation required the president to approve the constitution, a requirement not imposed on any previous state (McClory 2001, 22). Taft, the president at the time, vetoed the constitution because it allowed citizens to recall judges. Taft feared that the procedure would destroy the independence of the judiciary. The citizens of Arizona amended the constitution to remove recall of judges, and the constitution was passed by Congress and the president (McClory 2001, 31). Upon admission of Arizona to the Union as a state, the citizens of Arizona promptly amended the state's constitution to allow for the recall of judges (McClory 2001, 32).

8. For instance, the Republican River Compact settlement allowed a state to call a special meeting of the compact commission to address substantive concerns over the operation of the compact. All three states did not have to first agree to a special meeting (Final Settlement Stipulation 2002, 36).

9. Returning to the Republican River Compact settlement, the states devised several different conflict-resolution mechanisms. If the compact administration cannot settle a dispute, a single state may request non-binding arbitration. If non-binding arbitration fails to settle the issue, the states, by unanimous consent, may use binding arbitration. If unanimous consent for binding arbitration is not forthcoming, a state may still resort to the U.S. Supreme Court, but only after it has used the multiple conflict-resolution mechanisms afforded it under the compact (Final Settlement Stipulation 2002, 36–37).

10. Scholars and practitioners of watershed collaboratives often confuse or conflate scale and centralization, however. One of the oft-claimed benefits of watershed collaboratives is that they encompass watersheds. In practice, many do not; rather, they match segments of watersheds, such as the upper portion of a stream or creek, or the middle portion of a river.

11. Governments can, of course, be general-purpose—municipalities, counties, states, and the national government. As discussed in Chapter 5, they tend to have more extensive powers and more diverse sources of funding than do special governments. As general-purpose governments, they address, act on, balance, compromise, and make trade-offs among a whole host of issues. A general-purpose government may consider and attempt to balance a variety of water problems, and in turn, water problems are considered and balanced against transportation needs, economic development, and so forth. As general-purpose governments, and as foundational governments in the U.S. federal system, they provide the institutional structure around which governance is created. They provide the means by which governments and citizens within their jurisdictions create and follow common sets of laws and settle disputes.

12. New York City turned to the Delaware River Basin for water after towns, farmers, and other water users in the Hudson River Basin strenuously opposed further water supply projects (Albert 2005).

13. As Derthick (1974, 51) explained, "The executive branch maintained that the proposal would require the federal government to yield certain of its constitutional powers to 'a third form of government' responsible to neither the federal government nor the states."

14. The commission is guided in its licensing program by its comprehensive plan. The commission is required to approve licenses that do not conflict with the plan. The term "comprehensive plan" is somewhat of a misnomer since the plan does not consider the many dimensions of the watershed and human impacts on those dimensions. Also, it is not integrated—it does not attempt to balance and make trade-offs among the many different aspects of the watershed that it governs—and it is not prospective. Rather, the comprehensive plan is a loose compilation of the commission's standards, regulations, policy statements, operating rules for water projects, and licenses issued. The commission does engage in more prospective and integrated planning through what is called the Water Resources Plan. The Water Resources Plan, which was just completed in 2004 after an extensive public participation process, establishes a framework to guide the actions of the commission and the states for the next thirty years. The plan consists of five key results areas, with goals and objectives identified for each of the areas. The areas are sustainable water use and water supply, waterway corridor management, linking land and water resource management, institutional coordination and cooperation, and education and involvement for stewardship (DRBC 2004).

15. The Beltzville Reservoir, located on a tributary of the Lehigh River, holds up to 39,830 acre-feet of water. The Blue Marsh Reservoir on the Schuylkill River holds 14,600 acre-feet of water (Featherstone 1999, 67).

16. As Derthick (1974, 71) explains, "Unable to deliver commitments from the federal government or to state a unified position, the federal commissioner . . . typically reports the positions of federal agencies. He is an 'ambassador' rather than a 'commissioner.'"

17. For instance, once it became apparent that the federal government would not be building large water projects in the basin, the commission turned to other alternatives to expand water storage (Featherstone 1999). The commission decided to pursue the expansion of a reservoir by raising the dam. In order to pay for the expansion, the commission wanted to impose a tax on all basin water users, which required an amendment to the compact. The compact forbids imposing taxes on pre-compact water users. Although the commission and the states were prepared to support such a compact amendment, petroleum refineries and steel companies, who were major water users, managed to gain sufficient support in the U.S. Senate

to prevent congressional approval of the compact amendment. The companies believed that they would gain little from the reservoir expansion but pay the bulk of the expense (Featherstone 1999, 98).

7

A Rational Embrace?

An institutional structure that realigns but does not supersede existing authorities is emerging, together with a shared perception of the possibilities and conflicts implicit in managing resources whose requirements are partly incompatible. The goal is an ecologically sustainable salmon population coexisting with an economically sustainable hydropower system. An optimist sees in the still incomplete story of the Columbia basin a social system searching for a path to that goal of dual sustainability; a pessimist sees resistance to the changes needed before sustainability can be realized.

KAI N. LEE (1995, 214)

In the preceding chapters, we have paired analytical discussions of political topics in watershed management with case studies of the institutions that currently exist in certain locations in the United States. We begin this closing chapter with a consideration of those case studies as a group—what their similarities and differences reveal and how those lessons relate to the broader themes of the overall book, beyond the connections that were drawn in the particular chapters in which the cases appeared.

The cases do not represent "successes" and "failures" nor were they chosen for that purpose. It is not our intention to show that the institutions in some cases have worked well and those in other cases have worked poorly. All of the cases—the Santa Ana River watershed in Chapter 1, the Platte River Basin in Chapter 3, the Columbia River Basin in Chapter 4, the San Gabriel River watershed in Chapter 5, and the Delaware River Basin in Chapter 6—exhibit a mix of successes and shortcomings.

To say that is to invite questions of what we mean by successes and shortcomings and what criteria we are using for evaluation. As one might expect given the nature of resource management in a watershed or any other social and ecological system, a mix of criteria is involved. Some criteria for assessing success have to do with the conditions of the water resource per se—whether declining streamflows or groundwater levels have been stabilized or reversed, whether contamination incidents have been remediated and water quality protected or improved. Some have to do with the other natural resources associated with the water resource—the protection or restoration of fish populations or migratory bird habitat. Some have to do with the human communities associated with the water resource—whether conflicts over allocation of supplies are addressed and resolved, whether economic uses have been sustained, whether the watershed continues to support local communities. Some have to do with the political character of the watershed governance and management institutions themselves—whether they provide meaningful opportunities for addressing concerns, expressing values, participating in decisions, and holding decision makers accountable. Last and definitely not least, some criteria have to do with adaptability—whether people can modify the institutional arrangements as changes occur to resource conditions, the demographic and/or economic composition, or the political and cultural values within the watershed.

Such a multifaceted composite does not lend itself to a scale along which one could arrange the five cases from "best performing" to "worst performing." This type of assessment presumes a single evaluation criterion, which we do not have. Neither do watersheds, at least in the real world. Our conclusion that each case exhibits a mix of successes and shortcomings follows from our multiple evaluation criteria and from the particular selection of cases.

Why include multiple cases, if we cannot rate or rank them, and if each ends up as an amalgam of accomplishment and disappointment? Any reader might pose such a sensible question, and we offer two answers. First, each case has connected with points being made in the respective chapters—

Box 7.1 Case Studies Used in the Previous Chapters

Case	Principal issue highlighted in the case study	Distinct organizational feature
Santa Ana River watershed (Chapter 1)	Watershed complexity and dynamics	A joint-powers agency at the watershed scale
Platte River Basin (Chapter 3)	Politics of boundary definition, decision making, and accountability	An administrative agreement among states and the federal government
Columbia River Basin (Chapter 4)	Limits on human decision capabilities: bounded rationality and transaction costs	A congressionally created river basin council
San Gabriel River watershed (Chapter 5)	Specialization and coordination in a multi-organizational setting	Absence of any watershed-scale organization or agency
Delaware River Basin (Chapter 6)	Federalism and the challenges and possibilities of coordination among governments	A federal-interstate commission

about complexity and uncertainty (the Santa Ana River case in Chapter 1), about the politics of decision-making structures (the Platte River case in Chapter 3), about the challenges posed by bounded rationality and transaction costs (the Columbia River case in Chapter 4), about the prospects for differentiation by function and scale as an alternative to organizational integration (the San Gabriel River case in Chapter 5), and about the political capabilities and complications of federalism (the Delaware River case in Chapter 6). Second, each case presents both common and distinct lessons compared with the others.

LESSONS FROM THE CASES

No two cases among our five have the same organizational structures and institutional rules. Each therefore represents a distinct possibility for governing and managing a complex resource system. Thus, together they reinforce our overall position that the search for a best way of organizing watershed management is a misplaced undertaking.

Instead, common to all of the cases is a polycentric, indeed federal, style of governance. This polycentric, federal style features

- nested and overlapping jurisdictions (i.e., a mix of Type I and Type II governance structures);

- differentiation among organizations by function and by scale (i.e., multiple organizations participating in watershed governance and management that are not mere duplicates of one another);

- representation of diverse communities of interest through various public jurisdictions and private associations (sometimes implicitly but usually explicitly recognizing the politics of position and identity that are present within a watershed); and

- multiple nodes and pathways for data gathering, communication, deliberation, and participation in decision making (providing some redundancy as well as some coordination and means of accountability).

The fact that we can identify these common features of the polycentric, federal style of watershed governance is not at odds with our statement above that no two cases have the same organizational structures and institutional rules. Polycentric and federal systems can take a variety of forms in watersheds as in other political settings.

Another commonality among the cases is the dynamism of governing and managing complex adaptive systems. All of the cases are ongoing stories of the relationships between complex social and ecological systems, which have changed and are changing over time. In each case, human beings have managed to make some progress toward the "dual sustainability" Lee mentions in the quote at the beginning of the chapter, even though in each case, plenty of problems remain unsolved and challenges lie ahead. This point is worth some further discussion, with specific illustrations.

In each watershed, the natural resource management agenda has changed significantly over time, usually for a combination of reasons that include emerging problems, improved information, changed social values, and new opportunities. The loss of fish populations in the Santa Ana and Columbia Rivers, for example, and the threat to several species in the Big Bend region of the Platte River occurred during the twentieth century (and persist in the twenty-first), but the attention paid to those losses rose because of better information, increased public concerns, and legislative mandates. Groundwater contamination in the San Gabriel Valley, which had been developing for decades, came to the attention of the public and policy makers through improved information, and the efforts to remediate it (rather than simply abandon the groundwater basin as a source of supply) benefited from economic growth and technological advance. Plans for construction of flood control, water supply, and hydropower facilities on the Delaware and Platte Rivers were scaled back or canceled because of changing public attitudes, economic realities, and new opportunities to meet water demands through increased efficiency and conservation. River restoration efforts just getting under way in the San Gabriel River watershed reflect changes in public values for water resources, as a postindustrial population appreciates the recreational and aesthetic dimensions of river channels as much as their utility for disposing of municipal and industrial wastes.

None of this is meant to dismiss or minimize the ecological damage that has been done and continues in these watersheds; rather, the point is that in each watershed, both the ecological systems and the social systems changed, and the current state of affairs in each place emerges from the interactions of those social and ecological systems. In each case, institutional arrangements have been created and modified by people over time in response to changed awareness and understanding of problems, changes in the set of tools available for addressing them, and changing public attitudes and preferences. Some older institutions have been left in place, others modified, and others replaced. In each case, people have faced choices about whether to add new tasks to existing organizations or add new organizations; sometimes they have chosen the former and other times the latter. And in each case, the set of institutional arrangements in place at this moment is complex, with multiple public and private organizations working on different dimensions of watershed problems at different scales, with varying degrees of specialization, coordination, integration, success, and failure.

COMPLEX SYSTEMS, DECOMPOSITION, AND NONCENTRALIZATION

These observations relate to one of our broader themes. Although resources in a watershed are interrelated, watersheds are complex systems with somewhat decomposable features and problems, and people have often constructed institutional systems in ways that address or take into account that near-decomposability.[1] More precisely, people have used institutions to bound problems and recognize communities of interest within the watershed—establishing one set of rules for allocating flows on the main stem of a river, for instance, and other sets of rules for allocating extractions from one or more groundwater resources in the same watershed, or creating separate jurisdictions for the upper and lower areas of a watershed and then tying those jurisdictions together through a compact, court decree, or other institutional mechanism. These are political choices, but that does not mean they should be lamented or overturned. Using the San Gabriel River case as an example, it is just as reasonable to argue that (1) the pumpers from each of the four major groundwater basins in the San Gabriel River watershed, for instance, really are relevant communities of interest with respect to the allocation of pumping rights; while (2) the lower watershed area as a whole and the upper watershed area as a whole are the relevant communities of interest with respect to dividing the flows and monitoring the water quality of the river main stem; and (3) the municipalities and private water suppliers overlying the contamination plumes in the Main San Gabriel Basin really are differently positioned with respect to the costs and benefits of contamination remediation than others located elsewhere in the watershed. That different organizational structures have been devised for addressing these different problems and communities of interest within the San Gabriel River watershed is not necessarily fragmentation, or even mere political expediency; it can be seen instead as a combination of rational problem-solving strategy (decomposing a system into components that can be addressed more manageably by boundedly rational people) with political realism (to paraphrase the observation by Lebel et al. [2005] concerning the politics of scale, position, and place within a river basin: although everyone is in the same watershed, everyone is not in the same boat).

Each of the river basins and watersheds covered in the case studies is organized in ways that recognize and demonstrate the significance of communities of interest and identity, including ones that do not conform to the watershed's physical boundaries. In the basins where some form of basin-wide governance system was adopted—the Platte, the Columbia, the Delaware—already organized communities of interest have played significant roles, both in working with basin-wide efforts and in undermining basin-wide efforts. Furthermore, in each of those basins, the initial effort (or at least desire) to manage resources on a basin-wide scale has gradually given way to recognition of the necessity or preferability of organizing at least some efforts on a smaller scale. In the Columbia River Basin, fish and wildlife recovery programs are being decomposed to the sub-basin scale; in the Delaware River Basin, states eventually agreed to an institutional division of various reaches of the river so they could do their own planning for water-supply distribution; and in the Platte River Basin, each state took on the task of regulating the water-use behavior of its own residents in order to meet the states' obligations to one another and the objectives in the cooperative agreement. Thus, in all of the case studies, the tendency has been to create organizations at a variety of scales, sometimes moving toward and at other times moving away from a watershed-wide focus.

The principle of decomposition has been applied in these watersheds not only spatially but topically. Although fish and wildlife recovery is clearly linked to the operation of hydropower and flood-control facilities, or the control of groundwater withdrawals is linked to the flows of hydrologically connected rivers, or the remediation of contamination is linked to the availability of water supplies for municipal and industrial uses or for irrigation, and so on, people in the watersheds we included in this book have often chosen to create separate organizations and employ separate staff to focus on facility operation, groundwater use, fish and wildlife recovery, or the cleanup of underground pollution plumes. These choices have been affected to some degree by historical developments and/or jurisdictional jealousies (i.e., they are "path dependent"), but they also reflect a recognition of the limitations of human beings as information processors. As Chapters 1 and 4 particularly emphasized, the information requirements implicit in comprehensive integrated management of water or any other natural resources are enormous, and the information and decision-making capabilities of people are, well, not.

People are capable of a great deal of knowledge and creativity, but it is also well within the sensible judgment of boundedly rational people to decompose interrelated problems in a complex system and have different individuals or groups focus on them. Of course, when this option is chosen, mechanisms for communication, information sharing, and coordination must be devised, established, and maintained. There are risks of error proneness with either choice. When boundedly rational people attempt comprehensiveness and integration, they face risks of imperfectly understanding micro-level and subsystem patterns, selecting and paying attention to the wrong indicators of resource conditions, persisting in policies while system-scale indicators remain acceptable even though smaller-scale conditions are going awry, and so on. When boundedly rational people choose to institutionally subdivide a complex system and address its decomposable units separately, they face risks such as overlooking externalities and, among individuals in separate organizations, failing to communicate effectively with one another and coordinate actions.

There are substantial challenges of coordination in multi-organizational structure, but this needs to be viewed realistically in terms of trade-offs. It is simply not possible to trade in all the coordination problems of a multi-organizational system for a better-functioning single organization. Integrated organizations have coordination problems of their own (see Department of Homeland Security) and lack some of the advantages of polycentric structures. In a world where information, communication, coordination, and decision making are all costly and imperfect, there are always trade-offs between the costs and benefits of organizational integration on the one hand and organizational differentiation on the other. It is therefore to be expected that the balance struck between them will differ from one watershed to another, as it has in the cases in this book.

OBSERVATIONS ON FRAGMENTATION

We mentioned above that polycentric systems need not be dismissed merely as fragmentation. The relationship between fragmentation on the one hand and noncentralized, polycentric, or federal systems on the other bears some further discussion. There are four important considerations as we reflect upon the concern with fragmentation.

First, fragmentation is clearly a real problem in institutional design. For instance, the fragmentation of water resource responsibilities across so many federal agencies (such as the Corps, the Bureau of Reclamation, Fish and Wildlife, National Marine Fisheries Service, EPA) has presented real obstacles to progress in some of the cases we have described. Organizations in a watershed can indeed work at cross-purposes, failing to coordinate their actions and putting "turf" interests ahead of other concerns. As we have noted, the proliferation of agencies and organizations within a watershed is not an intrinsically good thing.

The second consideration concerns whether the presence of multiple organizations working on various dimensions of natural resource issues within a watershed constitutes undesirable fragmentation or sensible differentiation. This is an empirical question, not one with an a priori answer.

In examining the institutional landscape of a watershed, observers should not merely take a census of public and private entities but look at what they do and how they relate to one another. Looking at what they do, it is worthwhile to consider whether institutions and organizations have been created to address different geographic scales, distinct problems, or issues; to finance and operate specific projects; or to try to assess whether and to what degree multiple organizations merely duplicate one another or have been established to take advantages of specialization or scale. Looking at how they relate to one another, it is important to search for the connections as well as the distinctions between organizations. A simple census of public and private organizations in a watershed will not reveal whether there are also coordinating institutional mechanisms such as contracts, compacts, memoranda of understanding, stipulated judgments, court decrees, joint-powers agreements, and the like. Any conclusion about whether a particular watershed enjoys the benefits of an "institutionally rich environment" or is beset by "fragmentation and duplication"—or more realistically, where it is situated on a spectrum between those poles—depends on a closer examination. The case studies in this book illustrate some of the institutional arrangements that can connect organizations and coordinate activities in a watershed even in the absence of a comprehensive watershed management authority.

Third, some manner of fragmentation will be present no matter how natural resource management and protection is organized. In large part this is an unavoidable consequence of the presence of multiple communities of interest and identity in a complex social system. In Chapter 4, for example, we noted that each state in the Columbia River Basin has its own laws and regulations governing water use, logging, and fishing. Suppose as an alternative (another thought experiment, if you will) that rules for water use, logging, and fishing were set on a watershed-by-watershed basis rather than state-by-state. Now shift your focus to a state in the Columbia Basin, say, Oregon. Some of Oregon is in the Columbia Basin and some is not. If rules for water use, logging, and fishing were established on a watershed basis, Oregonians owning property, doing business, or pursuing recreation in different parts of the state would be subject to differing rules. Real communities of interest and identity, including states, tribes, cities, and counties as well as interest groups, exist in every watershed and need to be taken into account. Identified as "Columbia Basin dwellers," the community is subject to fragmented rules owing to the differences among states; identified as "Oregonians," the community would be subject to fragmented rules owing to the differences among watersheds. One can make a reasoned or even an impassioned argument that the latter type of fragmentation is preferable to the former, but one cannot argue effectively that one arrangement represents "fragmentation" and the other does not.[2]

Fourth and finally, in addition to the thought that watershed-by-watershed rule making would substitute one kind of fragmentation for another, there is the question of which watersheds "count." Staying with Oregon and the Columbia Basin, consider the watershed of the Willamette River. The Willamette flows into the Columbia—should the rules governing water use, logging, fishing, and so forth in the Willamette watershed be subsumed within the Columbia Basin, or is the Willamette "big" enough, "important" enough, "distinctive" enough to have its own governing body making rules for natural resource use and protection? Similar questions could be asked for tributaries of the Willamette, or for any other watershed nested within the Columbia, or for any other watershed within any other watershed anywhere in the United States. The answers to these questions are judgment calls. Neither science nor nature can answer them. As we noted in Chapter 1, we cannot just let nature do the choosing for us. The choice of boundaries for governing bodies for the management and protection of water, or any other natural resources, and the choice of organizational structures, decision rules, and so forth are political choices—unavoidably, inescapably, and essentially political choices.

The case studies in this book illustrate to a small extent the variety of political choices that are available in managing watersheds. As we have seen, even decision rules can vary, not only from place to place but from time to time and from one kind of decision to another. In some of the organizations in the Delaware and Columbia Basins, unanimity rules (consensus requirements) were modified over time to super-majority rules. In the Columbia, Platte, and Delaware Basins, the degree of agreement needed for major modifications to basin plans or cooperative agreements is different from the degree of agreement needed for day-to-day administrative decisions. In the San Gabriel River watershed, modifying the apportionment of river flows between the upper and lower areas is subject to a different decision rule than modifying the apportionment of pumping rights within any of the major groundwater basins, or modifying the funding and implementing of groundwater cleanup projects in the Main San Gabriel Basin, or approving river restoration projects through the Lower Los Angeles and San Gabriel Rivers and Mountains Conservancy.

A (SORT OF) BOTTOM LINE

From the theoretical arguments we have presented in the preceding chapters and from the case studies, it appears to us that effective management of watersheds cannot be comprehensive and integrated into a single jurisdiction, but neither can it be the job of nongovernmental collaborative partnerships alone. The former option is foreclosed by the limits on human capabilities and the complexity of natural resource systems and social systems and fails to take advantage of some of the benefits that can be gained through organizational diversity (i.e., advantages of functional specialization and scale differentiation). The latter option confronts problems of collective action that are familiar in political economy. Governmental power is often needed to overcome free-rider tendencies, to raise funds, and to make and enforce authoritative policies. Consensus-based collaborative processes can also lead to gridlock, as we noted in Chapter 3, when interests benefited by the status quo use their implicit "veto" by withholding their agreement and blocking consensus.

Collaborative partnerships are pretty heavily dependent on who chooses to be involved, and involvement is a challenge to sustain over time. And even with respect to initial involvement, there are a number of potentially vexing questions. Can someone (an individual, an interest group, a business, a municipality, etc.) opt in voluntarily and make their values and interests count in watershed decision making whether or not others think they should be involved? Can someone opt out voluntarily, escaping costs or other burdens borne by those who remain? Can a collaborative, perhaps even nongovernmental, watershed council or partnership *make* someone participate? How are voluntary partners/collaborators held to commitments?

Between the ideal of the integrated authority and the ideal of the collaborative partnership, what remains? The polycentric structures of federal systems and politics. In the "federal watershed," a mix of Type I jurisdictions and nongovernmental organizations may represent communities of identity and interest, and a number of Type II jurisdictions may be created and employed to pursue specialization and scale advantages. A combination of smaller (and more directly participatory) local arrangements with overlapping (and more likely representative rather than directly participatory) organizations at larger scales strives to balance the autonomy of local arrangements to do their own thing with the need to have some way of ensuring that actions by one local arrangement in one subsystem do not impose harm on other subsystems.

There is no single organizational model for this kind of combination. We are left instead with adding to, modifying, and subtracting from the organizational array in place at a given time as conditions (social and ecological) change, or as our understanding of them changes. But that is not a bad thing. Indeed, it makes sense that one must monitor complex adaptable institutional systems, just as one would closely monitor complex adaptive ecological systems, with an eye toward learning and an openness to changing course. As we observed in Chapter 6, federal systems depend heavily upon the presence of individuals who know what they are doing—not only with respect to the ecological sciences but the social sciences too. Fortunately, operating within a culture of federalism can also help cultivate those skills. People are capable of operating at multiple levels of action, playing different roles in diverse arenas, and coordinating their behavior with one another. In the federal watershed more specifically, this means finding and skillfully employing the kinds of mechanisms of inter-organizational coordination we have pointed to—memoranda of understanding; inter-organizational agreements, contracts, and compacts; stipulated judgments and court decrees; joint-powers agencies; decision rules that encourage consensus but allow matters to come to a vote if consensus is not reached.

TWO CHEERS FOR POLITICS

The preceding discussion is not intended to be a defense of the status quo in water resources management in the United States (or elsewhere). A great deal of both the past and the status quo is pretty indefensible. Important interests, values, and communities have been left out for too long, and some rules that made sense 150 years ago do not necessarily make sense today or looking toward the future (e.g., the first come, first served rigidity of the prior appropriation doctrine). The attraction of ideas such as grassroots environmental management and collaborative environmental management has a lot to do with overcoming past exclusion and bringing new interests and values into policy making on a more nearly equal footing with established ones.

One way to think about the governance of watersheds is in terms of constitutions. Earlier we referred to institutional arrangements as constitutions establishing numerous "water governments" in the United States. Constitutions, understood in this broader sense, establish and contain rules concerning who participates in decision making and how, how communities of identity and interest will be represented, how authority over various decisions is allocated among a number of different entities—in short, who can do what, under which conditions, and with what limitations. Constitutions embody commitments that allow individuals and communities to make decisions and allocate resources with some assurance about "the rules of the game." But any constitution worth having will also be adaptable, accommodating the establishment of new rules and entities when they are really needed. Constitutions can freeze in place rules that once made sense but no longer do. Our repeated references in this book to complex, *adaptable* systems of institutions were intended to convey precisely this point.

Constitutional questions and decisions are not merely political, or sort of political. They are *essentially* political. The politics of watershed management—the politics of creating new organizations alongside old ones and figuring out their boundaries and interrelationships, the politics of establishing and modifying representation and decision rules (one person–one vote, one community–one vote, hierarchy–consensus/unanimity, super-majority–majority, veto points–deference to experts, etc.), the politics of distributing benefits and costs, and, above all, the politics of establishing policy directions in an unavoidably multi-organizational setting—is frustrating, time-consuming, costly, and unavoidable.

Politics in the watershed, then, is not just some residue of the past to be overcome. It is also how we change the present and anticipate the future. Politics and institutions are not just how individuals and communities protect their interests. Politics and institutions are also how we accomplish change. The politics of watersheds is to be embraced, if not with joy, then with a reflective understanding that this is how imperfect people living in a complex social and natural environment have to deal with one another and their world. It is how we get things done.

NOTES

1. We mean near-decomposability in the same sense as Herbert Simon (1996); namely, that complex systems are composed of parts that themselves can be considered distinctly even while recognizing that they are connected to the other system components. Decomposability should not be confused with decentralization.

2. The only way to eliminate this kind of "fragmentation" (i.e., different sets of governing rules confronting people who can be identified as within the same community of interest or identity) is to replace both jurisdiction-by-jurisdiction and watershed-by-watershed governance with a single set of federal rules governing water use, logging, fishing, and so forth, an option that strikes us as neither likely nor desirable.

References

Adger, W. Neil, Katrina Brown, and Emma L. Tompkins. 2006. "The Political Economy of Cross-Scale Networks in Resource Co-Management." *Ecology and Society* 10(2):Article 9. http://www.ecologyandsociety.org/vol10/art9/.

Adler, Robert. 1995. "Addressing Barriers to Watershed Protection." *Environmental Law* 25:973–1107.

Aiken, J. David. 1999. "Balancing Endangered Species Protection and Irrigation Water Rights: The Platte River Cooperative Agreement." *Great Plains Natural Resources Journal* 3(Spring):119–158.

———. 2004. "The Western Common Law of Tributary Groundwater: Implications for Nebraska." *University of Nebraska Law Review* 83:541–595.

Albert, Richard. 2005. *Damming the Delaware: The Rise and Fall of Tocks Island Dam*. University Park: Pennsylvania State University Press.

Allee, David J., Leonard B. Dworsky, and Ronald M. North. 1981. "United States Water Planning and Management." In *Unified River Basin Management—Stage II*, ed. David J. Allee, Leonard B. Dworsky, and Ronald M. North, 11–42. Minneapolis: American Water Resources Association.

Barham, Elizabeth. 2001. "Ecological Boundaries as Community Boundaries: The Politics of Watersheds." *Society and Natural Resources* 14:181–191.

Barnard, Chester. 1938. *The Functions of the Executive*. Cambridge, MA: Harvard University Press.

Bates, Sarah, David Getches, Lawrence MacDonnell, and Charles Wilkinson. 1993. *Searching Out the Headwaters: Change and Rediscovery in Western Water Policy*. Washington, DC: Island Press.

Behrman, Robert. 1993. "Legal Issues Associated with an Integrated Watershed Management Approach." *Colorado Water* 10:6(December):11–12.

Berkes, Fikret. 2006. "From Community-Based Resource Management to Complex Systems: The Scale Issue and Marine Commons." *Ecology and Society* 11(1): Article 45. http://www.ecologyandsociety.org/vol11/iss1/art45.

Big Blue River Compact Administration. 1993. *19th Annual Report*. Topeka, KS.

———. 2002. *29th Annual Report*. Topeka, KS.

Bish, Robert, and Vincent Ostrom. 1973. *Understanding Urban Government*. Washington, DC: American Enterprise Institute.

Blatter, Joachim, and Helen M. Ingram. 2000. "States, Markets and Beyond: Governance of Transboundary Water Resources." *Natural Resources Journal* 40:2 (Spring):439–474.

Blomquist, William. 1992. *Dividing the Waters: Governing Groundwater in Southern California*. San Francisco: ICS Press.

———. 1994. "Changing Rules, Changing Games: Evidence from Groundwater Systems in Southern California." In *Rules, Games, and Common-Pool Resources*, ed. Elinor Ostrom, Roy Gardner, and James Walker, 283–300. Ann Arbor: University of Michigan Press.

Blomquist, William, K. S. Calbick, and Ariel Dinar. 2004. *Institutional and Policy Analysis of River Basin Management: The Fraser River Basin, Canada*. Policy Research Working Paper No. 3525. Washington, DC: The World Bank. www.worldbank.org/riverbasinmanagement.

Blomquist, William, Edella Schlager, and Tanya Heikkila. 2004. *Common Waters, Diverging Streams: Linking Institutions and Water Management in Arizona, California, and Colorado*. Washington, DC: Resources for the Future.

Blumm, Michael C. 1982. "Fulfilling the Parity Promise: A Perspective on Scientific Proof, Economic Cost, and Indian Treaty Rights in the Approval of the Columbia Basin Fish and Wildlife Program." *Environmental Law* 13:103–160.

————. 1983. "The Northwest's Hydroelectric Heritage: Prologue to the Pacific Northwest Electric Power and Planning Conservation Act." *Washington Law Review* 58:175–243.

————. 1984. "Implementing the Parity Promise: An Evaluation of the Columbia Basin Fish and Wildlife Program." *Environmental Law* 14:277–357.

————. 1986. "Reexamining the Parity Promise: More Challenges Than Successes to the Implementation of the Columbia Basin Fish and Wildlife Program." *Environmental Law* 16:461–513.

————. 1995. "Columbia Basin Salmon and the Courts: Reviving the Parity Promise." *Environmental Law* 25:349–363.

————. 1997. "The Amphibious Salmon: The Evolution of Ecosystem Management in the Columbia River Basin." *Ecology Law Quarterly* 24:653–676.

Blumm, Michael C., Michael Schoessler, and R. Christopher Beckwith. 1997. "Beyond the Parity Promise: Struggling to Save Columbia Basin Salmon in the Mid-1990s." *Environmental Law* 27:21–73.

Blumm, Michael C., and Andy Simrin. 1991. "The Unraveling of the Parity Promise: Hydropower, Salmon, and Endangered Species in the Columbia Basin." *Environmental Law* 21:657–744.

Bolte, John, et al. 1999. "Developing Methods and Tools for Watershed Restoration: Design, Implementation, and Assessment in the Willamette Basin, Oregon—Summary." In *Proceedings: 1999 Water and Watershed Program Review*, 5–6. EPA/NSF Partnership for Environmental Research. April 19–21, 1999. Silver Spring, MD.

Brandes, Oliver M., Keith Ferguson, Michael M'Gonigle, and Calvin Sandborn. 2005. *At a Watershed: Ecological Governance and Sustainable Water Management in Canada*. Victoria, BC: POLIS Project on Ecological Governance, University of Victoria.

Brunson, Mark W. 1998. "Social Dimensions of Boundaries: Balancing Cooperation and Self-Interest." In *Stewardship Across Boundaries*, ed. Richard L. Knight and Peter B. Landres, 65–86. Washington, DC: Island Press.

Buchanan, James, and Gordon Tullock. 1962. *The Calculus of Consent: Legal Foundations of Constitutional Democracy*. Ann Arbor: University of Michigan Press.

Caldwell, Lynton K. 1996. "Science Assumptions and Misplaced Certainty in Natural Resources and Environmental Problem Solving." In *Scientific Uncertainty and Environmental Problem Solving*, ed. John Lemons, 394–421. London: Blackwell Science.

Carpenter, Richard A. 1996. "Uncertainty in Managing Ecosystems Sustainably." In *Scientific Uncertainty and Environmental Problem Solving*, ed. John Lemons, 118–159. London: Blackwell Science.

Chaney, Ed. 1986. "The Last Salmon Ceremony: Implementing the Columbia River Basin Fish and Wildlife Program." *Idaho Law Review* 22:561–608.

Chisholm, Donald. 1989. *Coordination Without Hierarchy: Informal Structures in Multiorganizational Systems*. Berkeley: University of California Press.

Coggins, George Cameron. 2001. "Of Californicators, Quislings and Crazies: Some Perils of Devolved Collaboration." In *Across the Great Divide: Explorations in Collaborative Conservation and the American West*, ed. Phillip Brick, Donald Snow, and Sarah Van De Wetering, 163–171. Washington, DC: Island Press.

Coglianese, Cary. 1999. "The Limits of Consensus." *Environment* 41(3):28–32.

Coglianese, Cary, and Laurie K. Allen. 2004. "Does Consensus Make Common Sense? An Analysis of EPA's Common Sense Initiative." *Environment* 46(1):10–25.

Committee to Assess the U.S. Army Corps of Engineers Water Resources Project Planning Procedures. 1999. *New Directions in Water Resources Planning for the U.S. Army Corps of Engineers*. Washington, DC: National Academy Press. http://www.nap.edu/openbook/0309060974/html/7.html.

Cooperative Agreement for Platte River Research and Other Efforts Relating to Endangered Species Habitats Along the Central Platte River Nebraska. 1997 (July).

Coordinating Committee. 2004. *U.S. Army Corps of Engineers Water Resources Planning: A New Opportunity for Service*. Washington, DC: National Academy Press.

Cortner, Hannah, and Margaret A. Moote. 1999. *The Politics of Ecosystem Management*. Washington, DC: Island Press.

Costanza, Robert, Bobbi S. Low, Elinor Ostrom, and James Wilson. 2001. "Ecosystems and Human Systems: A Framework for Exploring the Linkages." In *Institutions, Ecosystems, and Sustainability*, ed. Robert Costanza, Bobbi S. Low, Elinor Ostrom, and James Wilson, 3–29. Boca Raton, FL: Lewis Publishers.

Derthick, Martha. 1974. *Between State and Nation: Regional Organizations of the United States*. Washington, DC: Brookings Institution.

de Tocqueville, Alexis. 1969. *Democracy in America*. Garden City, NY: Anchor Books, Doubleday & Company.

Doppelt, Bob, Mary Scurlock, Chris Frissell, and James Karr. 1993. *Entering the Watershed: A New Approach to Save America's River Ecosystems*. Washington, DC: Island Press.

DRBC. 2004 (September). "Water Resources Plan for the Delaware River Basin." Delaware River Basin Commission Web site (www.state.nj.us/drbc/BPSept04/cover.pdf). Accessed July 19, 2006.

———. 2006a. "Listing of DRBC Milestones and Accomplishments." Delaware River Basin Commission Web site (www.state.nj.us/drbc/milestones.hm). Accessed July 19, 2006.

———. 2006b. "DRBC Financial Struggles Continue." Delaware River Basin Commission Web site (www.state.nj.us/drbc/). Accessed July 19, 2006.

Duncan, Angus. 2001. "Of Time and the River." *Forum for Applied Research and Public Policy* 16:88–95.

Dworsky, Leonard, Ronald North, and David Allee, eds. 1988. *Water Resources Planning and Management in the United States Federal System.* Henniker, NH: Engineering Foundation.

Dzurik, Andrew A. 1995. *Water Resources Planning.* Revised edition. Lanham, MD: Rowman & Littlefield.

Echeverria, John D. 2001. "No Success Like Failure: The Platte River Collaborative Watershed Planning Process." *William and Mary Environmental Law and Policy Review* 25:559–593.

Elazar, Daniel. 1987. *Exploring Federalism.* Tuscaloosa: University of Alabama Press.

Featherstone, Jeffrey. 1999. "An Evaluation of Federal-Interstate Compacts as an Institutional Model for Intergovernmental Coordination and Management: Water Resources for Interstate River Basins in the U.S." Ph.D. dissertation, Temple University.

Final Settlement Stipulation. 2002 (December 15). No. 126 Original. In the Supreme Court of the United States. *State of Kansas, Plaintiff v. State of Nebraska and State of Colorado, Defendants.* Before the Honorable Vincent L. McKusick, Special Master.

Frant, Howard. 1993. "Rules and Governance in the Public Sector: The Case of Civil Service." *American Journal of Political Science* 37(4):990–1007.

Goldfarb, William. 1994. "Watershed Management: Slogan or Solution?" *Boston College Environmental Affairs Law Review* 21(3):483–510.

Gregg, Frank, Douglas Kenney, Kathryn Mutz, and Teresa Rice. 1998. *The State Role in Western Watershed Initiatives.* Research Report RR-18. Boulder, CO: Natural Resources Law Center.

Griffin, C. B. 1999. "Watershed Councils: An Emerging Form of Public Participation in Natural Resource Management." *Journal of the American Water Resources Association* 35:3(June):505–518.

Grumbine, R. E. 1995. "What Is Ecosystem Management?" *Conservation Biology* 8:27–38.

Gunderson, Lance H., C. S. Holling, and Stephen S. Light. 1995. "Barriers Broken and Bridges Built: A Synthesis." In *Barriers and Bridges to the Renewal of Ecosystems and Institutions*, ed. Lance H. Gunderson, C. S. Holling, and Stephen S. Light, 489–532. New York: Columbia University Press.

Gunderson, Lance H., Lowell Pritchard Jr., C. S. Holling, Carl Folke, and Garry D. Peterson. 2002. "A Summary and Synthesis of Resilience in Large-Scale Systems." In *Resilience and the Behavior of Large-Scale Systems*, ed. Lance H. Gunderson and Lowell Pritchard Jr., 249–266. Washington, DC: Island Press.

Haeuber, R. 1996. "Setting the Environmental Policy Agenda: The Case of Ecosystem Management." *Natural Resources Journal* 36(1):1–28.

Harkins, Joseph F., and Margaret A. Baggs. 1987. "An Alternative to Public Health–Based Environmental Protection: A Comprehensive Environmental Protection Concept." *University of Kansas Law Review* 35:2(Winter):431–441.

Harrison, David. 1980. "Basinwide Perspective: An Approach to the Design and Analysis of Institutions for Unified River Basin Management." In *Unified River Basin Management*, ed. Ronald M. North, Leonard B. Dworsky, and David J. Allee, 427–437. Minneapolis: American Water Resources Association.

Hart, Gary Warren. 1966. "Creative Federalism: Recent Trends in Regional Water Resources Planning and Development." *University of Colorado Law Review* 39:1 (Fall):29–47.

Heathcote, Isobel W. 1998. *Watershed Management: Principles and Practice.* New York: John Wiley & Sons.

Heikkila, Tanya, and Andrea K. Gerlak. 2005. "The Formation of Large-Scale Collaborative Resource Management Institutions: Clarifying the Roles of Stakeholders, Science, and Institutions." *Policy Studies Journal* 33(4):583–612.

Heywood, Andrew. 2004. *Key Concepts in Politics.* London: Palgrave.

Hinchcliffe, Fiona, John Thompson, and Jules Pretty, eds. 1998. *Fertile Ground: The Impacts of Participatory Watershed Management.* Sterling, VA: Stylus Publishers.

Holling, C. S. 1978. *Adaptive Environmental Assessment and Management.* New York: John Wiley & Sons.

———. 1986. "Resilience of Ecosystems, Local Surprise and Global Change." In *Sustainable Development of the Biosphere*, ed. William Clark and R. E. Munn, 292–317. Cambridge: Cambridge University Press.

Holling, C. S., and G. K. Meffe. 1996. "Command and Control and the Pathology of Natural Resource Management." *Conservation Biology* 10:328–337.

Holmes, Beatrice Hort. 1972. *A History of Federal Water Resources Programs, 1800–1960.* Washington, DC: U.S. Department of Agriculture, Economic Research Service.

———. 1979. *History of Federal Water Resources Programs and Policies, 1961–1970.* Washington, DC: U.S. Department of Agriculture, Economic Research Service.

Hooghe, Lisbet, and Gary Marks. 2003. "Unraveling the Central State, but How? Types of Multi-Level Governance." *American Political Science Review* 97:2(May): 233–243.

Horn, Murray. 1995. *The Political Economy of Public Administration.* Cambridge: Cambridge University Press.

Ingram, Helen. 1990. *Water Politics: Continuity and Change.* Albuquerque: University of New Mexico Press.

Ingram, Helen, Dean Mann, Gary Weatherford, and Hanna Cortner. 1984. "Guidelines for Improved Institutional Analysis in Water Resources Planning." *Water Resources Research* 20(3):323–334.

Jacobs, Sue-Ellen. 1978. "'Top-Down Planning': Analysis of Obstacles to Community Development in an Economically Poor Region of the Southwestern United States." *Human Organization* 37(3):246–256.

Joering, E. A. 1980. "The Ohio River Basin Commission: How to Manage a River Basin Without Threatening or Expanding Existing Authorities." In *Unified River Basin Management*, ed. Ronald M. North et al., 159–169. Minneapolis: American Water Resources Association.

Jones, Bryan D. 2001. *Politics and the Architecture of Choice*. Chicago: University of Chicago Press.

Jones, Bryan, and Frank Baumgartner. 2005. *The Politics of Attention: How Government Prioritizes Problems*. Chicago: University of Chicago Press.

Jordan, Carl F., and Christopher Miller. 1996. "Scientific Uncertainty as a Constraint to Environmental Problem Solving: Large-Scale Ecosystems." In *Scientific Uncertainty and Environmental Problem Solving*, ed. John Lemons, 91–117. London: Blackwell Science.

Kagan, Robert. 1997. "Political and Legal Obstacles to Collaborative Ecosystem Planning." *Ecology Law Quarterly* 24:871–876.

Karkkainen, Bradley. 2002. "Collaborative Ecosystem Governance: Scale, Complexity, and Dynamism." *Virginia Environmental Law Journal* 21:189–243.

Kenney, Douglas S. 1997. *Resource Management at the Watershed Level: An Assessment of the Changing Federal Role in the Emerging Era of Community-Based Watershed Management*. Report for the Western Water Policy Review Advisory Commission. Denver: Western Water Policy Review Advisory Commission.

———. 1999. "Historical and Sociopolitical Context of the Western Watershed Movement." *Journal of the American Water Resources Association* 35:3(June): 493–503.

———. 2000. *Arguing About Consensus: Examining the Case Against Western Watershed Initiatives and Other Collaborative Groups in Natural Resources Management*. Research Report No. 23. Boulder: University of Colorado Natural Resources Law Center.

Kerr, John, and Kimberly Chung. 2001. "Evaluating Watershed Management Projects." *Water Policy* 3:537–554.

King, Loren A. 2004. "Democratic Hopes in the Polycentric City." *Journal of Politics* 66(1):203–223.

Kingdon, John. 1995. *Agendas, Alternatives, and Public Policies*. Second edition. Boston: Little, Brown.

Kiser, Larry, and Elinor Ostrom. 1982. "The Three Worlds of Action." In *Strategies of Political Inquiry*, ed. Elinor Ostrom, 179–222. Beverly Hills, CA: Sage Publications.

Knott, Jack, and Gary Miller. 1987. *Reforming Bureaucracy: The Politics of Institutional Choice*. Englewood Cliffs, NJ: Prentice-Hall.

Komesar, Neil. 1994. *Imperfect Alternatives: Choosing Institutions in Law, Economics, and Public Policy.* Chicago: University of Chicago Press.

Koontz, Tomas M., Toddi A. Steelman, JoAnn Carmin, Katrina Smith Korfmacher, Cassandra Moseley, and Craig W. Thomas. 2004. *Collaborative Environmental Management: What Roles for Government?* Washington, DC: RFF Press.

Kopelman, Shirli, J. Mark Weber, and David Messick. 2002. "Factors Influencing Cooperation in Commons Dilemmas: A Review of Experimental Psychological Research." In *The Drama of the Commons,* ed. Elinor Ostrom, Thomas Dietz, Nives Dolsak, Paul Stern, Susan Stonich, and Elke U. Weber, 113–156. Washington, DC: National Academy Press.

Kraft, Steven, et al. 1999. "Understanding the Social Context for Ecological Restoration in Multiple-Ownership Watersheds: The Case of the Cache River in Illinois—Summary." In *Proceedings: 1999 Water and Watershed Program Review,* 10. EPA/NSF Partnership for Environmental Research. April 19–21, 1999. Silver Spring, MD.

Lackey, R. 1998. "Ecosystem Management: In Search of the Elusive Paradigm." *Human Ecology Review* 4:107–113.

Landau, M. 1969. "Redundancy, Rationality, and the Problem of Duplication and Overlap." *Public Administration Review* 29(4):346–358.

Lasswell, Harold. 1958. *Politics: Who Gets What, When, How.* New York: Meridian Books.

Leach, William, and Neil Pelkey. 2001. "Making Watershed Partnerships Work: A Review of the Empirical Literature." *Journal of Water Resources Planning and Management* 127(6):376–385.

Leach, William, and Paul Sabatier. 2005. "Are Trust and Social Capital Keys to Success? Watershed Partnerships in California and Washington." In *Swimming Upstream: Collaborative Approaches to Watershed Management,* ed. Paul Sabatier, Will Focht, Mark Lubell, Zev Trachtenberg, Arnold Vedlitz, and Marty Matlock, 233–258. Cambridge, MA: MIT Press.

Lebel, Louis, Po Garden, and Masao Imamura. 2005. "The Politics of Scale, Position, and Place in the Governance of Water Resources in the Mekong Region." *Ecology and Society* 10(2):Article 18. http://www.ecologyandsociety.org/vol10/iss2/art18.

Lee, Kai N. 1993. *Compass and Gyroscope: Integrating Science and Politics for the Environment.* Washington, DC: Island Press.

———. 1995. "Deliberately Seeking Sustainability in the Columbia River Basin." In *Barriers and Bridges to the Renewal of Ecosystems and Institutions,* ed. Lance H. Gunderson, C. S. Holling, and Stephen S. Light, 214–238. New York: Columbia University Press.

Levin, Simon A. 1999. *Fragile Dominion: Complexity and the Commons.* Reading, MA: Perseus Books.

Low, Bobbi, Elinor Ostrom, Carl Simon, and James Wilson. 2003. "Redundancy and Diversity: Do They Influence Optimal Management?" In *Navigating Social-Ecological Systems: Building Resilience for Complexity and Change*, ed. Fikret Berkes, Johan Colding, and Carl Folke, 83–114. New York: Cambridge University Press.

Lubell, Mark, Paul Sabatier, Arnold Vedlitz, Will Focht, Zev Trachtenberg, and Marty Matlock. 2005. "Conclusions and Recommendations." In *Swimming Upstream: Collaborative Approaches to Watershed Management*, ed. Paul Sabatier, Will Focht, Mark Lubell, Zev Trachtenberg, Arnold Vedlitz, and Marty Matlock, 261–296. Cambridge, MA: MIT Press.

Lubell, Mark, Mark Schneider, John Scholz, and Mihriye Mete. 2002. "Watershed Partnerships and the Emergence of Collective Action Institutions." *American Journal of Political Science* 46(1):148–163.

Ludwig, Donald, Brian H. Walker, and C. S. Holling. 2002. "Models and Metaphors of Sustainability, Stability, and Resilience." In *Resilience and the Behavior of Large-Scale Systems*, ed. Lance H. Gunderson and Lowell Pritchard Jr., 21–48. Washington, DC: Island Press.

Lutz, Donald. 1988. *The Origins of American Constitutionalism*. Baton Rouge: Louisiana State University Press.

MacKenzie, Susan H. 1996. *Integrated Resource Planning and Management: The Ecosystem Approach in the Great Lakes Basin*. Washington, DC: Island Press.

Mann, Dean E. 1993. "Political Science: The Past and Future of Water Resources Policy and Management." In *Water Resources Administration in the United States: Policy, Practice, and Emerging Issues*, ed. Martin Reuss, 55–65. East Lansing: Michigan State University Press.

Markman, Arthur, and Douglas Medin. 2002. "Decision Making." In *Steven's Handbook of Experimental Psychology*, Third edition, Volume 2, ed. Douglas Medin, 413–466. New York: John Wiley & Sons.

Martin, Roscoe C., Guthrie S. Birkhead, Jesse Burkhead, and Frank J. Munger. 1960. *River Basin Administration and the Delaware*. Syracuse, NY: Syracuse University Press.

McClory, Toni. 2001. *Understanding the Arizona Constitution*. Tucson: University of Arizona Press.

McCrea, James. 1980. "The Basin Overview: A Planning Tool and a Process." In *Unified River Basin Management*, ed. Ronald M. North, Leonard B. Dworsky, and David J. Allee, 459–468. Minneapolis: American Water Resources Association.

McGinnis, Michael Vincent. 1999. "Making the Watershed Connection." *Policy Studies Journal* 27(3):497–501.

Miller, Gary. 1992. *Managerial Dilemmas: The Political Economy of Hierarchy*. New York: Cambridge University Press.

Milon, J. Walter, Clyde F. Kiker, and Donna J. Lee. 1998. "Adaptive Ecosystem Management and the Florida Everglades: More Than Trial-and-Error?" *Water Resources Update* 113(Fall):37–46.

Moe, Terry. 1989. "The Politics of Bureaucratic Structure." In *Can the Government Govern?* ed. John Chubb and Paul Peterson, 267–329. Washington, DC: Brookings Institution.

———. 1990. "The Politics of Structural Choice: Towards a Political Theory of Bureaucracy." In *Organization Theory: From Chester Barnard to the Present and Beyond*, ed. Oliver Williamson, 116–153. Oxford: Oxford University Press.

Mossman, Stephen D. 1996 (December). "'Whiskey Is for Drinkin' but Water Is for Fightin' About': A First Hand Account of Nebraska's Integrated Management of Ground and Surface Water Debate and the Passage of L.B. 108." *Creighton Law Review* 30:67–100.

Naiman, Robert I., ed. 1994. *Watershed Management: Balancing Sustainability and Environmental Change.* Berlin: Springer Verlag.

Nakamura, Liane, and Stephen M. Born. 1993. "Substate Institutional Innovation for Managing Lakes and Watersheds: A Wisconsin Case Study." *Water Resources Bulletin* 29(5):807–821.

National Water Commission. 1973. *Water Policies for the Future: Final Report to the President and to the Congress of the United States.* Port Washington, NY: Water Information Center.

National Watershed Forum. 2001. *Final Report of the National Watershed Forum.* Arlington, VA: National Watershed Forum.

Nebraska Department of Natural Resources. 2004 (September). "Order Designating Overappropriated River Basins." http://metadata.dnr.state.ne.us/LB962/Notice/OverappropriatedOrder9-15-04.pdf.

Nemec, Kristine. 2005. "Beneath Ground Lies Treasure." *Lincoln Journal Star*, May 9, Section B, p. 1.

Newson, Malcolm D. 1997. *Land, Water and Development: Sustainable Management of River Basin Systems.* Second edition. London: Routledge.

New York Times. 2006. "A Chance to Reform the Corps." *New York Times*, July 19, Section A, p. 20.

North, Douglass, and Barry Weingast. 1989. "Constitutions and Commitment: The Evolution of Institutions Governing Public Choice in Seventeenth-Century England." In *The Origins of Liberty*, ed. Paul Drake and Mathew McCubbins, 16–46. Princeton, NJ: Princeton University Press.

Northwest Power and Conservation Planning Council. 2005 (May). *The Fifth Northwest Electric Power and Conservation Plan.*

Northwest Power Planning Council. 2000. *Return to the River 2.* http://www.nwppc.org/library/return/ch1.pdf.

Oakerson, Ronald. 1999. *Understanding Local Public Economies*. San Francisco: ICS Press.

Omernik, James M., and Robert G. Bailey. 1997. "Distinguishing Between Watersheds and Ecoregions." *Journal of the American Water Resources Association* 33:5(October):935–949.

Ostrom, Elinor. 1990. *Governing the Commons: The Evolution of Institutions for Collective Action*. New York: Cambridge University Press.

———. 1992. *Crafting Institutions for Self-Governing Irrigation Systems*. San Francisco: ICS Press.

———. 2005. *Understanding Institutional Diversity*. Princeton, NJ: Princeton University Press.

Ostrom, Vincent. 1973. *The Intellectual Crisis in American Public Administration*. Tuscaloosa: University of Alabama Press.

———. 1987. *The Political Theory of a Compound Republic*. Lincoln: University of Nebraska Press.

———. 1989. *The Intellectual Crisis in American Public Administration*. Second revised edition. Tuscaloosa: University of Alabama Press.

Ostrom, Vincent, Charles M. Tiebout, and Robert Warren. 1961. "The Organization of Government in Metropolitan Areas: A Theoretical Inquiry." *American Political Science Review* 55:4(December):831–842.

O'Toole, Laurence J., Jr. 1993. "Interorganizational Policy Studies: Lessons Drawn from Implementation Research." *Journal of Public Administration Research and Theory* 3(2):232–251.

Parks, Roger, and Ronald Oakerson. 1989. "Metropolitan Organization and Governance: A Local Public Economy Approach." *Urban Affairs Quarterly* 25 (September):18–29.

Pereira, H. C. 1989. *Policy and Practice in the Management of Tropical Watersheds*. Boulder, CO: Westview Press.

Platte River Draft Programmatic Environmental Impact Statement. 2003. Prepared by Bureau of Reclamation and Fish and Wildlife Service. U.S. Department of the Interior. http://www.platteriver.org/library/DEIS/TableContents.pdf.

Platte River Endangered Species Partnership Governance Committee. 2003 (December). Draft Recovery Implementation Program.

Platte River Whooping Crane Maintenance Trust, Inc. 2004. "Habitat Management and Research." www.whoopingcrane.org.

Radin, Beryl, and Barbara Romzek. 1996. "Accountability Expectations in an Intergovernmental Arena." *Publius: The Journal of Federalism* 26(2):59–81.

Reimold, Robert J. 1998. *Watershed Management: Practice, Policies, and Coordination*. New York: McGraw-Hill.

Reisler, Irwin. 1981. "The Federal Charter for Water Resources Planning and Management: An Overview." In *Unified River Basin Management—Stage II*, ed.

David J. Allee, Leonard B. Dworsky, and Ronald M. North, 47–52. Minneapolis: American Water Resources Association.

Reuss, Martin. 1992. "Coping with Uncertainty: Social Scientists, Engineers, and Federal Water Resources Planning." *Natural Resources Journal* 32(1):101–135.

Reynoso, L.A.E. Vicente Guerrero. 2000. "Towards a New Water Management Practice: Experiences and Proposals from Guanajuato State for a Participatory and Decentralized Water Management Structure in Mexico." *Water Resources Development* 16(4):571–588.

Rockloff, Susan F., and Susan A. Moore. 2006. "Assessing Representation at Different Scales of Decision Making: Rethinking Local Is Better." *Policy Studies Journal* 34(4):649–670.

Roe, Emery. 2001. "Varieties of Issue Incompleteness and Coordination: An Example from Ecosystem Management." *Policy Sciences* 34(2):111–133.

Romzek, Barbara. 1998. "Where the Buck Stops: Accountability in Reformed Public Organizations." In *Transforming Government: The Realities of Managing Change in Public Organizations*, ed. Patricia Ingraham, Ronald Sanders, and James Thompson, 193–219. San Francisco: Jossey-Bass.

Romzek, Barbara, and Melvin Dubnik. 1987. "Accountability in the Public Sector: Lessons from the Challenger Tragedy." *Public Administration Review* 47(3): 227–238.

Romzek, Barbara, and Patricia Wallace Ingraham. 2000. "Cross Pressures of Accountability: Initiative, Command, and Failure in the Ron Brown Plane Crash." *Public Administration Review* 60:3(May/June):240–253.

Ruhl, J. B. 1999. "The 'Political' Science of Watershed Management in the Ecosystem Age." *Journal of the American Water Resources Association* 35(3):519–526.

Sabatier, Paul, Will Focht, Mark Lubell, Zev Trachtenberg, Arnold Vedlitz, and Marty Matlock. 2005. "Collaborative Approaches to Watershed Management." In *Swimming Upstream: Collaborative Approaches to Watershed Management*, ed. Paul Sabatier, Will Focht, Mark Lubell, Zev Trachtenberg, Arnold Vedlitz, and Marty Matlock, 3–22. Cambridge, MA: MIT Press.

Sabatier, Paul, and James Quinn. 1999. "When Do Stakeholder Negotiations Work? A Multiple-Lens Analysis of Watershed Restorations in California and Washington—Summary." In *Proceedings: 1999 Water and Watershed Program Review*, 17. EPA/NSF Partnership for Environmental Research. April 19–21, 1999. Silver Spring, MD.

Sabatier, Paul, Chris Weible, and Jared Ficker. 2005. "Eras of Water Management in the United States: Implications for Collaborative Watershed Approaches." In *Swimming Upstream: Collaborative Approaches to Watershed Management*, ed. Paul Sabatier, Will Focht, Mark Lubell, Zev Trachtenberg, Arnold Vedlitz, and Marty Matlock, 23–52. Cambridge, MA: MIT Press.

Scharpf, Fritz. 1997. *Games Real Actors Play*. Boulder, CO: Westview Press.

Schattschneider, E. E. 1960. *The Semisovereign People: A Realist's View of Democracy in America*. New York: Holt, Rinehart, and Winston.

Senate Select Committee on National Water Resources. 1959. "Water Resources Activities in the United States: Reviews of National Water Resources During the Past Fifty Years." 86th Cong., 1st sess.

———. 1960. *The Impact of New Techniques on Integrated Multiple-Purpose Water Development*. Committee Print No. 31. 86th Cong., 2nd sess.

Simon, Herbert. 1955. "A Behavioral Model of Rational Choice." *Quarterly Journal of Economics* 69:99–118.

———. 1957. *Models of Man*. New York: Wiley.

———. 1983. *Reason in Human Affairs*. Stanford, CA: Stanford University Press.

———. 1996. *The Sciences of the Artificial*. Cambridge, MA: MIT Press.

———. 2005. "Foreword." In *Modularity: Understanding the Development and Evolution of Natural Complex Systems*, ed. Werner Callebaut and Diego Rasskin-Gutman, ix–xiv. Cambridge, MA: MIT Press.

Slaughter, Richard A., and John D. Wiener. 2007. "Water, Adaptation, and Property Rights on the Snake and Klamath Rivers." *Journal of the American Water Resources Association* 43:2(April):308–321.

South Platte River Compact. 1989. Colorado Proceedings. Reprinted by Groundwater Appropriators of the South Platte River Basin, Inc.

Stakhiv, Eugene Z. 2003. "Disintegrated Water Resources Management in the U.S.: Union of Sisyphus and Pandora." *Journal of Water Resources Planning and Management* (May/June):151–154.

Stanley, T. R. 1995. "Ecosystem Management and the Arrogance of Humanism." *Conservation Biology* 9:255–262.

Stetson, Thomas M. 1986. "Water Quality of the Main San Gabriel Basin." In *Hydrogeology of Southern California: Volume and Guidebook*, ed. Prem K. Saint. Los Angeles: Geological Society of America.

Stone, Debra. 1988. *Policy Paradox and Political Reason*. New York: HarperCollins.

Supalla, Raymond J. 2000. "A Game Theoretic Analysis of Institutional Arrangements for Platte River Management." *Water Resources Development* 16(2):253–264.

Swallow, Brent, Nancy Johnson, Anna Knox, and Ruth Meinzen-Dick. 2004. "Collective Action and Property Rights for Sustainable Development: Property Rights and Collective Action in Watersheds." Focus 11, Brief 16 (February). Washington, DC: International Food Policy Research Institute / Consultative Group for International Agricultural Research.

Swallow, Brent M., Nancy L. Johnson, and Ruth S. Meinzen-Dick. 2001. "Working with People for Watershed Management." *Water Policy* 3:449–455.

Tarlock, A. Dan. 2000a. "Putting Rivers Back in the Landscape: The Revival of Watershed Management in the United States." *Hastings West-Northwest Journal of Environmental Law and Policy* 6:167–195.

———. 2000b. "Reconnecting Property Rights to Watersheds." *William & Mary Environmental Law and Policy Review* 25(1):69–112.

Tobin, Mitch. 2004. "Frogs' Friend Could Face Federal Rap." *Arizona Daily Star*, May 16, p. A1.

Tucker, Robert K., et al. 1999. "Integrating Models of Citizen Perceptions, Metal Contaminants, and Wetlands Restoration in an Urbanizing Watershed—Summary." In *Proceedings: 1999 Water and Watershed Program Review*, 18. EPA/NSF Partnership for Environmental Research. April 19–21, 1999. Silver Spring, MD.

U.S. Advisory Commission on Intergovernmental Relations. 1987. *The Organization of Local Public Economies*. Report No. A-109. Washington, DC: U.S. Advisory Commission on Intergovernmental Relations.

United States Coastal America Organization. 1994. *Toward a Watershed Approach: A Framework for Aquatic Ecosystem Restoration, Protection, and Management*. Washington, DC: Executive Office of the President.

United States Environmental Protection Agency, Office of Water. 1991. *The Watershed Protection Approach: An Overview*. Report EPA/503/9-92/002. Washington, DC: U.S. Government Printing Office.

United States Environmental Protection Agency, Office of Wetlands, Oceans and Watersheds. 1995. *Watershed Protection: A Statewide Approach*. Report EPA/841-R-95-004. Washington, DC: U.S. Government Printing Office.

Walters, Carl. 1986. *Adaptive Management of Renewable Resources*. New York: Macmillan.

Walther, Pierre. 1987. "Against Idealistic Beliefs in the Problem-Solving Capacities of Integrated Resource Management." *Environmental Management* 11(4):439–446.

Wandschneider, Phillip. 1984. "Managing River Systems: Centralization Versus Decentralization." *Natural Resources Journal* 24(4):1043–1066.

Weber, Edward P. 2003. *Bringing Society Back In*. Cambridge, MA: MIT Press.

Weimer, David, ed. 1997. *The Political Economy of Property Rights*. New York: Cambridge University Press.

Wengart, Norman. 1981. "A Critical Review of the River Basin as a Focus for Resources Planning, Development, and Management." In *Unified River Basin Management*, ed. Ronald M. North, Leonard B. Dworsky, and David J. Allee, 9–27. Minneapolis: American Water Resources Association.

Wester, Philippus, and Jeroen Warner. 2002. "River Basin Management Reconsidered." In *Hydropolitics: A Southern Africa Perspective*, ed. Anthony Turton and Roland Henwood, 61–71. Pretoria, South Africa: African Water Issues Research Unit.

White, Gilbert F. 1998. "Reflections on the 50-Year International Search for Integrated Water Management." *Water Policy* 1(1):21–27.

Williamson, Oliver. 1985. *The Economic Institutions of Capitalism*. New York: Free Press.

Wilson, James M. 2002a. "Scientific Uncertainty, Complex Systems and the Design of Common Pool Institutions." In *Drama of the Commons*, ed. Elinor Ostrom, Thomas Dietz, Nives Dolsak, Paul Stern, Susan Stonich, and Elke U. Weber, 327–359. Washington, DC: National Academy Press.

———. 2002b. "Decision Making and the Environmental Arena." *Polycentric Circles* 8(2):6.

Wilson, James Q. 1989. *Bureaucracy*. New York: Basic Books.

Woolley, John T., and Michael Vincent McGinnis. 1999. "The Politics of Watershed Policymaking." *Policy Studies Journal* 27(3):578–594.

Yaffee, Steven L., Al Phillips, Irene Frentz, Paul Hardy, Sussanne Maleki, and Barbara Thorpe. 1996. *Ecosystem Management in the United States: An Assessment of Current Experience*. Washington, DC: Island Press.

Zimmerman, Joseph F. 2002. *Interstate Cooperation: Compacts and Administrative Agreements*. Westport, CT: Praeger.

.

Long Beach, 141, 146
Los Angeles and San Gabriel Rivers Watershed Council, 146
Los Angeles County: San Gabriel River watershed, 135–36, 141, 144; urbanization, 136–39
Los Angeles County Department of Public Works, 141, 146, 147
Los Angeles County Flood Control District, 143
Los Angeles River Basin, 145, 150

McConaughy, Lake, 76, 77
Main San Gabriel Basin, 136, 138, 140, 141, 149, 188; water quality issues, 142, 143–44; watermaster authorities, 144–45
Main San Gabriel Basin Water Quality Authority, 145
Metropolitan Water District (MWD) of Southern California, 131–32, 138, 149
Mining, Columbia River Basin, 104
Missouri River Basin, 33
Monongahela River, 36
Montana, 108
Monterey Park, 139
Multiple accountability mechanisms, 70–71
Multiple goals, of watershed management, 124–27
Municipalities, 104, 128; San Gabriel River watershed, 136–39, 141, 146
MWD. See Metropolitan Water District of Southern California

National Marine Fisheries Service (NMFS), 108, 117, 118
National Park Service, 33
National Planning Board, 30, 37
National Resources Board, viii, 37, 38
National Resources Committee, 37, 48
National Resources Planning Board, 38
National Water Commission, 29
National Watershed Forum, 24
Natural resource management, viii, 28, 60, 80; changing agendas of, 186–87; fragmentation of, 191–92; multiple-scale

organizations, 16–17. See also Resource management, integrated
Natural systems, 151–52
Nebraska: agriculture in, 79–80, 81; interstate compacts with, 155, 157, 158–59, 179(n6); Platte River Basin in, xiii, 57, 74, 76, 77–78, 84, 88(n4), 163–64
Nebraska Department of Natural Resources, 80, 164
Nebraska Game and Parks Commission, 77
New Deal Era, 28, 29, 32
New England River Basin Commission, 36
New Jersey, 166–68, 169, 170, 176
New York, 165, 166, 168, 169, 170, 176
New York City, 165, 166, 167–68, 169, 170, 181(n12)
NMFS. See National Marine Fisheries Service
North Platte, 76
North Platte Decree, 157
North Platte River, 74–75, 81
Northwest Power Act, 108; Congressional role, 111–13
Northwest Power Planning Council, xii, 91, 104, 121(n13); federal agencies and, 115–17; plan developed by, 113–15; policy analysis in, 162–63; role of, 108–10, 118–19

Ohio River Commission, 36
Olmsted Brothers, 145
Orange County Water District, 10
Oregon, Columbia River Basin, 108, 191–92
Oregon State University, salmon recovery, 118
Organizations, 2, 50; accountability in, 68, 69; coordination among, 132–34; hydrologically based, 23–24; multiple-scale management, 16–17, 190–91; overlapping, 160–61; polycentric structures of, 17–18, 134–35; voluntary, 159–60

Pacific Northwest Coordination Agreement (1964), 107